OUT OF THE JAWS OF VICTORY

And They All Laughed When I Sat Down to Play!

OUT OF THE JAWS OF VICTORY

by

JULES ABELS

HENRY HOLT AND COMPANY, New York

In Canada, George J. McLeod, Ltd.

FIRST EDITION

Library of Congress Catalog Card Number: 59-13594

80031-0119

Printed in the United States of America

TABLE OF CONTENTS

PREFACE

Why this book?

A Presidential election is important enough to deserve study. The election of 1948 with its totally unexpected outcome is the most perplexing, perhaps, in our history. Altogether the remarkable events in 1948 entitle it to be termed *Annus Mirabilis* in American politics. Whatever light this book can shed on those events, I feel, will be useful.

To Republicans 1948 is especially meaningful. Over a decade has passed since the great fiasco, but the regrets and bitterness still survive. Despite the two victories of Eisenhower and Nixon, many Republicans believe that the setback to the position of the Party has been a lasting one.

I have always been intrigued by the human experience involved in the objective event. Whatever one's appraisal of Harry Truman as President, he commands admiration for his indomitable courage through the election year. On the other hand, what happened to Dewey is a classic example of what the Greeks called *hubris,* the pride before the fall. Yet, there is no room for anyone to throw scorn or derision. All saw through the glass darkly in 1948. Circumstances contrived a gigantic comedy and pulled all like puppets. One can almost hear Puck in the wings, "What fools these mortals be." The experience should be a sobering reminder of human fallibility.

This book is written as we move to another Presidential election. The election of 1948 was the last close election we have had. It was also the first election in the postwar period and the environment is largely the same today as it was then. We still have the ideological split in the Republican Party with which Dewey was preoccupied, the disaffection of the South on civil rights continues to plague the Democratic Party, the cold war abroad and the inflation at home are our major national concerns. The psychological motivations and economic interests which elect a President are still a dark area that needs exploration. The election of 1948 is the best for case study on the subject.

The 1948 election is distant enough in time to give perspective. It is recent enough so that almost all concerned are still alive and still prominent in public and private life. This book has interwoven with secondary research materials the recollections and views of many persons connected with the political events of 1948.

The author interviewed three of the four Presidential candidates in 1948: former Governor Thomas E. Dewey, former Vice-President Henry A. Wallace, and Senator J. Strom Thurmond. Former President Harry S. Truman declined to be interviewed, but an account of the election is contained in his *Memoirs*.

The following persons intimately connected with the election gave their accounts in personal interviews: (their roles in 1948 are stated here only when they are not described in the book) former Senator Joseph H. Ball; Arthur Barnett; Elliott V. Bell; former Secretary of the Senate Leslie Biffle; former Senator Owen Brewster, who was a member of the Eightieth Congress; Representative Clarence J. Brown; former Attorney General Herbert Brownell, Jr.; Clark Clifford; General Bonner Fellers; Interstate Commerce Commissioner Abe McGregor Goff; former Republican National Chairman Leonard W. Hall; House Minority Leader Charles A. Halleck; Republican Campaign Director Robert Humphreys; former Senator William E. Jenner; former Secretary of Defense Colonel Louis Johnson; Victor A. Johnston; Edward Larson, who was Harold Stassen's campaign secretary.

Also, former Attorney General J. Howard McGrath; Judge

I. Jack Martin, who was Senator Taft's administrative assistant; Raymond Moley; Senator Karl E. Mundt; Merlyn S. Pitzele; former Republican National Chairman B. Carroll Reece; Representative James Roosevelt; Senator Richard B. Russell; Senator Hugh Scott; former Republican National Committeeman J. Russel Sprague; former Governor Harold Stassen; Dr. Rexford Guy Tugwell; former Senator Burton K. Wheeler; Chairman of the Federal Deposit Insurance Corporation Jesse L. Wolcott.

The following gave their views by letter: Former Congressman Howard Buffett; Dr. George Gallup; former Chairman of the House Agriculture Committee Clifford R. Hope.

In this book when an individual "says" something, "denies" something, or makes a similar assertion in the present tense, it means that the statement was made personally to the author. The responsibility for the accuracy of the statement is entirely that of the author.

OUT OF THE
JAWS OF VICTORY

[1]

TRUMAN TAILSPIN

THE SHADOW of the coming Presidential election lengthened over Washington in the closing months of 1947. Secretary of Defense James Forrestal recorded in his diary on October 6 that President Truman "remarked that he looked forward with deep misgiving to another four years after 1948 in the White House. And that if it were not for his duty to run again in the face of world conditions, the delay in getting the peace treaties with Japan, Germany, Austria, etc., he would like to step aside. He said he wanted to get a place for [General] Vaughan and that having accomplished that he would have taken care of everyone." Forrestal recorded on November 12 that the President made a similar statement to him about the duty he felt he owed to the country and the party. This overrode his reluctance to run arising from the fact that his family could not lead a normal life, a sentiment which Forrestal accepted as one of "complete sincerity."

In opening this narrative, it is important to note a fact that was soon to be smothered out of notice in the universal pessimism as to Truman's chances. At the end of 1947 the President was considered certain of renomination by his party and was rated as a formidable candidate in the national election. The Gallup Poll, then considered well-nigh infallible, showed that he would defeat the two leading Republicans,

Governor Dewey and Senator Taft, by decisive margins. A get-tough policy with Russia, first under Secretary of State James Byrnes and later under his successor General Marshall, had pushed up his popularity—the Marshall Plan proposed in 1947, his advocacy of Government action to curb high prices, and his toe-to-toe slugging match with John L. Lewis, in which the labor titan had been vanquished, all had boosted him in popular favor.

The November elections had brought favorable omens. A Democrat, Earle Clements, had been elected Governor of Kentucky and Democrats had won in many local elections. Senator Taft had said before the November elections, "The Kentucky election will reflect to a large degree which party will elect a President in 1948." An astute political commentator, David Lawrence, said on November 7, "The chances are less than even that the Republicans will win in 1948 no matter whom the Republicans select as their candidate."

But within four months President Truman was considered a certain loser as a Presidential candidate, so certain, in fact, that a drive was on to ditch him, backed by strong political leaders. Within that short period all events seemed to conspire to defeat him. Never has the political stock of a President fallen with such lightning-like rapidity.

It was taken for granted within the leadership of the Democratic Party that the election would be won or lost on domestic rather than foreign policy. J. Howard McGrath, newly elected Chairman of the Democratic National Committee, succeeding Robert E. Hannegan, says that he reminded the President at the end of 1947 that it was all very well to concentrate on winning the peace, but a national election was ahead. There was a special session of the Eightieth Congress (it was a Republican Congress) on November 17, which was devoted mainly to a domestic issue, the President's request for stand-by price-rationing controls to deal with the inflation. Congress, however, was in no mood to restore wartime controls.

On January 7, 1948, the President appeared in person before the second session of the Eightieth Congress to deliver his message on the State of the Union. The message was widely interpreted as the opening gun of his campaign. The reaction of Congress, according to the New York *Times,* was "extraordinarily chilly." Seven times the President paused, obviously for applause, and there was none. When he was halfway through his address there was handclapping, when the President pledged to carry out the Taft-Hartley labor law which Congress had enacted over his veto the year before. Then Senator Glen Taylor of Idaho, soon to be a running mate of Henry Wallace on a third-party ticket, applauded when the President proposed raising taxes on corporations. A staunch Democrat, Lowell Mellett, wrote: "The reception for Harry Truman was markedly like that given the Polar explorers by their immediate audience—a circle of correctly attired penguins. A few penguins on that cold day flapped their wings."

The message consisted of a long list of legislative recommendations without plan or pattern. "Everything including the kitchen stove," said political analyst Arthur Krock of the New York *Times*. Constructed on a "Crazy-quilt formula," echoed his colleague, James Reston. The President asked again for the ten-point, anti-inflation program recently rejected at the special session of Congress. He also asked for prompt approval of the European Recovery Program launched in a commencement address by Secretary of State Marshall at Harvard the previous June, which the President had presented to Congress during the special session.

The main emphasis of the message, however, was on a multi-pronged social program, including expanded social security, health insurance, Federal aid for education, Federal housing, extended farm supports and conservation of natural resources, and higher minimum wages. Although these were familiar New Deal objectives, they never had been pulled together in such an imposing array. There was one novel approach, put in at the last minute, which made the message newsworthy—the President proposed that every taxpayer should be able to deduct forty dollars from his tax bill for himself and each dependent. This was something uncluttered by mathematics, which every voter could understand.

There was silence from the Democratic ranks, but sharp attacks from the Republicans. House Majority Whip Leslie Arends commented that as he listened to the message, "It suddenly occurred to me for the first time I had the privilege of participating in the Democratic Convention." To the forty dollar tax-cut plan, Majority Leader Charles Halleck, harkening back to the Reconstruction slogan of "forty acres and a mule," exclaimed, "What, no mule!" Senate policy leader Taft toted up the bill at $10 billion and said, "The Federal Government comes forward again as Santa Claus himself." Newspaper comment was similarly unappreciative. The New York *Times* called the tax plan "The Voters' Bonus Bill of 1948," and the Washington *Post,* usually friendly to Truman, dismissed it as "unmitigatedly demagogic . . . explicable as a transparently political move."

The President, who up to this time had acted as a moderate, had now emerged fully clad in the Roosevelt mantle as a flaming New Dealer. Commentators on the left and on the right agreed on the reason—on December 29, only a few days previously, Henry Wallace had entered the political arena with a third party. The Truman program was designed to steal the thunder of Wallace's progressive platform with its appeal to New Dealers. As Raymond Moley put it, it was not unknown in the past for party platforms to be taken over by opposing parties, "but now apparently the Wallace issues are to be grabbed before he has a chance to have a convention. The infant is stolen from the delivery room."

The liberals were suspicious of the siren song. While welcoming it, Max Lerner noted that it was a "campaign document" and that "the Wallace candidacy has pushed Truman farther and more sharply left than he would have gone otherwise." As for the Old Curmudgeon turned columnist, Harold Ickes, he wrote that to call the "political harangue a State-of-the-Union Message is akin to slander. . . . The words purported to be that of the Roosevelt New Deal, but the voice was the voice of Esau."

The State-of-the-Union Message might fittingly be called the overture to the 1948 campaign since the President started in it to weave the pattern of themes on which he would wage his campaign. The audience at the time preferred to skip the overture. Typically, the Washington *Post* brushed it off as "merely sketching the Utopia he envisions for America," and Walter Lippmann said it was "a program for his successors." This was only the first instance of the astigmatism that was to afflict all observers of the national political scene in 1948.

The apparent fizzle of the State-of-the-Union Message coincided with a wave of criticism against the President from liberal sources for his dismissal of James M. Landis, head of the Civil Aeronautics Board, one of the few New Dealers of old vintage in a high post in the Administration. It was an unexpected dismissal because Sam Rayburn had been told forty-eight hours before that Landis would be re-appointed. The President: "You have been doing a fine job." Landis: "Thank you, Mr. President." The President: "But I can't re-appoint you. I have made a prior commitment to someone else."

So Landis departed without the customary word of thanks, but to far more munificent rewards in the employment of Joseph B. Kennedy. "Curt and ungracious" was the way the

Washington *Post* termed the manner of his dismissal. Although the cause for the dismissal was not disclosed, it was claimed by the *Nation* and the New York *Post* that Landis had offended large airlines by his insistence on safety regulations, his sympathy with new noncertified freight-carriers, and his position against mail payments as a form of subsidy. It was claimed that Commerce Secretary Averell Harriman was the executioner.

A few weeks later came another unexpected dismissal which caused further disgruntlement in the liberal faction that Truman had sought to win over in his State-of-the-Union Message. Marriner Eccles, who had been Chairman of the Federal Reserve Board for twelve years, was not redesignated as Chairman at the end of January. It was quite a shock to Eccles, since he had met with the President a month before, during Christmas, and had received no clue. In an interview the President declined to give Eccles any reasons. In his memoirs, *Beckoning Frontiers,* Eccles writes, "The reasons were best known to himself alone. It was evident that he did not want me to know what lay behind his action." The President wanted him to stay on. "Please stay and help me." He would designate him as vice-chairman. Eccles swallowed his pride and stayed on, but the vice-chairmanship never came through, probably for the same undisclosed reason that he lost the chairmanship.

It was widely believed that Eccles had been dumped because of Wall Street pressure. Ernest Lindley wrote in *Newsweek* that Eccles was a "symbol of opposition to New York control of the banking system and as such of special political value to an Administration which has become heavily staffed with men with a Wall Street background." Eccles himself doubts that Wall Street was responsible for his dismissal and believes that the pressure came from the West Coast and more particularly from the Giannini interests because of the efforts of Eccles to limit the activities of their Transamerica Company.

In contrast to the two shining symbols of the New Deal dismissed from their posts, two men close to the President in the same month of January became embroiled in a matter that tarnished slightly the reputation of the Administration. Their accuser was Harold Stassen, former Governor of Minnesota, an early contender for the Republican nomination. Appearing before the Senate Appropriations Committee, he charged that eleven Government insiders had made $4 million in killings on the commodity market, even though the President on October 5 had denounced "the greed of speculators" and had asked Congress for powers to control commodity exchanges. Stassen claimed that Edwin W. Pauley, a close friend of Truman and now a special assistant to the Secretary of War, had made a million dollars in commodity speculation and that he had been engaged in commodity deals while he entertained Agriculture Secretary Anderson and Democratic Chairman Robert E. Hannegan as his guests on Coconut Island in Hawaii. He also claimed that Brigadier General Graham, the President's personal physician, had lied when he said he had withdrawn from the commodity market shortly after the President's statement denouncing commodity speculation.

Stassen's information was close enough to the truth to demonstrate that he was the beneficiary of a leak from well-informed sources. Pauley in his testimony admitted a gain of $932,000 in commodity transactions but disclaimed any claim of impropriety (and none was proved). In fact, he said his strategy for making money was to go long on the market every time Secretary Anderson said there would be a break in prices. General Graham appeared in a far less favorable light. He had to admit that he had lied. His prior statement about withdrawing from the market was "not accurate." He had not "lost his socks" as he had said before, but he had doubled his money. As for speculating, he was only a country boy who didn't even know that cotton was a commodity and he didn't even know what margin was.

Pauley resigned shortly thereafter, but General Graham stayed on. The incident was more ammunition that was used against Truman. Harold Ickes, referring to "Landis-Graham day," said, "The difference in treatment accorded Landis and Dr. Graham has shaken to its foundations the morale of the whole Washington set-up."

A seemingly far more trivial incident caused a much greater furor. The President had decided to build a porch on the south portico of the White House. In 1946 he had sprung a plan to remodel the west wing into what was labeled something "midway between a pretentious railroad depot and the club house of a very exclusive Long Island golf club." Congress had squelched that plan. This time, he was not to be dissuaded from building his porch, even by the unanimous dissent of the Fine Arts Commission, which supervises the exterior construction of public buildings. An official of the Commission said that Truman had ordered secrecy in the project—but the news had nonetheless leaked out. There was a hue and cry. The President was reminded that he was only a temporary tenant—the President's reply was that all tenants were only temporary tenants. The President wanted privacy; he was reminded that the south portico was private enough for Woodrow Wilson to propose to Mrs. Galt. The President claimed that all innovations in the White House from the time of Millard Fillmore faced the same resistance, whether bathtubs, gaslights, or cooking stoves. The Washington *Evening Star* ran a front-page cartoon on the subject.

Thus ended the month of January, unhappy for the President, full of blunders and fizzles. He had gained no political capital out of balcony troubles, commodity-speculation probes, maladroit dismissals, or charges that his legislative proposals were early campaigning. Congress gave an immediate answer on the key Presidential request for a forty-dollar tax cut. The first and second Democratic ranking members of the House Ways and Means Committee refused to introduce the bill and so the third ranking member, Congressman Dingell, sponsored it. But it was turned down by the House Ways and Means Committee nineteen to five. After listening to Administration officials, Congress shelved again the President's plea that he be given authority to impose price ceilings

Why Not Put the Bathtub on the Balcony?

Berryman in the Washington Evening Star

and ration goods. The President fought with the Senate Armed Services Committee over his nomination of Major General Laurence S. Kuter to be Landis' successor as head of the Civil Aeronautics Board, insisting that the General be permitted to retain his $15,000 Army pay in the $10,000 civilian job. Permission was refused and the nomination was withdrawn.

The most momentous project facing the new Congress, the Marshall Plan, was slowly grinding its way ahead, but the initiative was now being taken by Republicans, Chairman Charles Eaton of the House Foreign Affairs Committee, and Senator Arthur Vandenberg, Chairman of the Senate Foreign Affairs Committee.

These were minor setbacks compared to the convulsions that occurred in the following month. A Presidential committee on Civil Rights had been set up in December 1946 under the chairmanship of Charles E. Wilson, president of General Electric. Its recommendations were drastic, and, as some northern critics pointed out, ignored the great progress the Negro had made in recent years. On the basis of its report, "To Secure These Rights," the President sent a message to Congress on February 2 recommending a permanent commission on civil rights and, among other measures, legislation to protect the right to vote, to outlaw lynching, the poll tax, and segregation in interstate commerce, and proposing the establishment of a Federal Employment Practices Commission similar to that which had operated during the war.

Immediately there was a roar of protest from Southern legislators. Senator Richard Russell of Georgia accused the President of trying to set up "an American OGPU." Representative Sam Hobbs attributed to the President a desire "to keep the South a conquered province," and Representative Eugene Cox said, "Harlem is wielding more influence with the Administration than the entire white South." Senator Connally of Texas said that it was a "lynching of the Constitution."

The President surely expected these repercussions. However sincere he was about civil-rights reforms, he most likely sprang his message early in 1948 in the hope that Southern tempers would be cooled long before the national convention. But the rebellion was wafted on a favorable gale. A conference of Southern governors was to be held at Wakulla Springs,

Florida, the following week with nothing on the agenda but an innocuous report on education. Now the conference had an opportunity to ponder and debate the President's message. This gave the revolt an organizational nucleus, a chance to gather momentum at the highest level in the South. The conference appointed a delegation of four governors headed by Governor J. Strom Thurmond of South Carolina and including Governors Jester of Texas, Cherry of North Carolina, and Laney of Arkansas to go to Washington to get some concessions from the President.

A spirit of moderation still prevailed in the councils of the South. The conference rejected a proposal for a South-wide convention in Jackson, Mississippi, to map a revolt, and instead adopted a forty-day cooling-off period. But cold threats were being made, and it seemed that something more serious than the regular quadrennial rumblings could be in the works. Senator Eastland of Mississippi, labeling Truman a "carpetbagger," declared, "All we have to do is to refuse to vote the [Democratic] ticket. . . . By withholding the electoral votes, the South can defeat in 1948 any Democratic candidate."

A far more serious blow for Democratic hopes came a few days later. The extent of the support for Henry Wallace had been an unanswered question. On February 17 there was a special election for Congress in New York City, in the 24th Congressional District in the Bronx, supposedly a stronghold of Democratic boss Ed Flynn. The American-Labor candidate backed by Henry Wallace, Leo Isacson, easily trounced his Democratic and Liberal opponents by a two to one margin. Wallace's appeal seemed to be stronger than had been expected and indicated that the Wallace strength could cost the Democrats New York and other Eastern States in the Presidential election.

The Democrats had pulled a boner by advertising this as a test of public opinion. They had been confident of victory, after making an all-out effort with bigwigs like Mrs. Roosevelt and Mayor O'Dwyer to plead for backing of Truman. Wallace had campaigned too in the district and he had been effective. The district was thirty-five per cent Jewish and Wallace proclaimed "Truman talks Jewish but acts Arab." Although the United Nations, under pressure from the United States, had pushed through a resolution for partition of Palestine on November 29, the United States had clamped down an arms embargo on December 5. Fighting was now in progress between Jews and Arabs and hundreds had already been killed.

Under the clouds of recent events, the President appeared before the party faithful at a Jefferson-Jackson Day dinner in Washington on February 19. There was no mention at all of civil rights; a discussion he had planned on his anti-inflation program was deleted because of a sudden, sharp break in commodity prices which made the headlines. He took the occasion to re-affirm the progressive viewpoint which permeated his State-of-the-Union Message. Surely the nation's voters would not turn over affairs to a "bunch of reactionaries who are trying to turn us back to 1896." He drew laughs with this sally, "These men who live in the past remind me of a toy I'm sure all of you have seen. The toy is a small wooden bird called the 'floogie bird.' Around the floogie bird's neck is a label reading 'I fly backwards. I don't care where I'm going. I just want to see where I've been.'" (This bird had a long pedigree, dating back to Roosevelt and Wallace on December 17 had referred to it in exactly the same terms as the "oozle finch.")

The atmosphere was grim. There was only a smattering of applause. A visible reminder of the burgeoning Southern revolt was an empty table right under the eyes of the President, bought by Senator Olin Johnston of South Carolina and his wife. They had refused to attend on the ground that since no segregation was enforced they might have to dine with Negroes. Mrs. Johnston had been on the arrangements committee for the dinner and thus picked a choice front table to administer the public slap in the face. A friend kept insisting, "We paid $1,100 to keep this table vacant," and vacant it remained. Governor Thurmond and his wife canceled their reservations. There were party dinners throughout the South but very little of the proceeds poured into the Democratic treasury in Washington. At Little Rock more than half of the 750 persons present walked out when Truman's voice came over the loudspeakers, and a proposal to send the $10,000 raised to Washington failed of a majority.

The next day more steam was added to the revolt when fifty-two House Democrats assembled to condemn Truman's civil-rights proposals, and asked for cooperation with the Governors' Conference. On February 23 the four Southern governors met with Democratic Party Chairman McGrath. The South had found a firebrand on the civil rights issue in Governor Thurmond. Refusing a seat, he paced up and down hurling his demands. In response to Thurmond's repeated insistence that he advocate a retreat from the civil-rights program, McGrath's answers shortened as the conference went on and wound up on a definite "I will not." Returning to their suite in the Mayflower, the governors issued a statement of defiance, "The Southern states are aroused and the Democratic Party will soon realize that the South is 'no longer in the bag.' "

Far from backing down, the President carried through an engagement which made his position more firm. He visited the Virgin Islands and dined with William Hastie, the first Negro governor. A banner across St. Thomas' main street read, "Welcome, President Truman, champion of human rights."

At the outset the inclination almost universally had been to discount Southern threats, in the words of one columnist as "merely toughening up vocal chords." But scoffing diminished as defections multiplied. Suggestions were cropping up that Truman should withdraw as a possible candidate. This undoubtedly accounted for his before-scheduled announcement on March 8, three days before the meeting of the Democratic Executive Committee, that he was a candidate for President. Republican Chairman Carroll Reece said that it hit "with the terrific impact of a poached egg on a featherbed." Senator John McClellan took the credit for being the first to say that Truman couldn't win and said, "I still say he can't win."

Within a week after the announcement of Truman's candidacy, a meeting of Southern governors at the Mayflower Hotel, a few blocks from the White House, boldly announced plans to deprive Truman of the South's electoral votes. If a candidate were nominated who advocated the invasion of state sovereignty, then the people of the South would "see to it that the electoral votes of the South are not cast for such nominee." It advocated that state conventions should not be held until after the national convention and that the Presidential electors should be instructed to vote in accordance with the orders of the state conventions.

By mid-March disillusionment with Truman's chances was so profound that a check of fourteen Democrats running for the Senate showed that only three were willing to say that they were Truman backers, Senator Theodore Green of Rhode Island, Senator Jim Murray of Montana, and Secretary of Agriculture Clinton Anderson, running in New Mexico. The desertion of outstanding Southern liberals was a bitter blow. Senator John Sparkman of Alabama, who previously had joined with Senator Claude Pepper in saying "The problem will be worked out within the Democratic Party," now said, "The Democratic Party will be cut to ribbons," and Senator Lister Hill, also of Alabama, said, "There cannot be Democratic unity under him." But there was no word of compromise from the President, who told Mrs. Lennard Thomas, Alabama's National Committeewoman, over coffee in the White House, "I take back nothing of what I proposed and make no excuse for it."

A widely reprinted cartoon of the Washington *Evening Star* (the President proudly kept the original) showed Truman's mood.

Berryman in the Washington Evening Star

Then came another event which seemed a crusher to Democratic hopes. On March 19 the United States announced withdrawal of its position in favor of partitioning Palestine which it had pushed through the General Assembly of the United Nations the previous November 29. The Administration urged a UN trusteeship to prevent chaos when the British ended their rule on May 15. The decision was a surprise although it had been foreshadowed by an earlier announcement that the United States was not in favor of force to make partition a reality, and since the Arabs were putting up a fight it seemed that force might be necessary. In the view of the New York *Times* the decision "comes as a climax to a series of moves which has seldom been matched for ineptness in the handling of any international issue by an American Administration."

The Palestine issue was deeply wrapped in votes. The previous November, at the time of the UN partition vote, Forrestal buttonholed Democratic Chairman McGrath and pleaded that the issue should be "taken out of politics." Forrestal cited indications of a division among American Jews themselves as to the wisdom of a Jewish state. McGrath replied by saying "that there were two or three pivotal states which could not be carried without the support of the people who were deeply interested in the Palestine question." On November 26 McGrath told him there were contributions from Jewish sources to the Democratic National Committee made "with a distinct idea on the part of the givers that they will have an opportunity to express their views and have them seriously considered on such questions as the present Palestine question." A week later Jimmy Byrnes commented to Forrestal that David Niles and Sam Rosenman were responsible for the President's decision in favor of partition, "that both had told the President that Dewey was about to come out with a statement favoring the Zionist position on Palestine, and that they had insisted that unless the President anticipated this movement New York State would be lost to the Democrats."

Forrestal got some encouragement in his "depoliticization" drive from a few Republicans such as Senator Vandenberg, but none at all from Dewey, with whom Forrestal talked at a Gridiron Club dinner in December. Dewey said, "It was a difficult matter to get results on because of the intemperate attitude of the Jewish people who had taken Palestine as the emotional symbol, because the Democratic Party would not be willing to relinquish the advantages of the Jewish vote." Bernard Baruch talked to Forrestal warning him to go slow, that he did not approve of the Zionists' actions but "the Democratic Party could only lose by trying to get our Government's policy reversed."

There is a good deal of independent testimony that the President was intensely irritated by heavy Zionist pressure. Henry Wallace says that Jewish admirers today would be surprised at some of the statements Truman made in his presence occasioned by the Palestine issue. Senator Burton K. Wheeler was closest to Truman while he was in the Senate and remained an intimate after his defeat in 1946. He says that he discussed the Palestine question with Truman in the White House in October 1947, one month before the decision for partition. Reminding him that he, Wheeler, had been accused of being anti-Jewish because of his prewar isolationism, Wheeler urged that the United States back the Zionist cause, that otherwise the Jewish vote would be lost in 1948. Truman replied, "Plenty of Jews will vote for me, such as Lessing Rosenwald." Wheeler answered that such Jews were in a minority, that he was referring to the mass Jewish vote that he needed to win the election. Truman reflected and then answered—"I don't know about that. I think that a candidate on an anti-Semitic platform might sweep the country."

The continued fighting in Palestine and election considerations put the Administration in a dilemma. On November 29 the partition resolution was pushed through the UN. On December 1 Truman told Forrestal that our armed forces would not be used to implement the resolution. In early February the President warned Chairman McGrath and Gael Sullivan, Executive Director of the Democratic Committee, not to interfere with the Palestine question or give encouragement to the Zionists. It was the position of Forrestal and of Loy Henderson, in charge of Near Eastern affairs for the

State Department, that the partition resolution was a "recommendation" that would be carried out only if it proved "just and workable" and did not contemplate the use of force.

Forrestal's argument went further. The deployable Army troops left in this country were less than 30,000 to which 23,000 Marines could be added, while the British needed 90,000 troops merely to police Palestine without trying to impose partition. Mid-East oil was important to us; without it the Marshall Plan could not succeed, and the auto industry would have to convert to four-cylinder cars. It would be dangerous to allow Soviet troops in the Mid-East oil fields. Partition was one of the few issues on which Russia had voted with us. Under it Soviet troops would get into the Mid-East. Forrestal told Franklin D. Roosevelt, Jr., that he was tired of hearing about how the Democrats might lose three states and that someone should consider "whether we might not lose the United States."

The President, putting political considerations aside and responding to his convictions as to the national interest, finally swung over to the Forrestal and State Department position for a retreat from partition and adoption of the temporary position of trusteeship.

The political impact of the new policy was shattering since it seemed certain to throw away the normally Democratic Jewish voters. Paul Fitzpatrick, Chairman of the Democratic Party in New York State at the time of the Jefferson-Jackson Day dinner, had spent hours with Secretary of Defense Forrestal, pleading with him to lift the arms embargo. Jacob Arvey, Democratic leader of Chicago, broke with Truman. Senator Scott Lucas of Illinois said he was "shocked and surprised," and Democratic Congressman Emanuel Celler from Brooklyn called the move "wicked and iniquitous." Max Lerner voiced the sentiment of many liberals, "One would have to go back to Munich to recall a sell-out as cynical, as bedraggled, as contemptible. . . . A man has to have a genius for blundering to have done so complete a job of stripping himself of the support of so many varied groups." Senator Murray shied away from the Truman candidacy, saying that there was time to make the choice at the convention, and Senator Pepper of Florida, one of Truman's very few remaining supporters in the South, took the same stand.

It was generally believed now that only a disaster or a miracle could secure the President's election. The Gallup Poll did a flip-flop and now showed Truman far behind Dewey and Stassen in popularity. Chairman Reece, voicing the jubilation of the Republicans, said, "With the Moscow wing departed and the racially intolerant ring now threatening to go off in another direction, it looks like the Pendergast wing will be alone next November." It was in fashion to gibe at the political gaucherie of the President. Governor Laney of Arkansas said, "We don't want to run a race with a dead Missouri mule." Doris Fleeson in her nationally syndicated column reported a favorite cocktail-lounge joke in Washington—in a smoke-filled room some Democratic leaders were discussing the crisis in the party; one said, "I wonder what Truman would do if he were alive." A newspaper referred to Truman constantly as "Thruman." The Martha Taft quip "to err is Truman" was widely repeated.

The end of March marked the nadir of Truman's popularity and a move was under way to deprive him of the nomination.

How could optimism as to Truman's chances of election swing to bleak pessimism in a few short weeks?

John Hay had once defined the Democratic Party as "a fortuitous concurrence of unrelated prejudices." During the Roosevelt period the prejudices were a good deal more unrelated than during Hay's era. The party was an amalgam of a conservative South, a progressive organized labor movement, big-city machines, moderates, liberals, idealists, radicals,

Jews, and newly-won Negroes—all fused together by the peculiar political genius of Roosevelt, which was regarded as a peculiar personal kind of necromancy.

The new Wallace party and the Southern revolt seemed to signify that the amalgam was now dissolving. A long-time political writer, Marquis Childs, wrote on March 9, "We may well be watching the liquidation of one of the major parties." Had the vast majority in the big Northern cities been voting Democratic in the past fifteen years or had they been voting Roosevelt? Had the conservative South been held only by the commanding Roosevelt personality?

The conviction that Truman was a dead duck was due basically to a cliché, a generalization that political analysts had been proclaiming for some time—that the dissolution of the Roosevelt coalition was inevitable. Now that there was a strong radical movement in the North and a Southern revolt, it looked like *der Tag* had arrived, proving to analysts that they had been right all along. To a large extent, the swift decline in Truman's political strength was sophisticated political thinking which became ingrained in the public psychology. After a while, the premise for the certainty of Truman's defeat was forgotten, but the certainty remained—an *idée fixe*.

There was more mechanistic reasoning on the part of the analysts which seemed to foreordain the direction of the mass mind. The Republicans had won a resounding victory in the Congressional elections in 1946 and except for the Hayes-Tilden election of 1876 every time a party had lost control of Congress it lost the election two years afterward—in 1884, 1892, 1896, 1912, 1920, and 1932. Then, too, Democratic administrations had been in power for sixteen years; the longest previous span since the Civil War had been for eight years. Time and again political analysts wrote that it was only the war which had prevented a change of administration in 1940 and 1944—a statement that was as impossible to challenge as to substantiate.

Third parties have never survived in our history, but they have been responsible for electing Presidents, such as Lincoln in 1860 and Wilson in 1912. The Bull Moose Party in 1912, which polled twenty-seven per cent of the vote, and the La Follette Progressive Party in 1924, which polled seventeen per cent of the vote (it got five million votes, capturing Wisconsin, as well as displacing the Democratic Party as the runner-up in twelve States) have made impressive showings in recent times. Even the Populist vote in 1892 was nine per cent of the total and Debs had gotten as high as six per cent on the Socialist ticket.

Henry Wallace looked like the man to crack the Roosevelt coalition. His was a name with luster—his career included posts as Vice-President, Secretary of Agriculture, and Secretary of Commerce—he was far more closely identified with Roosevelt than Truman had ever been and could claim to be his spiritual heir. His antiwar and progressive stands were considered sure magnets for votes; his personality personified Americana. As William Harlan Hale, who worked for Wallace when he was editor of the *New Republic* and who resigned in protest when Wallace continued as a contributing editor of the magazine after the announcement of his candidacy, wrote: "Here is grass roots morality and intellectual eagerness, applied Christianity and a keenness to experiment, an unusual combination of Iowan folksiness and world ranging curiosity. Fighting militarism, monopoly, and race hatred, he embodied much of what was best in America's tradition."

At first, seasoned political observers scoffed at the new party. Democratic Senator Scott Lucas of Illinois said, "He won't get enough votes to wad a shotgun." Writer Frank Kent said that the only result would be that it would be easier for the regular parties to raise funds. Chicago machine chief Jake Arvey predicted that it would serve only to rally anticommunists, a shrewd observation.

But the Isacson victory had a ballooning effect on all assessments of his strength. In April, Marquis Childs said that a vote of ten million for Wallace was quite possible. As astute a politician as Jim Farley saw a minimum of six million votes. Soon after he launched his candidacy Wallace had said that he would withdraw "if either of the major parties should become a peace . . . party before the election." Wallace himself did not consider that a real possibility and had no thought of withdrawing. Some of his lieutenants like Robert Kenny of California had hoped that he would merely try to stop Truman from getting the Democratic nomination. But after the Isacson triumph all chance of withdrawal was gone. In the *New Republic* of April 19 it was stated, "The new party has raised its sights. Ten million votes seem so clearly in view to the Wallaceites that they have decided to try for twenty million."

More closely examined, the Isacson victory should not have been as disheartening to the Democrats as it was. The pessimism overlooked some features of the election—the fact that the radical American Labor Party was more effective in special elections than in general elections. The 24th was the most strongly ALP district in New York except for the Brownsville District. The victory, moreover, was unique, since there was no chance in this district that a split in the Democratic vote could elect a Republican candidate. Therefore, a most effective argument for voting Democratic, to prevent a Republican from being elected, could not be used.

The Wallace movement turned out to be a fiasco in the end because of the elements behind it and because of the vulnerability of the man himself. We shall discuss the Wallace movement in greater detail in a later chapter. Here we shall point out that the new party put its main emphasis on foreign policy. On May 29, 1948, the Communist National Committee openly took credit for the party in a draft resolution for its national convention released through the *Daily Worker*: "The Communist Party was the only force in American political life which instantly grasped the whole reactionary imperial essence of the Marshall Plan. . . . Acting upon this understanding, it boldly proclaimed the need for such a new party."

Before this, on April 28 at a Convention of the Textile Workers Union, Phil Murray, head of the CIO, denounced the Wallace party and said that its inception was at a Communist Party meeting in October 1947. He gave no details. The Washington *Post* ran a lead article by Alfred Friendly on May 2, which may have gotten its facts from Murray's source. Friendly said that the Wallace campaign was a Moscow inspiration to foment labor opposition to the Marshall Plan. On October 15, 1947, the CIO, after listening to a speech by Secretary Marshall, had endorsed the broad principle of the Marshall Plan. A few days afterward, there was a meeting of the Communist Central Committee with William Z. Foster as chairman, Eugene Dennis, executive secretary, and John Williamson, chief official for labor, which decided that an attempt should be made to force the CIO to reverse its stand. This was followed by a December 15 meeting of Communist-minded unions around New York, in which the most active member was Robert Thompson, chairman of the New York party. There the die was cast for the Progressive Citizens of America to call on Wallace to head the new party in a Presidential contest.

An example of Communist pressure was the experience of Mike Quill, head of the Transport Workers Union. After expressing his admiration of Wallace, he got a call from Eugene Dennis asking his support for the party. He said no, it would split his union. He then got a call from Foster, who said that a split was in line with his objective, to form a federation of the United Electrical Workers, the Maritime Union, and the Transport Workers. When Quill still said no, he faced a Communist-led revolt in his union.

Far from winning labor support as expected, the Wallace

candidacy was to solidify labor in the camp of Truman. Within a month of his candidacy, the CIO voted on the Wallace party. Phil Murray asked what Wallace had done for labor at crucial cabinet meetings. He accused the leftists of political dishonesty, saying that he had been denounced for advocating Roosevelt's renomination in 1940 but they had "put a halo around my head" after the Germans invaded Russia. The vote was thirty-one to eleven against the third party and the board then voted approval of the European Recovery Plan. Harry Bridges said that Truman didn't have the chance of a snowball in hell to be elected and that he would continue to fight for Wallace. He was thereupon ousted as regional director in northern California for the CIO, which started an energetic crackdown against dissident locals.

Prominent liberals turned their backs on Wallace. He was denounced in a statement by the Americans for Democratic Action and was deserted by Dr. Frank Kingdon, Max Lerner, Raymond Walsh, Mrs. Roosevelt, and even the newspaper *PM*, which had built him up. Walter Reuther, who had just become president of the United Auto Workers on an anti-Communist platform, denounced him as an "agent of Stalin." The powerful Amalgamated Clothing Workers deserted the radical American Labor Party in New York, which gave Wallace its support. Al Whitney brought 220,000 members of the Brotherhood of Railroad Trainmen back into the Democratic fold. In 1946, after Truman had appeared before Congress and asked for a draft of railroad workers to prevent a strike, Whitney had denounced Truman as a "political accident," and pledged millions of dollars to defeat him. Now there was a peace meeting in the White House to the evident delight of Democratic Chairman McGrath. This lack of labor support might have been expected to dispel the fear among Democrats and the conclusion of analysts that the Wallace bolt might cost the election. But the idea had become deeply rooted.

The Wallace movement had a close connection with the Southern disaffection. Truman's civil-rights message was motivated, in part at least, by a desire to offset Wallace's appeal to the Negroes. The timing of the message suggests it, and Wallace believed it himself.

The attempt on the part of the Truman Administration to head off the Wallace bolt ignited smoldering resentment among Southern Democrats who felt that their loyalty had been too long taken for granted. If Truman was willing to cater to Wallace in his shift to the left in his State-of-the-Union Message, then why should he not be willing to strike a bargain with the Southerners on civil rights? The Wallace bolt might make the time ripe for a bargain to restore the two-thirds rule which formerly gave the South a veto power over the Democratic nominee at the convention. At the Wakulla Springs meeting of the Southern governors in February Governor Caldwell of Florida remarked that the South's troubles started in 1936 "when we laid our necks on the log and gave up the two-thirds rule." Governor Folsom of Alabama said that since the rule change "we have been treated down here as stepchildren. The Democrats know they have got us and the Republicans know they can't get us."

Democratic Chairman McGrath saw the connection. After his meeting with the four Southern governors in February, he said to his publicity chief, Jack Redding, "They see in the present situation, with Wallace already an avowed third-party candidate and with the Palestine situation hurting us so deeply, an opportunity to make us bow to their will."

There was another factor that played a part in the calculations. If the Democrats were sure to lose because of the Wallace bolt, then the real issue was one of party control. At the end of February Senator George of Georgia sat calmly amid the ruckus and said that it would be possible to reorganize the party after the 1948 election on the basis of "sound principles and good government."

Politically it would have been suicidal for Truman to repudiate his civil-rights message or show any willingness to retreat. The report of the President's Committee had been greeted with wild enthusiasm among Negroes. The Baltimore *Afro-American* called it "one of the most significant documents of all time." The Pittburgh *Courier* said, "It will be on the basis of the committee report and recommendations that candidates will be weighed, Democratic or Republican." Walter White, executive secretary of the NAACP said the report was "the most uncompromising and specific pronouncement by a Government agency on the explosive issue of racial and religious bigotry. . . . The report puts Congress and particularly the Republican-Southern Democratic bloc squarely on trial."

A book written by H. L. Moon on the Negro vote and published in early 1948 told the story in its title, *Balance of Power*. He estimated that in at least seventy-five Congressional districts in eighteen northern and border states the Negro votes could be the decisive factor. In the 1944 election the 50,000 votes which Baltimore Negroes cast for Roosevelt were more than double the 22,500 votes by which he carried the state. Negro voters of five New Jersey cities cast 28,700 votes for him, more than his plurality of 26,450. Negro voters gave him a margin of 52,000 votes in Philadelphia and Pittsburgh, half of his winning margin in the state. Truman needed to keep that Negro vote in 1948.

[II]

TRUMAN FIGHTS BACK

IN THE DARK DAYS in the spring of 1948, Dr. H. H. Brummall, a dentist of Salisbury, Missouri, wrote to Truman urging him to withdraw. Truman replied, "I was not brought up to run from a fight. A great many of you Democrats in 1940 ran after a certain governor who was trying to cut my throat and he didn't do it successfully. They are not going to succeed this time either."

This was an expression of the President's credo in putting up a good fight. On another occasion he said, "I do not scare easily," and again, "I do not depress." His fighting spirit came through during his trip through Arizona in June when he said that the best epitaph he knew was in Tombstone, "Here lies Jack Williams. He done his damndest." Truman added that whenever a man does the best he can, then that is all he can do.

He had in the past been considered a hopeless underdog and had emerged on top. In the Brummall letter, he was referring to the fight for the nomination to the Senate in 1940 in which Governor Stark was his chief opponent. In a three-way contest, Truman was considered a sure loser, but pulled it out by a small margin. He mentioned this often. In Forrestal's diary, after the Presidential election, we have this passage, "The President recited tonight a most interesting analogy of the 1948 election. He recalled that in 1940, when he was up for renomination as Senator from Missouri, he attended a meeting in St. Louis at which a number of Democratic Party leaders tried to dissuade him from entering the primary contest on the ground that he could not possibly be elected. He said he listened to them until three o'clock in the morning at which time he announced he would go into the primary and wage the best campaign he knew how even if the result was only a single vote, which would be his own, cast for him."

The President viewed the picture with more perspective than the frightened party members. His personal popularity, which was high at the time he succeeded Roosevelt, was at its nadir by the time of the 1946 Congressional elections when it was felt that for the good of the party he should stay discreetly in the wings. His popularity had bounced back sharply during the succeeding year. Now his popularity had plummeted again, but there could be another rebound. Confidants said that he compared the situation to that of Lincoln, who was implored repeatedly in early 1864 to withdraw from the fight for re-election on the ground that it was a hopeless battle.

He was confident that he could not be denied renomination. In his *Memoirs,* he writes that a President is able to get a renomination if he so desires. "When the President is sitting in the White House, the National Convention of his party has never gone against his recommendations in the choice of a candidate or in the formation of a platform on which that convention is to operate." He repeated that statement to Adlai Stevenson in early 1952 when he offered him the Presidential nomination.

History refutes that statement. Of the six Vice-Presidents who had succeeded by death to the Presidency, only two had been renominated—Coolidge and Theodore Roosevelt. As for the influence of the President, Grover Cleveland was not for the nomination of William Jennings Bryan or for free silver in the platform of 1896.

In the twentieth century, as contrasted with the nineteenth century, Presidents have been able to control the party conventions. Truman writes only of the power to name the chairman and control the machinery of the convention, but strangely does not mention the patronage, multiplied many times in modern times, which gives the President control of the party machinery through the hierarchy down to the lowliest precinct worker, and enables him to corral delegates to the convention. There is a stronger accent today, too, on the President as the party's political leader, and it becomes more dangerous to dump him and thereby repudiate the record of the party. For modern times there is little doubt of the accuracy of Truman's conclusion, "When I had made up my mind to run, those in the party who turned against me could do nothing to prevent it."

Those who are awed with Truman's political skill in the 1948 campaign should bear in mind that the challenge to Harry Truman was a challenge to an old professional on the grounds he knew best. His trade was politics. For twenty-five years before he went to the Senate, Truman had toiled in the precincts of a big-city machine. In the Senate he was a protégé of Senator Wheeler who was Chairman of the Interstate and Foreign Commerce Committee. Wheeler says that Truman claimed special knowledge on only two subjects—he had read books on military history and strategy and claimed to know about that, and he claimed to know politics. In expressing disgust with nonelected officials in the Administration, he would say, "What do they know about elections; what do they know about getting votes?" Senator Russell sat next to Truman for years and had many talks with him on the subject of politics. He says that Truman showed a profound understanding of the subject, particularly bloc voting. That is high tribute from one of the Senate's most brilliant minds.

Chairman McGrath, also a fine politician, says that he was convinced from the beginning that the election could be won only by grabbing the states in the North with the big electoral votes. The Democrats had to gamble that the South would go along. Thus, the civil-rights message. Truman and McGrath were confident that the South would not break away. Surely the Southern leaders in Congress would not risk the loss of their seniority rights and patronage. In 1928 there was a grassroots rebellion against the Catholic, Tammany, anti-prohibitionist Al Smith, but the state democratic organizations remained firm and after the election punished the deserters. The election of 1928 was a lesson to the South, too, that one could not count on a "controlled avalanche" since many Democratic Congressional and local posts were lost in Southern states which went for Hoover.

As for Henry Wallace, there is agreement among Truman intimates that from beginning to end they were not frightened about him no matter how much the threat was blown up in newspapers by political experts and sources outside the Administration. On domestic matters his vote appeal would be matched by the appeal that the Administration would have made anyway in the normal course of events in order to get the big-city vote. Clark Clifford, Truman's legal adviser and chief speech-writer, denies that the State-of-the-Union Message was influenced by the Wallace candidacy. The approach had been worked out weeks before. The Democratic Party had nowhere to go but in the New Deal direction. On the foreign side, Wallace was a positive asset since he gave the President a perfect opportunity to emphasize his own anti-communist position, which was sure to win votes.

The international situation and the President's handling of it strengthened the President's political position. A violent Soviet coup in Czechoslovakia on February 24 shocked the Western world. A model Democratic country from World War I had suddenly become a Soviet satellite. Representatives from the small, helpless state of Finland were ordered to Moscow for negotiations for a new treaty. It seemed that Russia was moving up its timetable for taking over Western Europe. A crucial election was to take place in Italy in April and a Communist victory there would outflank Greece and imperil our lifeline to our Mid-East oily supply.

Not only did the country have a spell of war jitters, but there was genuine fear of war within the Administration itself. Forrestal reveals that on March 5 a top-secret telegram from General Clay in Berlin said, "I have felt a subtle change in Soviet attitude which I cannot define but which gives me a feeling that it [war] may come with dramatic suddenness." On March 16 the Central Intelligence Agency was able to give the President only a tenuous assurance of peace, an estimate from the State Department and the Armed Services that war was not probable within the next sixty days. Congress was alarmed. A young Congressman who was to come into public attention in 1948, Richard Nixon, urged that Congress by resolution should "give solemn warning to the conspiracy in the Politburo that any further step of aggression, internal or external, will be resisted by every means at our disposal."

The President had planned to urge Universal Military Training at a St. Patrick's day dinner engagement he had on March 17, but when Secretary Marshall said this was not a proper forum and the Joint Chiefs insisted on a revival of Selective Service, he decided to appear before Congress.

On March 17 the President addressed a Joint Session of Congress and, eschewing diplomatic niceties, for the first time identified Russia by name as a "growing menace." "The Soviet Union and its agents have destroyed the independence and democratic character of a whole series of nations in Eastern and Central Europe. . . ." Russia has "actively sought to prevent" peace. . . . "The will for peace must be backed by the strength for peace. . . . There are times in world history when it is far wiser to act than to hesitate." The President urged that the European Recovery Program be rushed through Congress without further delay, and that Congress enact a new draft and Universal Military Training. The message was effective in sounding the tocsin of national alarm. Congress responded by rushing through the Marshall Plan by April 2 with an authorization of over $6 billion for the next twelve months. Passage came only one day after the deadline that the Administration had fixed. Sixteen days later the crucial Italian elections, to our intense relief, went against the Communist parties.

The presence of Henry Wallace in the fray was beginning to pay political dividends. A contest of ideas is always more comprehensible and dramatic when the ideas are embodied in living forms. *Voila l'ennemi.* The sentiment of the country was crystallized behind Truman's firm anti-Communist stand and against Wallace as the exponent of the Communist line. For some time Truman had ignored the existence of Wallace, but then shot from the hip when it counted most. Wallace says that Truman got votes throughout 1948 by using him as a convenient "lightning rod."

After his message to Congress Truman flew to New York to review the St. Patrick's day parade, the first time a President had done so. That night he brought 2800 Sons of St. Patrick to wild applause when he interjected in his prepared speech, "I will not accept the public support of Henry Wallace and his Communists." By that time there was no prospect that such support would be forthcoming. He chose an equally favorable forum for another animadversion to the enemy. Before a Greek fraternal society in New York, after being compared by the Chairman, Dean Alfange, to Demosthenes as an apostle of peace, Truman compared Wallace to Alcibiades, a Greek demagogue who tried to curry favor with the people but came to ultimate disaster. Wallace "ought to go to the country he loves so well and help them against his own country if that's the way he feels." All these attacks were welcomed by Paul Fitzpatrick, New York Democratic chief, who long had favored a direct assault on Wallace by name.

As an advocate Wallace was singularly inept. He blamed the Communist coup in Czechoslovakia on our US Ambassador Steinhardt. This was obviously impossible, since Steinhardt did not return to Czechoslovakia until February 19 and the grab began on February 17. Apart from the dates, Steinhardt seemed to be unaware of what was going on in Czechoslovakia and, in fact, had stated that Communism had no roots there. When Wallace was called to book on the physical impossibility that Steinhardt could have been responsible by his presence, Wallace answered that Steinhardt's expressed hope that the country could benefit from the Marshall Plan was a "provocative statement." Then Wallace adopted the Communist line that far from a retaliatory action by Russia, the event was a purely internal move to prevent a rightist coup. The suicide on March 10 of Foreign Minister Jan Masaryk, son of the founder of the Republic and former Ambassador to the United States, was news that was profoundly shocking here. Wallace surmised that the suicide may have been due to cancer four days after the *Daily Worker* took that line.

Originally Wallace had been in favor of the Marshall Plan. It "sounded good to me when it was delivered." It was "what I have been advocating all along," but when Russia turned down our offer of aid, he turned, too, and found that it was "designed to hem Russia in." In the January 12 issue of the *New Republic* he said, "Greek children still cry for milk while the American-trained Greek army parades the severed heads of Greek guerillas through the streets. The peoples of the world must see that there is another America than the Truman-led, Wall Street dominated, military-backed group that is blackening the name of American democracy all over the world. . . . The so-called European Recovery Program is a plan to interfere in the social, economic, and political affairs of countries receiving aid. We are saying 'We will help you if you have our kind of government, and subordinate your economy to ours.'" As a substitute for the Marshall Plan, Wallace backed a world relief plan to be administered through the United Nations and with no strings attached. Russia and her satellites having suffered the worst damage in the war would get the lion's share.

Wallace became more stinging in his criticism of the strong foreign policy of the Administration during the early months of 1948 when the nation appeared to face a deadly danger abroad. Testifying before a House committee in late February, he claimed that the Marshall Plan was backed by "big bankers, monopolists, and militarists." After the President's message, Wallace attacked the men who were running our Government: "They have recognized the peoples of the world are on the march. They know that the peoples of France, Italy, Czechoslovakia, yes, and the people of China and Greece want to try a new approach. They are afraid of this demand for change. They are standing against it." Later, before the Senate Armed Services Committee, he said that "the security of the United States is not threatened except from Washington." The Truman program was breeding a "deliberately created crisis" and "death and taxes for the many and very handsome profits for the few." At a third party conference in April in Chicago he condemned "the efforts of our Government to interfere in the April 18 election [in Italy] and to dictate the outcome."

Senator Glen Taylor had become the running mate of Wallace. He said that he was going to reject the bid until Jim Landis had been fired. Then he said he would consult historian Charles Beard "to get his ideas from the way history is going as to whether war is likely sooner or not." Finally, he announced his decision to bolt. "I am not leaving the

Democratic Party. It left me. Wall Street and the military have taken over."

Stalin showed his interest in the American election in May. Moscow announced that Russia had accepted an American offer for a discussion to settle difficulties between the two nations. There was a misunderstanding and Truman denied that the United States had made such an offer categorically, saying that differences must be settled in the United Nations. Ambassador Bedell Smith had merely acted on his instructions to express our hopes for an accommodation between the two powers. General Marshall said, "General Smith did not ask for any general discussion or negotiation. We had a long and bitter experience with such efforts." Russia would have to have a change of heart for talks to do any good.

But the subject was not dropped. Stalin personally announced that he was agreeable to an agenda for discussions contained in a letter to him from Wallace. "It is," said Stalin, "the most important document of recent times. . . . As far as the USSR is concerned it considers that Mr. Wallace's program could serve as a good and fruitful basis [for agreement]." A reference by the head of a state to a proposal by a private individual is extraordinary, not to speak of the glowing terms used by Stalin. Wallace himself seemed to be dazed at being recognized as a US spokesman. When the United States let Wallace down by again refusing talks, Wallace announced that it was proof General Marshall had decided to continue the cold war.

Were it not for the by-now ingrained conviction that Truman didn't stand a chance, it would have been evident that the President by his anti-Communist position was recovering a great deal of ground. Now Truman took an action which recouped some of the damage done when he had repudiated Palestine partition. The Jews in Palestine had taken matters into their own hands and, inflicting defeat after defeat on the Arabs, set up a state by force of arms and asked for recognition. The President overrode the State Department, which said that it was customary to wait for the new government to start to function. The request for recognition was supposed to come on May 14 simultaneously with the proclamation at 6:00 PM of the new state. It didn't arrive. The President waited impatiently only twenty minutes and then announced recognition at 6:20 PM. Eighteen hours later came the request for recognition.

That evening, at a meeting of Young Democrats, Chairman McGrath said, referring to the recognition, "God bless you for that," and Truman in his reply said, "During the next four years there will be a Democrat in the White House and you are looking at him."

Truman had taken the issue out of the hands of the State Department. The decision was made on the advice of Clark Clifford and Administrative Assistant David Niles. Truman shows considerable bitterness in his *Memoirs* toward the State Department, accusing elements within it of cottoning to the Arabs because of their oil reserves and of inclining to anti-Semitism. He quotes Under Secretary of State Robert Lovett as saying after the recognition, "They [the career men] almost put it over on you." He implies that he had been "sold" on the trusteeship idea which had been properly construed by the Jews as abandonment of partition, and was thus at odds with his real policy which was always in favor of partition. His statements on Palestine are clouded with inconsistency—thus, while arraigning the career officials of the State Department, Truman states the advantages of trusteeship in gaining time for a solution of the problem.

Truman's political thermometer nonetheless stayed at freezing. All popularity polls showed that his strength had disintegrated. The Gallup Poll, which in retrospect showed a marvelous capacity for mirroring widely held assumptions in statistics, put him behind Dewey and Stassen. Only thirty-six per cent of the people approved him as President compared with fifty-five per cent a few months before.

Southern Democrats, liberal and conservative, were proposing General Eisenhower as the Democratic nominee—in January Eisenhower had refused to allow his name to be entered in the New Hampshire Republican primary. Northern liberals were also getting behind Eisenhower. Two of Franklin D. Roosevelt's sons, Franklin, Jr., and Elliott; former OPA head Chester Bowles; leaders of the CIO, Phil Murray and Jim Carey; the Liberal Party in New York headed by Adolf Berle, which had previously promised Truman 400,000 votes; the Americans for Democratic Action, a recently formed organization of anti-Communist liberals of New Deal stripe—all were backing Eisenhower.

Enthusiasm was nowhere evident but only apathy or resentment that the party was saddled with this sure loser. At a Jefferson-Jackson Day dinner at Los Angeles National Chairman McGrath in his speech said that Truman was "trying to do what Franklin D. Roosevelt is calling to him from heaven to perform. Can we ask for more than this in a leadership?" The crowd clanked silverware and roared back "Yes." McGrath finished amid boos. Then State Chairman James Roosevelt followed with a speech praising Eisenhower. At a fifty-dollar-a-plate dinner by the New York State Committee, aside from a toast to the President there was not a single allusion to him all evening.

But the President was getting the delegates from the party faithful, and that was what counted. On April 11 there was a meeting of delegates from eight Midwestern states which was supposed to ignite a prairie fire when the national committeeman from Kansas was to put forth the Eisenhower name—but it did not materialize and 156 delegates were pledged to Truman. Maine had given its delegates to Truman the day before. From there on it was a steady procession. By early May, of 620 delegates named, the President had 423 pledged to him, only 195 short of a majority and many of the unpledged could be expected to vote for him. Weeks before the convention Truman had the nomination in the bag.

We now come to a central theme of 1948—the President's vendetta with the Eightieth Congress. This was an arrant fiction contrived out of thin air by a master politician. Senator Russell says, "As a matter of fact, President Truman got along well with the Eightieth Congress. He got along with the Eightieth Congress about the same as he did with the Seventy-ninth and Eighty-first Congress," no better and no worse. But he sensed what Russell had discovered in his years in the Georgia state legislature, that the people distrust and are disposed to blame their elected legislative body collectively even though they have no fault to find with this or that member. Clifford says that at this time Truman was impressed with a facet of our constitutional government—that the President and Vice-President are the only two persons elected by the whole people and represent all the people—all others in this country are elected by sectional or "special" interests. Here we have two of the psychological bases from which the issue was launched into the political ether.

The explosion against the Eightieth Congress came suddenly in June. During the first five months of the session of 1948 from January through May, there were no signs of any unusual acrimony between the President and Congress, only the normal friction on domestic affairs. In April Congress passed over the President's veto a tax reduction bill of $4.7 billion. The President called it an "evil in disguise" and "inequitable" but, as the New York *Times* said, he had undercut his own position against the principle of tax relief by offering a tax cut of his own at the beginning of the session. Against the President's wishes for a three-year extension, the House was putting through a bill for a one-year extension of the Reciprocal Trade Agreements Act. He engaged in a fight against making available the loyalty file of Edward Condon, head of the National Bureau of Standards, whom the House Un-American Activities Committee called the "weakest link in our security"; the House had passed a bill to compel the Executive to produce information demanded by Congress.

The President waved a red flag in the face of Congress when he sent to the Senate a five-year reappointment of the controversial David Lilienthal as head of the Atomic Energy Commission; a one-year appointment would have been acceptable to Lilienthal. In a nonpartisan vote Congress jammed down the throat of the Administration a seventy-group Air Force raised from the previous fifty-five group Air Force. In the House there were only three "nay" votes and two of them were from Marcantonio and Isacson, Wallace supporters.

The fireworks began when the President set off on June 3 in the eighteen-car *Presidential Special* on a cross-country jaunt. The ostensible purpose was to accept an honorary degree at the University of California, but the President in passing through eighteen strategic states was to make five major speeches, in Chicago, Omaha, Seattle, Berkeley, and Los Angeles. It was labeled as a nonpolitical trip, and as proof, Chairman McGrath was not to be on the train; since it was nonpolitical it was not to be defrayed by the impoverished Democratic National Committee, but from the Presidential expense account. "If I felt any better, I couldn't stand it," said the President as the train pulled out.

The timing of the trip was certainly injudicious if the President wanted to prod accomplishments from Congress, since he was not slated to return until June 18, the day before scheduled adjournment. Senator Vandenberg, who had carried a major burden in getting the Marshall Plan through Congress and was now trying to prevent a slash of twenty-five per cent in the appropriation for the first year of the European Recovery Plan, criticized Truman for "a self-serving political vacation at a moment when the whole Government should be on the job in Washington." The Washington *Post* editorialized, "To have the President himself extending the period of interparty strife by making a campaign tour in early June seems particularly out of keeping with his responsibilities."

Poinier in The Detroit Free Press

"Daily Workout."

It did not take long for politics to become the first order of business. At Pittsburgh, Mayor David Lawrence, national committeeman for Pennsylvania, boarded the train; at Crestline, Ohio, the President quipped with the crowd about "this nonpartisan, bi-partisan trip we are making," and expressed hope that former Governor Frank Lausche, beside him, would be successful in his race in November for the governorship; in Indiana Frank McHale, national committeeman, and former Governor Henry Schricker, a candidate for the governorship in November, got aboard; in Chicago he conferred with the political powers of the state, Senator Lucas, Mayor Kennelly, and Jake Arvey. Press Secretary Charlie Ross now explained that the nonpolitical part of the trip was the fact that no speech was to be delivered under political auspices.

Truman was making many impromptu rear-platform speeches. After making a prepared speech to the American Society of Newspaper Editors in April, he had spoken for twenty minutes off the cuff on foreign-policy problems and it had gone over big. It was discovered that the President was dull in his canned speeches, but he packed plenty of punch when he talked extemporaneously. On this trip the President showed the remarkable folksiness and local appeal that was to mark his Presidential campaign speeches. In Idaho he spoke of the GI confined to barracks for refusing to peel Maine potatoes and in California he said of the sunshine, "This is the real thing. It makes Florida look like thirty cents." (Floridians retorted that he was talking in terms of the Truman dollar worth thirty cents.)

At every stop on the way West, Truman would tell his audience he was on his way "fur to get me a degree." In one talk he made an enigmatic statement which reporters interpreted as a reference to his link to Pendergast. "If they can prove it on you, you are in a bad fix, indeed. They have never been able to prove it on me." Thereupon, columnist Tom Stokes wrote a ditty which became a theme song of the trip, to be sung to "Oh, Susanna."

> They can't prove nothing. They ain't got a thing on me,
> I'm going down to Berkley, fur to get me a degree.

At first the President was restrained if not diffident. He said, "They have been telling you a lot of things about your President, that he doesn't know what goes on, that he can't handle the Government . . . about my ability or inability, my intelligence or lack of it." He made the Eightieth Congress a target from the beginning, but the tone was moderate. At Gary, Indiana, he attacked it for not doing anything to curb the cost of living, in Chicago before a crowd celebrating the Pioneer Swedish Centennial he took Congress to task on its approach to the problem of admitting displaced persons. The speech was dull and Carl Sandburg on the platform fell asleep. In Omaha he was critical of Congressional inaction on farm measures.

At Omaha there was a real fiasco. Arrangements were entrusted for the rally to "Big Ed" McKim, a Battery D pal of the President, who was at odds with the local organization. Only 1200 persons showed up in the Ak-Sar-Ben Auditorium seating 12,000. The President seemed rattled when he appeared in the cavernous void facing acres of empty seats. Photos taken from the rear and widely reprinted in the press re-created the chilling experience, showing a small fringe around the President, and the rest darkness. Then the Democratic Chairman of Nebraska, William Ritchie, bolted Truman, claiming that he had gotten "the bum's rush." He said, "I am convinced that he cannot be elected. He has muffed the ball badly. He seems to prefer his so-called buddies to the persons who have done the work and put up the money for the party."

At Carey, Idaho, came the worst of the contretemps. In dedicating a local airport, the President had been badly briefed, was misled by the bunting and decorations, and misread "Wilma" for "William." He dedicated it to the "brave boy who died fighting for his country." When apprized that it was a girl, he said that he was "more honored to dedicate the airport to the young woman who bravely gave her life to her country." At this point he was told that the girl of sixteen had been killed in the crash of her sweetheart's plane while joyriding.

Such mishaps would try any man's soul. To observers the President's usually cheerful frame of mind seemed to desert him, and he became morose. It is plausible that there is a connection between these misfortunes and the aggressiveness and invective which characterized his attitude from this point on. Getting gifts of spurs and riding boots, he said he would use them to ride Congress. In Butte, Montana, he was greeted by a tremendous throng and said of Senator Taft, "I guess he'd let you starve. I'm not that kind." At Bremerton, Washington, he discarded all pretense of nonpolitics. "They're going to Philadelphia [for the convention] to tell you what a great Congress they have been. If you believe that you are a bigger sucker than I think you are."

In Spokane there was an impromptu interview which was historic. The interviewer was Rhea Felknor, a cub reporter on the Spokane *Spokesman Review,* getting his first by-line. Senator Magnuson handed Truman, on the observation platform of the train, a copy of the paper headlining the Butte reception. Felknor asked the President, "How does it feel to invade a Republican stronghold?" Felknor wrote Truman's answer this way:

> Raising his head to glare down on the lone newspaperman he asked, "Do you work for this paper, young man?" The President's voice became raspy for virtually the only time during his appearance here as he declared,
>
> "The Chicago *Tribune* and this paper are the worst in the United States. You've got just what you ought to have. You've got the worst Congress in the United States you've ever had. And the papers, this paper, are responsible for it."

The President enlarged on this thought during the day. The papers had contributed to this "worst" Congress by attacking previous Democratic Congresses. He hedged by conceding that the Thad Stevens Reconstruction Congress was the "worst," but then as he stood on the road overlooking Grand Coulee with Governor Wallgren he decided to stick to his first appraisal.

On June 11 Arthur Krock in the New York *Times* said that in the spring of 1946 Truman had referred to the Seventy-ninth Congress as "the worst since (President) Andrew Johnson's Congress." He had now found a new "worst." The epithets were now dismissed by Krock, "Nothing in the record of the Eightieth Congress as of the Seventy-Ninth justifies the scathing comparison" with the Reconstruction Congress in which President Johnson had been called on the House floor "that dead dog in the White House."

Truman kept blazing away, the crowds were enormous and local politicians told him that he had struck fire. He assumed the position of the fighting champion of the people against special privilege, a role he was to continue until election day. In Tacoma he said that Congress was "interested in the welfare of the better classes" and had passed a "rich man's tax bill." At Olympia he said, "If you want to continue the policies of the Eightieth Congress, it'll be your funeral." He built up a charge of Congressional antagonism toward the West, saying that the Republican Congress "believed in the theory of Daniel Webster that the West is no good and there is no use spending money on it."

At Berkeley, California, in a prepared commencement address before 50,000 he made a fine speech on foreign policy attacking Russia for its policies of "obstruction and aggression." Before he reached California, at Eugene, Oregon, he made a *faux pas* of which he was to be frequently reminded. In an impromptu speech he said of Stalin, "I like old Joe. He's a decent fellow but he's a prisoner of the Politburo."

In Los Angeles a million people greeted him between the railroad station and the Ambassador Hotel. After Dinah Shore sang, "You Made Me Love You," he made a speech demanding the enactment of price controls and social-welfare measures. State Chairman James Roosevelt had second thoughts about supporting Eisenhower, saying after his speech, "He hit the Republicans where it hurts." At San Bernardino, Truman accepted a gift of eggs. He said that he appreciated them in view of the high cost of living, but "I wouldn't throw *fresh* eggs at Bob Taft." At Albuquerque, he promised a crowd, "I'll keep pouring it on." In several places on the return trip the President reiterated his theme. "There is just one big issue. It is the special interests against the people, and the President, being elected by all the people, represents the people."

This preview of the election campaign impressed most observers as vaudeville rather than statesmanship, as the comments of the two leading Washington papers which were friendly to Truman indicated. The Washington *Evening Star* said, "The President in this critical hour is making a spectacle of himself on a political junket that would reflect discreditably on a ward heeler." The Washington *Post* said, "It would not be surprising if Democratic chieftains were beginning to echo that apt Goldwynism, 'He should have stood in bed.' "

The reaction of individual members of Congress to the label of "worst" was "so are you." Republican Majority Leader Halleck said, "There are a lot of people who find Truman is the poorest President since George Washington," and Congress had gotten from him the "worst cooperation" in the history of the Presidency. In the House, Representative Cliff Clevenger of Ohio said, "High-tax Harry, like a nasty little gamin, has dropped his hands in the mud and dirt and planted it all over our new buggy. There will be some Congress-tanned Missouri jackass hide on the Christmas market come November." Democratic leader Rayburn rose to call this an "amazing" remark and Representative Lawrence Smith, a Republican of Wisconsin, said that he felt Rayburn was right.

"We ought not to sink to his [Truman's] level." Senate Chaplain Peter Marshall seemed to be talking topically, as he often did, when he prayed, "Since we shall be judged for every idle word, let us speak carefully with a deep respect for the truth that cannot be twisted." He reminded the Senate of "the record that has eternal implications far beyond the next election."

Senator Taft, if he did not coin it, at least publicized the campaign term "whistlestopping." In a speech on June 11 to the Union League in Philadelphia, he said that Truman should not go "blackguarding Congress at every whistle station." In view of Truman's attitude toward Congress, "There is little use in our working day and night to complete constructive programs." The Democratic National Committee thereupon wired twenty-three places where the President talked, asking their reactions to Taft's use of "whistle stop." Civic pride was wounded. "Very poor taste," said the Mayor of Gary, and "The term hardly applies," said the Mayor of Los Angeles.

The battle with Congress reached a high pitch on the legislative as well as the polemic front. Congress passed three bills over the President's veto in the last week of the session, the Reed-Bulwinkle bill to exempt rail-rate agreements from the antitrust laws, a bill to transfer the United States Employment Agency from the Labor Department to the Federal Security Agency, and a bill to exempt 750,000 salesmen and independent contractors from social security. Three Presidential vetoes overridden in four days are an all-time record. There were seven bills passed over his veto in the whole of Truman's first Administration and five in the second. "The fact that Truman was off politicking 3,000 miles away did not help matters," commented the liberal *New Republic*. The bill to transfer the US Employment Service was an appropriation bill carrying $975,000,000—a veto of an appropriation bill is rare and Truman must have counted on an overriding of the veto.

There was a rush of business facing Congress in its closing days. Including the special session of the previous November, Congress had been at work for seven months, and the pace was tiring. Senate Chaplain Peter Marshall intoned on June 12, "We are only human. We grow tired." The Saturday

Justus in The Minneapolis Star

June 19 deadline had to be met because of the Republican Convention the following Monday. In the middle of May Speaker Martin had suggested that Congress return after the two political conventions and Senator Taft had suggested returning between the two conventions. The Republican House Steering Committee rejected the idea on June 10—so what could be done had to be done quickly. It was an error that the Republicans would rue.

A House move by conservative Republicans to slash the appropriation for the newly formed Economic Cooperation Administration below the authorized figure of $6 billion for the next fiscal year was defeated because of a fight by leading liberal Republicans. Senator Vandenberg said that its effect would be "to repeal by indirection." On June 11 the Senate passed Senate Resolution 239, the Vandenberg Resolution, sixty-four to four, marking the end of American isolation forever. The United States would enter into regional security pacts under Article 51 of the UN Charter "based on continuous and effective self-help and mutual aid." This was the foundation for NATO.

Through the night of June 19 and the following morning, Congress worked to put finishing touches on pending legislation. Bills were enacted calling for a new draft of men between the ages of nineteen and twenty-five, admitting 205,000 displaced persons from Europe in the next two years, extending fixed farm supports for one year and then introducing a sliding farm-support system, creating a secondary market for home mortgages. The House, which was ahead of the Senate, had a short recess, and then a carnival atmosphere and high-jinks reigned on the floor. The Senate remained in continuous session for forty-three and one-half hours, the galleries were jammed with men and women in evening dress until, at 7:00 AM in early dawn, the Senate finished and the Eightieth Congress closed up shop.

In signing bills passed by Congress, Truman did not spare the rod. In signing a pay-raise bill for Federal employees, he called the inequities "ridiculous" and said "The Act meets neither the needs of the employees nor those of the Government." In an appropriation for the TVA he called a refusal to include $4 million extra for its steam generator plant a "reckless and irresponsible decision," pointing out that TVA supplies Oak Ridge. In signing a bill to extend the term of AEC Commissioners for two years, he said, "Politics and atomic energy do not mix. . . . The refusal of the GOP leadership to put the public interest first, invests the Atomic Energy Program with an aura of uncertainty and party politics." The farm bill only went "part of the way to meet the needs of American agriculture." In signing the housing bill, the President said that Congress had "failed miserably" to meet housing needs.

The elemental struggle between good and evil has been portrayed through the ages in many contexts and many climes. Harry Truman recognized that to be effective this struggle must show absolute good waging war against absolute evil. He was drawing the battle line in terms of light and darkness between himself and the now-famous Eightieth Congress.

[III]

DEWEY WINS OUT OVER STASSEN AND TAFT

As Truman slid downhill, the Republican nomination appeared to be tantamount to election. The struggle for the nomination is, in essence, the chronicle of the rise and fall of Harold Stassen. This introduces the first "if" of many in the 1948 story, since it is widely believed in the Republican Party that if Stassen had been nominated, he would have been elected.

At the outset the leading candidates were Governor Dewey and Senator Taft with Stassen as the underdog contender. Opinion polls showed that popular sentiment within the party was far stronger for General Eisenhower than for any of the other candidates. Defense Secretary Forrestal sat next to Dewey at a dinner in New York on October 14, 1947, and recorded in his diary, "He is obviously concerned about General Eisenhower's candidacy and certain that he, Eisenhower, could dispose of it very quickly if he wanted to and cited Marshall's action. He said Ike was obviously campaigning." However, the General on January 23, 1948, wrote a strong letter to Leonard V. Finder, publisher of the Manchester *Union-Leader,* that he was removing himself from the New Hampshire primary, in which his name had been entered, and from the entire race. This cleared the road for the other contestants. On March 9 in the New Hampshire primary, Dewey won six delegates to two for Stassen. It was to be Dewey's last victory for a long time.

Then Stassen came to the fore.

The first big primary was in Wisconsin on April 6. The overwhelming favorite was General MacArthur, a native son, who had allowed his name to be entered. MacArthur as proconsul in Japan, of course, could not campaign, although there was no doubt of his eagerness to win, and he had the support of former Governor Philip La Follette. Dewey originally had intended to do little or no campaigning, but he altered his plans and went to Wisconsin to make a few speeches. The Stassen campaign managed by Vic Johnston was an all-out attempt. Stassen received strong organization support from Senator Joseph McCarthy and Tom Coleman, the closest thing to a state boss. The primary as effectively disposed of General MacArthur as it had disposed of Wendell Willkie four years before. Stassen won ninteen delegates to eight for MacArthur, while Dewey got none.

The next primary was in Nebraska on April 13. It was actually a popularity poll. All seven potential candidates were entered without their say-so in a free-for-all—Stassen, Dewey, Taft, Warren, MacArthur, Joe Martin, and Senator Vandenberg. Three of those entered, Stassen, Dewey, and Taft, electioneered seriously. Taft was persuaded by Senator Butler to make a campaign since the Butler organization was so strong in the state. Taft found that the support was not transferable.

As in Wisconsin, Stassen here had another effective campaign manager, Fred Seaton (now Secretary of the Interior). Stassen had toured the state from one end to the other, laying the groundwork for victory many months before. His "Paul Revere Riders," buttonholing and pleading, swarmed over the state from neighboring states in such droves that Senator Butler protested against the "dramatic and extravagant circus tactics of the Minnesota carpetbaggers." Stassen won easily, polling forty-three per cent of the vote to thirty-five per cent for Dewey and eleven per cent for Taft.

In the primary in Pennsylvania on April 27, no candidates were entered, but 74,000 wrote in Stassen's name to 41,000 write-ins for Dewey.

At this point Stassen was being hailed as the Republican Lochinvar from the West. The Gallup Poll, as in the case of Truman, did a remarkable flip-flop. On March 28 it had shown thirty-four per cent of Republicans for Dewey to fifteen per cent for Stassen, but it registered less than a month later an amazing advance for Stassen, putting him in the lead. *Business Week* in its issue of April 17 began its Washington news pages, "Your Next President: Harold Stassen. Two months before Philadelphia, six months before Election Day, it looks as if you can say that."

Stassen seemed to have captured the public imagination. The elements of Stassen's success as a candidate resided partly in the man himself—he was young, only forty-one, and appealed to young veterans. His drive and physical massiveness betokened strength and purpose. He seemed to possess the charisma of a leader, attracting to him young lieutenants with dedicated zeal. He was an internationalist suiting the temper of the times, having served as a delegate to the first United Nations conference in San Francisco in 1945 and having been one of the first to advocate large-scale foreign aid. He seemed to be bold and forthright, as the title of his book, *Where I Stand,* proclaimed. In the age of anxiety when there was a deep distrust of politicians, here was a new, unorthodox, and forceful personality who exuded the confidence to cope with the problems of the times.

His success was also due to hard campaigning which dwarfed all previous campaign drives. He had made a career of campaigning, crisscrossing the country in his personal DC-3 equipped with mimeograph machines, press aides, and other paraphernalia. Bryan covered 18,000 miles in his frenzied drive for election in 1896. Stassen announced himself as a candidate in December, 1946, and from that time up to April, 1948, *Newsweek* computed that he had covered 160,000 miles; in 476 days he had made 325 major addresses. His campaign was well financed. Possibly a million dollars went down the drain. Chief fund-raisers were two young Minnesotans, Al Lindley and George Crosby; wealthy Minnesota industrialist Dan Gainey was a heavy contributor and contributions came from New York sources including John Hay Whitney and Alfred Vanderbilt. Then there were dollars collected by "Neighbors for Stassen," "Paul Revere Riders for Stassen," "Lawyers for Stassen," "Doctors for Stassen," etc.

Why did this massive effort fail? The answer to this lies in the man himself. His vaulting ambition overreached itself.

There are few men who from early years are continuously animated by a fixed purpose. There are few indeed whose fixed purpose is to become President of the United States. One of these few was Harold Stassen. In 1938 he reached the first step in his goal when he was elected Governor of Minnesota at the age of thirty-one, the youngest governor in the country. He was a good governor but no starry-eyed liberal. The *Nation* said, reviewing his record, "He has managed to combine in a remarkable degree liberalism in the abstract with conservatism in the concrete." Minneapolis had been strife-torn for years and he was responsible for a harsh anti-strike law which required ten days' notice of a strike and then a thirty-day cooling-off period. Labor claimed he had catered to business by lowering the iron-ore tax to which the Mesabi iron-ore interests had objected.

In 1940 a significant incident occurred. He was anxious to be keynote speaker at the Republican Convention. He promised Dewey that if he would back him for keynote speaker, he would give his delegation to Dewey. He promised the Taft side that if he were the keynoter he would take no part in the selection of the nominees. On the eve of the convention he stunned Dewey when he told him that he was delivering the delegation to Wendell Willkie. After the keynote speech he stunned the Taft people when he became Willkie's floor leader. This was never forgotten by professional politicians. In 1948 he needed to score smashing victories in the primaries to overcome their distaste for him.

He was re-elected in 1940. In 1942 when he ran again, he told the voters that if elected he would resign to enter the armed services and Ed Thye, who was running for Lieutenant-Governor, would serve. This was the "unorthodox," a Stassen trade-mark. While he was in the Navy he ran against Willkie in the Wisconsin primary in 1944. Previously, he had pained Willkie with sharp comments on his book, *One World,* when he reviewed it for the New York *Times,* and now Willkie felt that his poor showing in Wisconsin, which finished his candidacy, was due to Stassen's turning against him. In the days before his death Willkie was bitter about his erstwhile supporter.

After he left the Navy Stassen took counsel as to his future. The logical thing to do was to run for the Senate in 1946, but he decided against it and let Ed Thye have the seat. Stassen says in explanation that his talents are as an administrator, not a legislator. Others say that it did not consort with his ambitions to be a lowly freshman Senator. Instead he chose to be a self-appointed evangel for internationalism, a "liberal" ready to do battle with the Old Guard of the party, and a *pater familias* of the party. In the last-named role in 1946 he backed a slate of sixty new faces for the Eightieth Congress, forty of whom won. Among these was Richard Nixon, for whom Stassen spoke at the Shrine Auditorium in Los Angeles.

And now in the spring of 1948 Stassen was on the road to the Presidency—but then came his mistakes. The first mistake occurred in Ohio. He chose to test his prowess in the May 4 primary against Senator Taft; he entered candidates for twenty-three out of fifty-three delegates, picking his spots carefully to cover the big city areas where labor was strong. The Taft people professed to be confident of victory but resented the prospect that the distinguished Ohioan would have to take time out from his duties in the Senate to campaign. Taft had contacted Stassen and in a long discussion at the Statler Hotel in Washington tried to persuade him not to run. Stassen would get few delegates, Taft said, and would alienate conservatives throughout the country, particularly by appearing to align himself with labor against Taft.

Robert Taft was completely without guile. When he told Stassen that he would lose in Ohio, that is what he believed. To Stassen it was only a confession of weakness and he determined to go ahead. In retrospect Stassen admits that, perhaps, the most serious error was in making the race only in selected districts. "Forthright" is the adjective that Stassen always associates with himself. Picking only the favorable districts was not "forthright," it was "tricky."

As soon as the Stassen troupe hit Ohio, they realized that they had made a mistake. Sentiment for Taft was evident everywhere, and they realized that their time would have been better spent working in the Oregon primary. Taft campaigned hard in Ohio, often for seventeen hours a day. His victory, while not overwhelming, stripped Stassen of the aura of invincibility. Stassen won only nine delegates; he had expected twelve at least. His lone candidate for delegate-at-large, a prestige name, former Chief Justice Carrington T. Marshall, trailed behind the nine candidates for Taft, a slate headed by Senator Bricker.

It was more than the vote that hurt Stassen in Ohio. Pitted against Taft, it was clear that Stassen tried too hard to play both sides of the fence. Taft had injured his chances for the nomination by an excess of candor in calling a spade a spade. By coming out against terminal leave pay he alienated the veterans' lobby; by suggesting at the Omaha Livestock Exchange in February that farm support prices should be reduced, he had alienated the farm lobby; and by co-authoring the Taft-Hartley law he had wittingly taken on the labor lobby. Expediency, to Taft, had to be subordinated to his feeling of responsibility. His outspokenness should be contrasted with the reticence of Dewey, who, though titular leader of the party, refused to take any stand on the burning issues of the day throughout 1947 on the ground that he was too busy in state affairs. In fact, he had urged Senator Ives of New York to stay off the Senate Labor Committee for fear of embarrassing him.

Taft pointed out that Stassen talked only in "general principles," that he had taken the easy way out by choosing not to run in Minnesota for Senator in 1946, that the business of translating "general principles" into legislation as a member of the Senate was quite a different matter from talking "general principles."

Stassen had written a book, *Where I Stand,* but it was difficult to find out where Stassen stood. His position on most matters, as one journalist put it, was "more than nothing but less than something." Columnist Tom Stokes reported that when Taft was asked how he stood on the Universal Military Training bill he said, "I'm against it"; when Stassen was asked the same question, he put himself on all sides of the issue.

Taft said, "Stassen thinks he is more liberal than I, but I've never found out what he thinks a liberal is." Again he said, "Everyone goes around calling himself a liberal. When he speaks of others as liberal, he means little except these so-called liberals agree with himself." Taft seemed justified in raising the question. Stassen favored a fifty-per-cent limit on the progressive income tax, a strange position for a liberal. Taft was successful in putting through the Senate in 1948 the Taft-Wagner-Ellender housing bill providing up to $160 million of Government funds a year to build 500,000 low-cost housing units. Stassen had taken the position in *Where I Stand* that "to subsidize housing is to tinker with the economic system. . . . Rent for the indigent should be handled just like every other facility needed by the indigent." The remedy would be more housing for the upper-income groups so that the poor could move into the premises vacated by them. Stassen claimed to be an internationalist, but he favored cutting off Marshall Plan aid to Britain unless it halted its nationalization ventures, a position never favored by Taft. Taft conceded that isolationism was dead and opposed only a "too lavish distribution of American dollars"; an unfriendly critic, the *New Republic,* said, "With Taft in vigorous opposition there would have been scant chance of any decent kind of European aid."

For Taft the meaning of liberalism was clear. It was freedom, which was a real issue. For all it meant lower taxes; for business it meant freedom from controls, for the worker and employer it meant the restoration of equality in collective bargaining, and for the union member freedom from union oppression. It meant equality of opportunity—thus, Taft changed his position and backed an aid-to-education bill which he pushed through the Senate. Too much government was bad. "You reach a diminishing point of return with government." The role of government was to guarantee decent minimums so that equality of opportunity should not be destroyed. After the Congressional session, *Time* magazine labeled Taft as a "progressive." (June 28th issue)

The primary in Oregon wrecked Stassen's hopes. Coming to Oregon on May 1, Dewey found his work cut out for him. Polls showed Stassen way ahead in the race for the twelve delegates; his barnstorming tactics had been a great crowd-pleaser on his previous tour. Dewey decided on an all-out effort, invading every hamlet, no matter how isolated, speaking at rural crossroads and wringing hands in hamburger stands. One journalist commented that Dewey was the greatest explorer of Oregon since Lewis and Clark.

Back in February a Madison political writer, Rex Karney

of the *Wisconsin State Journal,* had spoken to Stassen about a debate with Dewey. The idea would be to have it on the University of Wisconsin campus, with the huge Stassen tower-

Seibel in The Richmond Times-Dispatch

"The spirit of '48."

ing over his middle-sized opponent. Stassen went for the idea and challenged Dewey to debate on any of a long list of issues, including atomic energy, the Taft-Hartley law, strengthening the UN, and hydroelectric development. Dewey declined but the debate became an obsession with Stassen. He must debate with Dewey.

One day in early May at a Stassen war council in the Waldorf in New York a wire came from Dewey accepting the bid to debate in Oregon but "on conditions" set by Dewey. Stassen impetuously accepted. "But what are the conditions?" one of the Stassen advisers wanted to know. His question was brushed aside. When the conditions were announced, Stassen felt like withdrawing but was afraid the public would not understand. (In retrospect he thinks that it was a mistake not to withdraw.) Dewey had outfoxed him. The two conditions were that the debate was to be over the radio in a studio without an audience, and Dewey was to make the closing argument.

The subject of the debate was whether the Communist Party should be outlawed. In question-and-answer periods after speeches, encouraged by the applause, Stassen had nudged closer and closer to the position that the Communist Party should be outlawed, finally embracing it when he found that it seemed to go over big as in Nebraska. This was hardly in line with the mantle of the "liberal" that Stassen tried to wear. It was hard to reconcile with his opposition to the Taft-Hartley provision requiring anti-Communist affidavits. He said that the government was going too far in requiring them.

The debate was held on Station KEX in Portland on May 17, four days before the primary. Dewey ripped Stassen to shreds in the closing. Stassen's preparation was poor, he was dog-tired from his campaigning, and he was up against a better legalistic brain. Dewey scored with the argument that the proposal to outlaw Communists was un-American and it would be futile anyhow to try to shoot an idea with a law. "As I have watched the repeated proposals of this easy panacea for getting rid of ideas we do not like by-passing a law, I have been increasingly shocked. . . . I will never seek votes that way from free Americans."

Legislation to control Communism was being considered at

the time in Congress. The Mundt-Nixon bill, which passed the House, as its main feature compelled the registration of Communist and Communist-front organizations, thus flushing them into the open. It made the advocacy of totalitarian dictatorship a crime and stripped the Communists of certain privileges. One of the peculiar features of the Dewey-Stassen debate was that both men endorsed the bill, Dewey because it would not outlaw the party, Stassen because it would. Dewey's clinching argument was, "Mundt himself says that the bill does not outlaw the party. Therefore, Stassen has surrendered." This was all casuistry and mental gymnastics. The opinion of William Z. Foster, Chairman of the Communist Party, was more relevant: the Party would have to go underground. Richard Nixon was fully justified in his comment that the real winner of the Dewey-Stassen debate was the Mundt-Nixon bill. Stassen believes to this day that he was right and that his policy was carried out—the Mundt-Nixon bill was substantially enacted in the Internal Security Act of 1950 and the Communist Party today is at least two-thirds underground.

On primary day Stassen lost to Dewey by 9000 votes out of 200,000.

The Oregon victory was important to the Dewey cause, psychologically, in breaking a string of reverses. Before the primary, Dewey had spoken frankly to his lieutenants about the possible end of his political career. As for Stassen, the Oregon primary finished him. Delegates who had been on the fence now moved away from him. Stassen says now that even if he had won in Oregon, the odds against him were heavier than political analysts reckoned, because of the leanings of uncommitted delegates. But the best opinion is that if Stassen had stayed out of Ohio and had won in Oregon, he could not have been stopped.

Both Dewey and Stassen say that the debate has been overemphasized. People believe that Dewey won the primary on the strength of the debate. Dewey says that the fact is that he won it before. Stassen cites the poll of *The Oregonian* of Portland which showed him as strong at primary time as before the debate. But the poll did show a decline for Stassen right after the debate so that it had an effect. At any rate, the debate was broadcast nationwide over hundreds of stations and it convinced the public that Dewey was the better man.

Stassen lost in Oregon because of the heavy Dewey vote piled up in Multnomah County (Portland). A good deal of money poured in; there was persuasion exercised on businessmen, lawyers, and doctors; labor organizers from New York came to Portland to put in their oar with the labor unions. Discussing this power emanating from lower Manhattan, Stassen says, "I have always suffered from the fact that I never had a solid business base." There is no doubt that the "New York influence" is a potent factor in Republican conventions as it was in the Oregon primary and thereafter in winning delegates for Dewey. Lawyers in outlying areas get fees on cases assigned by the big New York law factories; businessmen and bankers are responsive to the extending or tightening of credit by New York banks. Alden Hatch in "The Men Around Dewey" in the October 1948 issue of *Harper's* wrote, "The bankers headed by Winthrop Aldrich were especially energetic; as one man put it, 'They really put the screws on the boys in Oregon.' " These are among the arts of subtle persuasion that will continue as long as economic power is concentrated in New York.

After Oregon there was no band-wagon rush to Dewey. At the time of the convention he had no more than 350 delegates in the bag, lacking 200 for the nomination. There was another candidate who had a bloc of delegates—Governor Earl Warren of California.

The party conclave opened in Philadelphia on June 21, only a matter of hours after the adjournment of Congress the day before. There was a universal conviction that the convention was choosing the next President of the United States. Walter Lippmann looking forward said, "The problem is not how to beat Truman, but how to preserve the victory beyond 1948." There is "not yet the kind of majority they can count upon holding together for two years, that is to say for the Congressional and state elections of 1950."

The keynote speech of Governor Green of Illinois was the usual bellowing hyperbole. H. L. Mencken, doing his last year of reporting for the Baltimore *Sun* at the conventions, wrote, "The most earnest clapper-clawing, save at the end, followed the honorable gentleman's solemn promise that the new Republican President will clean out all the dubious characters who now hog at the public trough, feasting upon the taxpayers' vitals and disgracing the human race. . . . Most of the delegates and alternates have been pining and panting for office for fifteen long years and their pulses race every time they hear that succor is at hand."

The convention, despite the conventional hoopla, seemed an uninspired affair. As one journalist put it, the Republicans demonstrated their capacity for "boredom from within." But beneath the surface there was a bitter contest for control between the old and new wings of the party. To those on the inside it was a high-spirited convention. Even though Dewey had more delegates than any other candidate, there was a strong party tradition against nominating a one-time loser, on the Alice Longworth principle that "you can't make a *soufflé* rise twice." Resentment was also keen among conservative party members against the "me too" campaign he had waged in 1944. Taft was the candidate of the conservative faction—while he had done much to close the gap in the Eightieth Congress between the two seemingly incompatible factions, isolationist and internationalist, Old Guard and New Guard, he was still cherished by the conservative wing. While all respected his intellect and character, many felt that he lacked vote-getting appeal and therefore if he were nominated, it would jeopardize the sure victory for the GOP. The diminished prospects for the new party of Henry Wallace hurt the Taft movement. The GOP could not take the gamble many believed would have been warranted if Wallace's stock had not dipped by this time.

On the opening day of the convention a Taft-Stassen alliance to stop Dewey seemed in the making. Then these anti-Dewey forces got a jolt when the Credentials Committee voted to seat the pro-Dewey Harry Sommers delegation from Georgia by a vote of twenty-six to twenty-four. Taft had been so confident that he had refused a deal to split the delegation on an even basis. There were surprising defections from the anti-Dewey forces—from Illinois where the delegation was first for Governor Green and then second for Taft; from Tennessee where Republican Chairman Reece held a pro-Taft delegation; from Iowa where Harrison Spangler headed a Stassen and Taft delegation. The Illinois vote to seat the pro-Dewey delegation was cast by Val Washington, who joined the Republican National Committee soon after, where he still holds a high position. The Taft forces claim that offers were made of Federal judgeships which the recipients of the offers could not resist. Mississippi's Negro delegation was headed by Perry Howard, a Taft man, but his delegate voted the other way. The story is that after the vote the delegate ran for a train and died of a heart attack on it. He had $1500 in fresh money on him and the delegation claimed that it should be divided up among them.

The ballroom of the Bellevue-Stratford was given over to a continuous Dewey jamboree with door prizes and even a fashion show. On the eighth floor the Dewey lieutenants with smooth precision went to work on the delegates—Herbert Brownell, Jr., a New York lawyer who was national chairman in 1944, J. Russel Sprague, New York national committeeman and boss of Nassau County, and Edwin F. Jaeckle, from Buffalo, former state chairman. Wherever possible a card file was kept on each delegate who was worked on. It was no easy job getting the nomination for Dewey, but this group was as skillful a group of operators as ever manipulated a convention. The modus operandi was conducted so skillfully that it was said that the Dewey forces "could have won even with Taft."

The Taft forces under Representative Clarence Brown were bumblers by comparison. They were limited by Taft's incapacity for promises. A typical case was the visit of a group of Utah delegates led proudly by Vernon Romney to discuss water conservation. Taft said frankly that he didn't know too much about the subject and might be against their position after he studied it. Romney left crestfallen. "Why did you have to say that?" said Brown. "Why couldn't you say that you appreciated the importance of the subject and that they could all rest assured that your views would be communicated through your great friend, Vernon Romney?" Taft replied that he gave an honest answer and that was all he could do.

The log jam broke up when Senator Ed Martin of Pennsylvania with Joe Grundy support switched his Pennsylvania votes to Dewey and agreed to make the nominating speech. The Governor Duff and Joe Pew faction called this a "double cross" and held out against Dewey, but Martin was able to deliver forty-one out of the seventy-three votes for Dewey on the first ballot. Governor Driscoll delivered to Dewey the votes of New Jersey, and Charlie Halleck those of Indiana. Stassen professed to be for Vandenberg as his second choice, but skeptics claim that Stassen was only for Stassen and nurtured the hope, as he did in 1952, that there would be a deadlock and then a call for Stassen. Taft lieutenants spoke to him of a Taft-Stassen ticket to stop Dewey, but he always replied, "Let's wait."

Stassen speaks of another move by himself, Senator Henry Cabot Lodge, and Mrs. Ogden Reid to block Dewey. They tried to contact General Eisenhower at Columbia, but he could not be reached.

On the second ballot Dewey came within thirty-three votes of the majority. A motion for a recess was accepted by the New York delegation, which was a surprise because it appeared that the recess would be beaten by an aye and nay vote which had been ordered. Russ Sprague had heard the Connecticut delegation behind him trying to break loose from Senator Baldwin, who was anti-Dewey, and decided that there was no harm in waiting. On the third ballot Senator Bricker for Taft, Senator Knowland for Warren, and Stassen, in turn, delivered their votes to give Dewey the nomination by acclamation.

Now let us turn to the Vice-Presidential candidate. The original ticket the Dewey forces had in mind was Dewey and Governor Green of Illinois, who would gladly have accepted the bid. But Colonel Robert McCormick of the Chicago *Tribune,* who was at Yale for a class reunion, was advised and hurried to Philadelphia to squelch the ticket. Illinois would go for Taft, not Dewey.

On Wednesday, the day before the balloting, there was a meeting in Dewey's suite. Charlie Halleck was seated on a bed and standing around him were Sprague, Brownell, Jaeckle, and Congressman Len Hall from Nassau. Sprague did the talking. "Charlie, do you believe that if we promise something we can deliver?" Halleck agreed. Then Sprague said, "Well, you look to us like *the* Vice-Presidential nominee." (Italics supplied.)

Halleck's eagerness rose. What did he have to do? "You will have to deliver the Indiana delegation," said Sprague.

"I think that I can deliver most of it," said Halleck, "but I'm not sure of some like [Ralph] Gates and [Raymond] Willis."

"No, no, Charlie," said Sprague, "part won't be enough. It must be all."

Two hours later Gates and Willis with broad grins were wearing Dewey buttons in the lobby. Halleck had assembled the Indiana delegation and told them that he could have the Vice-Presidency if Indiana went for Dewey.

After his nomination Thursday night at a session concluding at 10:30 PM, Dewey could have notified the party leaders of his choice of Halleck. He did not do so. At midnight on Thursday night a conference was held in room 808 with over twenty-five bigwigs. In addition to Sprague, Brownell, Hall, and Jaeckle, those attending included John Foster Dulles, Senator Saltonstall, Senator Henry Cabot Lodge, and Governor Bradford of Massachusetts, Governor Driscoll of New Jersey, Mason Owlett, national committeeman from Pennsylvania, Senator Vandenberg, Roy Roberts of the Kansas City *Star,* Lou Wentz, national committeeman from Oklahoma, and Barak Mattingly, national committeeman from Missouri. The purpose of the conference was to choose a Vice-Presidential nominee.

Dewey first brought up the name of Governor Green, but immediately dismissed him. "Let's not be mealy-mouthed about this. We can't take him." Then Dewey said, "We should have notes," and turning to Dulles, "Why don't you take notes?"

Then Halleck was considered. The sentiment was strongly against him. Vandenberg and Saltonstall were particularly outspoken. When their turn came, Brownell and Sprague were silent. Hall and Owlett held out for Halleck. "We have a commitment," Hall said. After each had spoken, Dewey said, "Halleck won't do." Other candidates were considered and Governor Warren was approved. He was called to the Dewey suite at 4:30 AM to be told the news.

Who was to break the news to Halleck? Dewey said he would do it alone, but then assembled his New York lieutenants for the dawn meeting. It was one that would never be erased from the memory of those present. Halleck was first speechless with disbelief and then overcome with emotion. He became quite voluble. "I can work for you and talk for you, but I can't run with you!" Dewey through the torrent of words was impassive, "stony-faced." "You're running out on the Eightieth Congress, and you'll be sorry," was his parting shot, according to Halleck. After Halleck left, Len Hall said to Dewey, "I don't know how I can face Charlie Halleck again," and Dewey replied, "Oh, I don't see that you did anything."

There was no doubt in the minds of Sprague, Hall, and Halleck at the time of the Wednesday meeting that a contract was being made. Dewey was in the next room and was advised of every word said. Dewey says of the Halleck affair: He instructed his lieutenants that they were to tell Halleck that he "looked like *a* Vice-Presidential candidate." (Italic supplied.) Halleck was considered on that basis as a potential candidate by a party conference and rejected. Dewey is undoubtedly right in saying that he would have had to buck strong disapproval within the party to have taken Halleck.

Halleck, Carroll Reece, and others believe that Dewey's mind was considerably influenced by an editorial which appeared in the New York *Times* on Friday morning, about which Dewey must have been apprized early Thursday evening. On the other hand, a Warren representative, Kyle Palmer of the Los Angeles *Times,* was conferring with Dewey at the same time as the Halleck negotiations were going on, so the decision may have been set many hours before. The *Times* editorial warned of the loss of the independent vote:

SURELY NOT MR. HALLECK!

Mr. Halleck would bring into the campaign the perfect record of a Republican isolationist.

Mr. Halleck voted against repeal of the arms embargo when the war broke out. . . .

Mr. Halleck voted against Selective Service in the summer of

> 1940. He voted against the extension of Selective Service a year later. . . .
>
> Mr. Halleck voted against Lend-Lease. He voted against the repeal of the ban on arming American merchant ships. He voted against the British loan. He voted against the Hull reciprocal trade program in 1940. . . . With Mr. Taber he led the fight to cut appropriations under the Marshall Plan. . . .
>
> Does the Republican Party want to saddle Mr. Dewey with the job of defending Mr. Halleck's record?

In his own defense Halleck says that he steered the Greek-Turkish aid program, the interim aid program, and the Marshall Plan through the House. As for his prewar record he says that even Vandenberg was an isolationist then. It was the first time since Lincoln that the Midwest was not represented on the ticket. It would have been hard for the Republican Party to have chosen anyone prominent from the Midwest except Vandenberg who would not have been tagged as an isolationist.

"*L'affaire* Halleck" may have been a fateful one. It is a moot point whether Halleck would have cost electoral votes in the East; it is indisputable that the loss of the Midwest cost the victory. The Warren nomination seemed a bull's-eye at the time, but Warren soon turned out to be a monumental disappointment to Dewey. Halleck with his forceful personality might have changed the tone of the Dewey campaign and certainly the issue of the record of the Eightieth Congress would have had to have been met heads on.

At a Gridiron Club dinner a few years later Halleck was recounting the incident to a group when Dewey appeared behind him. "Charlie, did I ever promise you the Vice-Presidential nomination?" Dewey asked. "No," Halleck replied, "but Sprague and Hall did." "But I never did, did I?" Dewey said. The argument against Halleck, as one politician puts it, is that on this matter "he should have talked to the horse."

After the Dewey victory, Clarence Brown found Taft in his room, seated on his bed, his head cupped in his hands. "I didn't measure up, Clarence," he said, taking full blame, "I'm sorry, I didn't measure up." He soon swallowed his disappointment and pledged his full aid to Dewey. There was some question as to how well the *rapprochement* with the Taft wing would proceed. Carroll Reece, a Taft man, was stripped of the national chairmanship and ousted from the Executive Committee. There were to be photographs of Dewey shaking hands with the outgoing chairman, but they were canceled as a matter of bad policy, for which advice Reece blamed Brownell.

As the new chairman, Hugh Scott, a Congressman from Philadelphia, was chosen. His selection has been ascribed to a deal with the Martin-Grundy forces as the price of their support, but there was no such deal. Scott was acceptable because he was young, forty-seven, a veteran, from a key state, with a liberal enough voting record in the Eightieth Congress, having supported tariff reduction and public-housing legislation. The real national chairman, in fact, was to be the campaign manager, Herbert Brownell, Jr.

There are certain characteristics of the Dewey nomination which should be noted in relation to the behavior pattern of the campaign. It was the end-product of a well-organized and scientifically managed campaign. Great emphasis was put on band-wagon convention psychology.

In his speech of acceptance, Dewey said, "I come to you unfettered by a single obligation or promise to any living person." There was an almost audible gasp from the delegates. That, too, is a campaign motif that should be borne in mind. Literally, it was correct but did not exclude commitments made by Dewey representatives. One recalls Lincoln's unsuccessful admonition to his friends in the 1860 convention not to bind him. Dewey says that no offer of a Cabinet post was

Jacob Burck in The Chicago Sun-Times

"You take the high road."

ever made and, in fact, there have never been rumors of any such offer in the convention or campaign.

Then, the "high level" content of the speech, which did not dwell on particulars, is another motif. "Our people . . . yearn to move to higher ground, to find a common purpose in the fine things which unite us. . . . The unity we seek is more than material. . . . Spiritually, we have yet to find the means to put together the world now broken in pieces, to bind up its wounds, to make a good society, a community of men of good will that fits our dream."

The lack of enthusiasm for Dewey was noted. He was not "well liked." *Time* magazine said that opposition to Dewey was that he was "too mechanistically precise to be liked, too watchfully unbending to be confided, too coldly ambitious to be loved." Dorothy Thompson wrote that Dewey's success "represented the success of political techniques and the managerial revolution. . . . Yet I had the impression by no means unique to myself that the man who so quickly rolled up a majority of votes had fewer real friends than any other leading candidate and that if he had been defeated more people would have been pleased with themselves."

But the combination of Dewey and Warren seemed unbeatable, East and West linked by the governors of two states which together contributed 72 of the 266 electoral votes required. And Dewey, as one of his advisers told the press, "would not have to fight the champ this time," but only Harry Truman and a split party.

[IV]

DEMOCRATIC PRELUDE— EISENHOWER FOR PRESIDENT

IN POLITICAL ANNALS it would be hard to find an incident as bizarre as the movement to make General Eisenhower the Democratic nominee in 1948 in place of Truman.

In November 1947, President Truman, wanting General Eisenhower to withdraw as Chief of Staff, brought General Bradley to the Army from the Veterans Administration. The President told Forrestal that "he thought he [Eisenhower] would take the hint." Ike did and resigned in February 1948, to become President of Columbia University in June. In the meanwhile he would be at Columbia writing his war memoirs.

At that time Ike was considered a Republican and led in popularity polls for President in that party. In his letter of January 23 to Leonard Finder, publisher of the Manchester *Union Leader* in New Hampshire, he removed himself from the race. "I am not available for and could not accept nomination to high political office." (General Eisenhower told Forrestal that he wrestled hard over the text of the letter since, as a symbol to American youth, he did not want to appear to shirk a duty.) His statement was accepted at face value by the GOP and by political writers, and at the Gridiron Dinner in early April, referring to the General's imminent job as President of Columbia University, a ditty ran:

You can offer me what you like
But I'll still be Professor Ike.

Then followed the period in which Truman became a pariah to all factions of his party. The name of Eisenhower as a potential Democratic nominee cropped up among Southern Democrats. Senator Russell said after suggesting that Truman should withdraw, "I would be happy to see General Eisenhower step in as Democratic Presidential nominee." Russell says that the idea occurred to him because he had had many talks with Eisenhower in Europe and was convinced that he was a firm believer in states' rights. (He was subsequently disillusioned.) Russell was astonished at what followed. The idea clicked with the Northern liberals who were afire with zeal to dump Truman. The CIO, the Liberal Party of New York, the Americans for Democratic Action, and assorted political bosses like Jake Arvey joined in the parade. Russell had not seen anything in Eisenhower's background to make him an ADA candidate.

The General had definitely renounced any political aims in January and there was no indication that he had changed his mind. On March 26 General Eisenhower tried to dissuade Franklin D. Roosevelt, Jr., from endorsing him as the Democratic nominee telling him it "might be interpreted abroad as implying failure to support the President at this critical time." In April Roy Roberts of the Kansas City *Star* and an intimate of Ike's said, "Of course, Eisenhower is not going to take a Democratic nomination or any other nomination. That's final." In May, Eisenhower at Columbia said to the press, "I slaved hard writing that letter and I meant every word I said. So far I know of nothing that has changed my conviction in that regard." But the Ike boosters professed to see hope. Senator Pepper, who was to prove the most valiant of all, said, "He may be pulling the door a little close to him, but I didn't hear the door click."

Throughout May there were many visitors at Eisenhower's office at Columbia, sounding him out on the Democratic nomination. There is no indication that he gave them anything more than a gracious hearing. In early June I met Leon Henderson, chairman of the ADA, who had spent some time with Eisenhower that afternoon at Columbia. He said that he had visited Ike several times, getting in by saying that surely the General would not refuse the free services of a personal economist. There was no doubt in Henderson's mind as to Ike's attitude. "He just joshed me," Henderson said, "and said he was sure there were a lot of Democrats the party could turn to without turning to him." In an unusually pensive mood Henderson mused why Ike was unwilling to accept the bid.

Nonetheless, the draft-Eisenhower movement picked up momentum immediately after the GOP convention. Jimmy Roosevelt announced that party leaders from eighteen states would meet on Saturday, July 10, two days before the convention, "to seek the ablest and strongest man available," obviously a draft-Eisenhower move. The list of persons who signed the call was impressive. In addition to Jimmy, who headed the California delegation, there were Northern liberals like Mayor Hubert Humphrey of Minneapolis, and Chester Bowles; city bosses like Jake Arvey, and Mayor O'Dwyer of New York; and Southerners, Governor Thurmond of South Carolina, Governor Laney of Arkansas, Governor Tuck of Virginia, Governor Jester of Texas, and Senator Hill of Alabama.

The movement snowballed. Mayor Frank Hague of Jersey City deserted Truman and delivered the 36 votes of New Jersey to Ike. Virginia and Georgia delegations were instructed for Eisenhower. Senator Byrd said, "I hope that Virginia Democrats will cast their votes for Eisenhower and lead the Democratic Party to victory." The Georgia convention resolved that Eisenhower is "the one man, the only proper man to lead the people in their fight against Communism, tyranny, and slavery." Tennessee was ready to join in. At this point Eisenhower had 150 sure votes.

Then Eisenhower punctured the balloon. In a statement on July 5 (which he drafted with George Allen and General Lucius Clay), he said, "I will not at this time identify myself with any political party and could not accept nomination for any political office." Truman, obviously relieved when told of the declaration on a journey back to Washington, said, "General Eisenhower is an honorable man." (In his *Memoirs* Truman said that he had earlier received assurance from Eisenhower in a visit to the White House that he would stand by his January 23 letter.)

Politicians who were now out on a limb would not accept the "no." Jimmy Roosevelt said that Ike had refused only to "seek partisan political office but will answer a call to political duty," and Jake Arvey said, "It's a people's draft, not a political draft." Senator Pepper then made the most amazing proposal in all the annals of political desperation—that the Democratic Party should hand itself over lock, stock, and barrel to Eisenhower. "The Democrats must be prepared to let General Eisenhower be a purely national President." The General would choose his own running mate and write his own platform. In notifying the General of this proposal, Pepper said, "I neither expect nor desire an acknowledgement or reply." He did get one, a decisive Sherman-like refusal, that the General would not take the nomination under any "terms, conditions, or premises." That administered the coup de grace to the Eisenhower boom, and Jimmy Roosevelt, arriving at Philadelphia, capitulated, calling off the projected anti-Truman caucus.

The Eisenhower episode of 1948 is most enigmatic. How could Southerners and Northern liberals be in the same camp since the liberals were dead set for the civil rights which the Southerners were fighting to a man? Walter White of the NAACP called it a "startling alliance." The South had no positive clue to Eisenhower's position on civil rights. It seems fair to assume that the detestation of Southern leaders for

Truman was such that they were ready to displace Truman even with an unknown quantity like General Eisenhower.

The attitude of the Northern liberals is equally hard to understand. They were bleeding for principle but the General's philosophy had not been disclosed. He did not turn down the Republican bid on the ground that he did not want to be considered a Republican. Jake Arvey said of Ike, "He is the kind of a liberal with whom we could win," but then how did Arvey know whether Eisenhower was a liberal or a McKinley conservative? The CIO-PAC mailed out a pamphlet with Eisenhower's views on democracy, religion, peace, free press, and others. All of these Ike approved. Eisenhower was the man for the Presidency on the Democratic ticket because, "American labor rightly shares in the laurels won by American troops on the battlefield."

With nothing to go on, there was difficulty in articulating the case for Eisenhower. Thus, Max Lerner, "His brilliantly phrased will-not-run letter of last January was one of the clearest anti-militarist documents in our history. He has given ample proof that the habits of a military life have not enslaved his mind and that it is a literate, thoughtful, distinctive mind." And again, "The one big thing he stresses is national unity and the sense of togetherness." Jonathan Bingham, head of the New York ADA, praised Ike because of "his devotion to the ideals of the United Nations, his abiding hatred of war, his conviction that different government systems can exist peaceably side by side in the world but that aggression cannot be appeased, his friendly attitude toward labor." What more could be asked? He went on to say that Wilson was considered an archconservative before he was elected, Lincoln did not know his own views (both untrue statements), and Franklin Roosevelt was elected on an economy platform. So why not buy a pig in the poke?

The AFL in contrast to the CIO took a sober view of Ike. President William Green expressing his wonderment over the boom said, "Labor does not know the economic, social, or industrial views of General Eisenhower." The New York *Post,* which never could go along with the idea, said after it was over, "There was a curious fascination to be found in this dream which had little or nothing to do with the man himself, his desires, his equipment, or even his party affiliations, if any."

If Eisenhower was at the time an unknown, then why Eisenhower? Since he was a newcomer to politics, his mind was virgin and perhaps could be impressed with the right kind of thinking, but in any event he could win and carry in a Democratic Congress. In what appeared to be the twilight hour of the Democratic Party, dignity and adherence to fixed principle were thrown to the winds. Max Lerner conceded that Eisenhower was a "gamble." He said that the main factor in the boom was "the certainty that he could win." A Washington report on May 9 to the Chicago *Sun-Times* and New York's *PM* said, "The dump-Truman-draft-Ike talk is based largely on one consideration, selecting a sure-shot candidate who would sweep into office a Democratic Congress with an unmistakable progressive stamp. The social and economic views of General Eisenhower which he has kept well concealed up to now do not overly concern the labor leaders who want him at the head of the ticket." Dale Kramer in the *New Republic* wrote, "Democratic politicians are not concerned about Eisenhower's views. What they want is a winning candidate who will carry local candidates to victory."

Weeks before the convention any illusion that the General would head the ticket must have disappeared from ADA ranks and the draft-Eisenhower boom must have had another objective. Raymond Moley wrote, "The whole Eisenhower movement was phony. The great name of the General was used as a stopgap until anti-Truman sentiment could find someone else." It is known that in May and June the ADA raised considerable money using hints that Ike would consent to run. On July 7 the New York *Star* (successor to *PM*), which was in intimate contact with the liberal wing, had this comment, "If General Eisenhower had waited only a few more days Leon Henderson and his ADA might have brought it off. Henderson believes that every vote he had for the General was tranferable for the Justice [Supreme Court Justice William Douglas]." It is significant that immediately after the first "no" Henderson plumped for Douglas.

Could Ike have gotten the Democratic nomination by a Willkie-type blitz if he had wanted it? Truman in his *Memoirs* says that he could not—that Eisenhower would have had to lead a bolt in "a four-way split in the party." He is undoubtedly correct since Truman had the majority of the delegates. Democratic Chairman McGrath says that even though there was some uneasiness earlier, "The Eisenhower boom at convention time was pure nonsense—the party could never have gone into the campaign after repudiating its leader and his record."

The numerical strength for Eisenhower was less than it appeared to be. Jimmy Roosevelt admits that he had no more than half of the California delegation with him and that there was a rumpus on the train all the way East between his faction and the pro-Truman faction. (Incidentally, all delegates had signed affidavits that they were for Truman before the California primary.) He also says that his position was largely influenced by the fact that the Ed Pauley faction was a rubber stamp for Truman and he was in a fight for control with Pauley. Roosevelt says that he would have expected Eisenhower to come out with a liberal manifesto if he wanted the nomination. If he had done so that certainly would have reduced his strength in the conservative South. Jake Arvey had less than a majority of the Illinois delegation; Mayor O'Dwyer, alone, in New York was against Truman, and he was for Douglas, not Eisenhower.

If one is credulous enough to believe that Eisenhower

could have had the nomination without a struggle, one should recall 1952 and the dogfight that the General had to undergo for months to wrest the Republican nomination from Taft, a man entrenched with the party faithful. That reflects the difference between popularity and delegate votes.

Since the enterprise was chimerical at best and the motives for the boom were suspect, there have been questions raised as to why Eisenhower's firm declination did not come sooner. The answers are many—Ike did not believe that anyone could misunderstand his January statement, he thought it presumptuous to refuse a nomination not offered to him, and, being human, he could not help being flattered by all the attention paid to him until the boom assumed serious proportions.

After Ike bowed out, the New Dealers did not give up. They switched their support to Justice Douglas, thus graduating in effect from chasing a phantom to wrestling with a moonbeam. Douglas had no popularity base—the latest Gallup Poll showed that he was the choice of two per cent of Democratic voters compared with sixty-seven per cent for Truman. As for the Southern bloc he was definitely persona non grata since it was reasonably certain that he was by instinct more pro-civil rights than Truman himself. Jimmy Roosevelt was not interested. Douglas' only following was the garrulous ADA minority which controlled less than a hundred votes in the convention. H. L. Mencken wrote that the Douglas supporters are "chiefly very young men who seem to be innocently unaware that nominations are made by the votes of delegates and not by the distribution of buttons."

Walter Reuther nonetheless called Douglas a man who "can unite the Democrats." Behind Douglas were Max Lerner, publisher Michael Straight of the *New Republic,* and Ted Thackrey, editor of the New York *Post.* Max Lerner now dismissed Eisenhower as merely "a catalytic agent, the essence of the movement lies less in him than in the straining for a coalition." But Douglas bowed out, "I never was a-running, I ain't a-running, and I ain't going to." Mayor O'Dwyer finished off the Douglas affair by his call that "our Democracy unite for President Truman."

A final event proved that there is only one step from the sublime to the ridiculous. Senator Pepper magnanimously offered himself for self-immolation as the party candidate. "The delegates have been looking for someone representing the policies and principles of Franklin D. Roosevelt. . . . I accept the challenge." The strongest point for him was that he had Drew Pearson behind him. David Karr, Pearson's assistant, told a group of delegates, "I can assure you that Drew Pearson is even more enthusiastic in his support of Pepper than he is in support of Eisenhower or Douglas." But even Florida would give no help to Pepper, and his candidacy lasted from Sunday to Tuesday, the second day of the convention.

Accompanying all the attempts to put over any candidate but Truman were the dirge-like reiterations that Truman was a hopeless cause in November, such as Mayor Hague's prediction that Truman would lose New Jersey by at least 300,000. Wrote Lowell Mellett, "A stranger convention there never was. Man and boy, I've been seeing them now for close to a half-century but I've never seen one quite like this . . . never one in which so many delegates worked so hard and at such cross-purposes with seemingly but a single intent—how to make sure that the man nominated should not be elected." Jim Farley issued a rebuke to the detractors of Truman. He was "thoroughly disgusted with the attitudes and actions of some of our leaders who have no appreciation or understanding of what the party has done for them." But Walter Lippmann thought that these goings-on were quite astute. "In addition to certain defeat this year, the party would have made it much more difficult for those who cannot support Truman now to remain Democrats for the future. . . . The new generation of Democrats will not be ready and available for some years to come."

Why were the Northern liberals so eager to dump Truman—so eager that they went to extremes that made them look ridiculous? Far from inviting an estrangement, the President had courted them with his veto of the Taft-Hartley law, he had vetoed three tax-reduction bills on the ground that they were unfair to lower-income groups, he had backed a strong civil-rights program, price controls, and public housing, among other measures. In the words of Samuel Grafton of the New York *Post,* Truman was a "dreamboat of vocal liberalism." Then why the vitriolic opposition?

Undoubtedly, the most important reason was that the Northern liberals were sure he could not win and they, like the Southerners, were engaged in a fight for party control. The ADA statement in April calling for another candidate made the indictment bluntly, "We cannot overlook the fact that poor appointments and faltering support of his aides have resulted in a failure to rally the people behind policies which we wholeheartedly support." The New York *Post* said a few days before his nomination that if he were chosen "the party might as well immediately concede the election to Dewey and save the wear and tear of campaigning."

A second cause for disgruntlement was the feeling that Truman was too small a man to deal with the world crisis. The "father-image" of Roosevelt was strong. Labor opponents of Truman said openly that his biggest handicap was that he followed F.D.R. A large sign in Tulsa during the preconvention campaign read, "Truman said he wasn't big enough to be President and he ain't." The liberal *Nation* put it this way, "A deep process is going on and political molds are breaking and reforming. . . . In America as in the rest of the world one senses a shift towards left and right. Wallace has come to represent the pressures towards change; Truman is hardly more than their victim, a small neutral figure who has lost meaning for liberals and conservatives."

A third and quite strong reason was that the liberals were skeptical that Truman was really their man—the ADA was filled with New Dealers who had no participation in this Administration. Truman's intimates were not New Dealers but moderates of the type of John Snyder, John Steelman, and Clark Clifford, or third-raters like General Vaughan or Matt Connelly. Harold Ickes reflected the scorn felt about Truman's intimates, "The political figures who surround the President . . . could all be blown out by one sure breath, as are candles on a birthday cake." New Dealers most emphatically did not hold the latchkey to the White House and were resentful. As one New Dealer put it, "Would you expect the Pope to run the Catholic Church with Baptist cardinals?"

His appointments reflected his middle-of-the-road philosophy. Men like Jim Landis, Wilson Wyatt, Will Davis, Wendell Berge, Chester Bowles, Francis Biddle, and others had been axed or found it expedient to resign. Walter Lippmann put the gap between words and action this way, "Truman's solution of the conundrum has been to get rid of New Dealers and to be what he really is, no New Dealer at heart but a politician who appreciates the voting strength of the Roosevelt combination."

Many black marks in the Truman record were disinterred to prove the charge that his professions of liberalism were only lip service. He had scuttled the excess-profits tax immediately after V-J Day. He had not held the line on inflation controls when he granted the steel price boost in 1946 which forced Chester Bowles to resign as Economic Stabilization Director. He had asked of Congress, in a fire-eating speech, the power to draft striking railroad workers into the Army. When he had found his housing program in hot water with Congress in 1947, he had dumped Wilson Wyatt and the program. When he had found price controls unpopular, he first found it expedient to kill meat controls on the eve of the 1946 election and afterward all price ceilings. In neither case had he drawn the battle lines with Congress.

Berryman in the Washington Evening Star

Truman regarded himself as sincere and all these shenanigans of the Northern liberals made him cold with anger. "He never thought much of the ADA," says Clifford, "but now he was disgusted with it." He wrote to Jimmy Roosevelt, "Here I am trying to carry out your father's policies. You've got no business trying to pull the rug out from under me." Explaining his support of Ike, Jimmy Roosevelt says that Truman did not follow in his father's footsteps by 1948 but did become a true Roosevelt liberal later on. The cleavage between the Truman of preconvention and postconvention 1948 is not visible to the naked eye.

The second phase of the convention was distinctly different. The northern Democrats closed ranks after the unsuccessful attempt to find a candidate to oust Truman. Mayor O'Dwyer and Jake Arvey now praised Truman for the "dogged and sincere fight" that the President had waged for liberal principles. Then the battling spirits of the liberals were directed into a new channel, a fight on the civil-rights issue against the South.

The unfolding of the Southern bolt in 1948 is something of a puzzle, too. As late as June, Frank Kent, veteran analyst of the Baltimore *Sun,* said, "The southern Democrats are engaged in an obviously futile battle. . . . The act they are putting on is based on a defensible principle. Perhaps their own self-respect compels them to put it on. But it is an act just the same."

It turned out to be more than just an "act." To understand the intensity of feeling of the South one must realize that the Truman civil-rights program was a sharp break with the past, not a continuation of the Roosevelt approach. In his *Memoirs* Truman reports being told of a conversation at the Democratic convention. When Thurmond was reminded by a reporter that Truman was only carrying out Roosevelt's platform, he replied, "I agree, but Truman really means it." Thurmond does not recall the remark. In any event the cause for the Southern revolt was that Truman in his civil-rights message went far beyond anything Roosevelt proposed. Roosevelt never proposed Federal action to enforce civil rights. That is the distinction Southerners make in evaluating 1948.

The gratitude of the Negro to Franklin D. Roosevelt was profound as H. L. Moon points out in *The Balance of Power.* W. E. B. DuBois, a race spokesman, said that he felt "without the slightest doubt that Franklin D. Roosevelt has done more for the uplift and progress of the American Negro than any President since Abraham Lincoln." The relief programs, the public-housing program which allotted one third of all units to Negroes, the wartime FEPC, the lifting of some restrictions against Negroes in the Armed Forces, and the appointment of a liberal Supreme Court which outlawed the white primary in the South—all these were great steps forward.

But at the same time there was dissatisfaction in Negro ranks with F.D.R. At times his hand had to be forced. For example, when A. Philip Randolph, head of the Brotherhood of Sleeping Car Porters, threatened to lead a march on Washington, it persuaded Roosevelt to issue Executive Order 8802 establishing the FEPC soon after Pearl Harbor. Neither in 1940 or 1944 did the Democratic platform favor a permanent FEPC, antilynching or anti-poll-tax legislation. The Pittsburgh *Courier* said, "Thousands of Negroes who distrust the Democratic Party but who have confidence in President Roosevelt are finding that even the great office of President has not been able to cope with the malignant influence of the South when the Democratic Party is in power."

The bitterness of the South toward Truman was increased by the recollection that he came from a border state and owed his nomination in 1944 to the South. Thus, the delegate nominating Senator Russell in the convention was to say, "If it wasn't for the vote of the South four years ago, Henry Wallace would be sitting in the White House today."

The problem facing the South was how to maintain party regularity, so precious in the South, and yet organize a revolt. One answer was the half-bolt. The people cast their vote not for the Presidential candidates but for electors and there is no constitutional prohibition against the electors exercising their free will to vote for anybody they choose. Since 1824, electors have always voted in accord with the expressed preference of the voters, but there are precedents to the contrary. In the election of 1912 even though there was no Bull Moose candidate in South Dakota, the Republican electors announced that they would vote for Theodore Roosevelt if the Republicans carried the state, and they did.

In 1944 the idea of having electors vote independently blossomed out as a means of repelling the threat of a strong civil-rights plank in the platform. A slate of unpledged electors, the Texas Regulars, were chosen by a Democratic state convention in Texas, but the Supreme Court of the state on a writ of mandamus gave official sanction to the slate of electors chosen by a rump convention who were pledged to vote for Roosevelt; in the November election the unpledged electors ran third. Revolts along similar lines failed in South Carolina and Mississippi.

The South started experimenting with the half-bolt early in 1948. Within a few weeks of the civil-rights message, in the 150-year-old capitol where Jefferson Davis had his offices, Governor Tuck of Virginia, a protégé of Senator Harry Byrd, asked his state legislature to approve a bill barring Truman's or the national candidates' names from the ballot and providing that the electors vote on the instruction of a state convention. "The people of the South have been put on the sacrificial altar to appease racial and minority fringe votes," Governor Tuck said in his request. From the time of the Confederacy the prestige of Virginia has been commanding and this type of law could have set a pattern for the other states. But there was opposition to it in the legislature and the Governor did not have his way. The bill was passed in a considerably toned-down form which allowed the names of the Democratic national candidates to appear on the ballot but permitted the state committee, if it chose to act, to place additional names on the ballot.

In early May there was a very significant election in Alabama. All eleven electors who were chosen pledged that they would not cast their votes for a civil-rights candidate. The state chairman announced that the Democrats were not bolting but merely "refusing to affiliate with the national Democratic Party." In 1860 Alabama had led the walkout from the Democratic convention in Baltimore which nominated Stephen A. Douglas.

On May 10 there was a conference of Southerners in Jackson, Mississippi, which decided tentatively to hold a rump convention in Birmingham immediately after the Democratic convention if Truman were nominated. Governor Laney of Arkansas was given authority to set up a campaign committee. The South would unite behind one candidate in the Democratic convention. Senator George of Georgia, Senator Russell, or Senator Byrd were likely choices. Signs of fission already appeared at this time in the solid Southern front; Georgia withdrew from the Jackson meeting and her delegates stayed on only as observers.

Hopes for a reconciliation were not gone when the convention opened. The appointment of two Southerners in charge of the machinery of the convention, House Minority Leader Rayburn as permanent chairman and Senator Barkley as temporary chairman who would make the keynote speech, were obvious moves to appease the Southern bloc. The Administration's plan which read, "We believe that racial and religious minorities have the right to live, develop, and vote equally with all citizens and share the rights that are guaranteed by our Constitution. Congress should exert its full constitutional powers to protect these rights."

This best-laid plan went agley. The boom first for Eisenhower and then for Justice Douglas put steam behind a coalition of liberals and raised their crusading zeal to a high pitch. Instead of venting their spleen on Truman, they would attack the South.

[V]

TRUMAN NOMINATED—SOUTHERN SPLIT

IT WAS NOW SET. The Democratic Party was to commit suicide to satisfy the inordinate vanity of Harry Truman, who wanted to continue as President. The Alsops cited a comparison of Truman and King Henry Christophe of Haiti, who ordered his army to march off the battlements. Since he had been repudiated by practically every Democratic leader, "If Truman is nominated he will be forced to wage the loneliest campaign in recent history."

Labor leaders were conspicuous by their absence. Victor Riesel wrote, "For the first time in 16 years a man can run on the Republican ticket without fear of real opposition from the political machines run by labor chiefs throughout the country. . . . The labor leaders are simply not going to campaign for Harry Truman, they'll simply go through the motions—slow motions. In labor circles this convention will go down as the big snub of 1948—with the labor leaders doing the snubbing." Phil Murray refused to address the convention or even attend it—David Dubinsky, John L. Lewis, Walter Reuther, and Dan Tobin were absent. Al Whitney of the Railroad Trainmen was the only major leader present. Lesser lights were present—Jim Carey of the Electrical Workers, Joseph Keenan of the AFL, David McDonald, then secretary-treasurer of the Steelworkers, and

James Petrillo, head of the Musicians Union, who, as a fellow musician, was the most ardent supporter of Truman.

Jack Kroll, head of the CIO's Political Action Committee, commented to the press, "Has it occurred to you that we can sit on our hands in this campaign?" After the demise of the Eisenhower and Douglas booms, Kroll called for an open convention "in a democratic manner"—the nominee must be chosen "free of interference from those holding high office or the strings of political patronage."

There was a lull just before the opening of the convention. H. L. Mencken wrote, "With the advancing Confederate Army still below the Potomac Philadelphia was steeped in the nervous calm that fell upon it in the days before Gettysburg." The Truman forces were in open command. Leslie Biffle, Secretary to the Senate minority, the sergeant-at-arms, passed out tickets carefully to prevent any packing of the galleries for anti-Truman demonstrations. In a meeting of the national committee, Chairman McGrath taunted Senator Johnston of South Carolina, who had been scheduled to offer a resolution asking Truman to withdraw, but, "No," said the Senator, "I have no resolution to offer at this time."

The Southern forces were determined to hold out to the end. They assembled in caucus to map a program. Said Governor Thurmond, Truman has "stabbed us in the back with his damnable program. . . . We have been betrayed and the guilty shall not go unpunished." It was agreed that the South should unite behind Senator Russell of Georgia, and Russell, who was at his home in Georgia, consented to let his name be presented.

The attendance at the caucus was not too encouraging for the revolters. "The count of bayonets," as Mencken put it, showed that while there was good attendance from Mississippi, Alabama, and Florida, there were only twelve delegates from Virginia, two each from Georgia and Louisiana, and one from Oklahoma. "Then Governor Laney asked if any copperheads were present and one Trumanocide from Indiana showed up."

Senator Barkley, Minority Leader of the Senate, delivered a rousing keynote address to the convention, sparing nothing in his invective against the opposing party, but notable for the fact that it did not predict victory. It was full of the choice Barkley humor—sample: When the Hoover Administration came to an end even the spiders in Washington "were so weak from undernourishment they could barely weave the cobwebs needed to drape the stricken government offices." Again, "A bureaucrat is a Democrat who holds some office that a Republican wants." He was given a rousing demonstration.

In this worst-managed of conventions everything seemed to go wrong. At a memorial service for the war dead on Tuesday night, Lawrence Tibbett sang the *Star-Spangled Banner* and the organ was pitched so high that his voice almost strangled, then dropped a full octave. Mayor O'Dwyer had to plead with the delegates who were buzzing with conversation, "We are having a service for the war dead. Won't you give us your attention." When taps were sounded, many of the notes were obviously off key. It was an ordeal and at the end, there was enormous relief.

The battle between the Roosevelt Democrats and the unregenerate South was coming to a slow boil. A resolution was offered by the South for the restoration of the two-thirds rule, which, as expected, was defeated. Mencken wrote, "The defeated army retired in good position to a prepared position on the swamps bordering the Swanee River." On Tuesday night, the Credentials Committee offered a resolution seating the Mississippi delegation, which was anti-Truman. A Negro delegate from Missouri, George Vaughn, rose to protest on the ground that the delegation was pledged to walk out if a strong civil-rights plan was adopted. "Three million Negroes have left the South since the outbreak of World War II to escape this thing." It had been agreed in the committee that there would be no floor vote, but demands were heard all over the floor from Northern delegations demanding a vote. Barkley pushed through the resolution seating the Mississippi delegation on a voice vote—protests demanding a ballot were cut off by the microphone going dead.

On Wednesday came the platform debate. The Resolutions Committee under Senator Myers of Pennsylvania offered the majority report with a civil-rights plank along the lines of the 1944 platform which was framed in general terms. The radical faction composed mostly of the ADA group proposed a stiffer plank which explicitly praised Truman for his civil-rights message and said, "We call upon the Congress to support the President in guaranteeing these basic and fundamental rights: (1) The right of full and equal political participation; (2) the right of equal opportunity of employment; (3) the right of security of person; (4) the right of equal treatment in the service and defense of our Nation."

In a better-managed convention the differences might have been patched up in the Resolutions Committee or prevented from coming to a vote, but not in this convention. Mayor Hubert Humphrey of Minneapolis, slated to run against Senator Ball in Minnesota, and former Congressman Biemiller of Wisconsin fought for the minority plank. Humphrey came into national prominence at this convention. Humphrey orated, "I say the time has come to walk out of the shadow of states' rights and into the sunlight of human rights." The vote was a sensational upset. The Americans for Democratic Action and their cohorts scored a great victory for the minority plank by 651 to 582, when Northern delegations led by a switch in Pennsylvania voted for it.

A circle of political pygmies had engineered a coup in the convention which had wrecked the Administration's harmony plan. The Mississippi delegation and half of the Alabama delegation, thirty-five delegates, walked out. The chairman of the Alabama delegation said, "We will never vote Republican, never vote for Truman, and never accept the civil-rights program. We therefore bid you good-by."

As the strategy on civil rights didn't pan out, the strategy of the Administration to have a young liberal as a running mate for Truman came to grief. On the Friday before the Monday opening the convention, Truman called Justice Douglas and asked him to be his running mate. Clark Clifford called Mrs. Roosevelt and asked her help in trying to persuade Douglas. Douglas put off the decision until Monday. The Truman circle had great hopes that Douglas would accept although Tommy Corcoran, as Douglas' emissary, had visited McGrath a week before and had asked that pressure not be put on him. Douglas definitely had the political bug. He had been Roosevelt's first choice for Vice-President in 1944, but practical reasons had forced Roosevelt to drop the idea. Douglas was tempted now, and the forlorn chances of Truman were undoubtedly the commanding reason for his saying "no," that he preferred to stay on the Supreme Court. Ed Flynn proposed Wilson Wyatt as the candidate. McGrath vetoed Senator O'Mahoney because as a Catholic he might be held responsible for Truman's defeat.

On Sunday Leslie Biffle, Secretary to the Senate minority, had been called out of a political meeting by an AP man with the news of the Douglas bid. Senator Barkley was Biffle's boss and his choice, and he set to work to organize support for him among Democratic Senators. After the keynote, Barkley sentiment mounted higher. Truman called Barkley on Tuesday morning to congratulate him on the keynote speech and then referring to the boom, said, "Why didn't you let me know you were a candidate?" The abruptness of the query jolted Barkley and then and there he considered bowing out. In his *Memoirs* Truman has a version that would put a different complexion on the matter—that Barkley and Biffle called him and asked him for permission to make the try, which he gave. The most qualified sources say that if Barkley as a running mate was not forced on Truman, at least he was reluctant to have him. There was a coolness between the two and Barkley though Senate Minority Leader had not been invited to the White House for months at a time. The reason is ascribed to "jealousy"—Truman could not abide a strong and popular figure in the party other than himself.

As a Kentuckian, Barkley might have appeal to the South. But he was seventy years old. Many looked on him as the caretaker after the anticipated defeat. Walter Lippmann commented, "If the party had expected to elect Truman, it would not have turned to an elder statesman as his running mate."

On Wednesday night Truman was nominated 947 to 263 to Senator Russell, who received all the votes of the South except for twelve from North Carolina. In nominating Russell, Charles J. Bloch of Atlanta said the South "will no longer be the whipping boy of the Democratic Party. . . . You shall not crucify the South on the cross of civil rights." For the first time in years the nomination was not made unanimous. Barkley was nominated by acclamation.

At 9:00 PM the President had arrived at Convention Hall and waited with Senator Barkley in a suite below the convention floor with a balcony overlooking Philadelphia. He was visited by assorted dignitaries such as Jimmy Roosevelt, Mayor O'Dwyer, and the only representative of the South, Senator Sparkman. It was strange for the President to be in the Hall before the convention made up its mind on what was ostensibly its free choice, but then this was a strange convention in a strange year. "They may be mad at me," the President said to visitors, "but I'm not mad at them. I believe in Christ." In his *Memoirs* Truman devotes pages to his reveries on the history of the Presidency during the long wait while the candidates were officially nominated. There was little time for reveries. In Jack Redding's account in *Inside the Democratic Party,* Truman himself annotates, "Barkley and I had a reception all evening."

At two o'clock in the morning the President appeared before the convention to accept the nomination. A flock of pigeons released from beneath a Liberty Bell made of flowers strafed all and sundry and perched all over the place. In this grotesque setting, the President experienced his first moment of triumph—he had conquered in his determination that his party should not repudiate him. All the efforts of New Deal Democrats, Southern Democrats, and city bosses to topple him had resulted only in building up his stature. A conservative commentator, Frank Kent, wrote in tribute that a Scotch ballad fitted him,

> "I am wounded," Sir Anthony Barton cried, "but I am not slain.
> I'll lie down and bleed awhile and rise and fight again."

After Barkley's brief acceptance came the historic acceptance speech of President Truman, brimming over with confidence and determination. Instead of being an anti-climax, it electrified the delegates and gave them their first surge of hope. The President spoke effectively from eighteen pages of notes compiled by Clark Clifford and Samuel Rosenman. He bluntly recorded the debt owed to the Democratic Party by the workers and farmers. Farm income had jumped to 18 billions a year from 2.5 billions in 1932 and labor income to 132 billions from 29 billions, and "they would be the most ungrateful people in the world if they would pass the Democratic Party by this year." He excoriated the Republican Congress for inaction and would call it back into special session on Turnip Day in Missouri, July 26. If the Republicans meant what they said in their platform, they would pass legislation on aid to education, national health programs, civil rights, raising of the minimum wage, extension of social security, revision of the Displaced Persons Act, and others.

"Now, my friends, if there is any reality behind that Republican platform we ought to get some action out of a short session of the Eightieth Congress. They can do this job in fifteen days if they want to do it. They will still have time to go out and run for office. . . . What the worst Eightieth Congress does in its special session will be the test. . . . The American people . . . will decide on the record."

Thus ended the Democratic convention of 1948. The Constitution gives the President the right to call together the Congress on "extraordinary occasions." Never before had a President in a contest for re-election done so. The reaction of Republican members of Congress to the Truman call was bitter. "This sounds like the last hysterical gasp of an expiring administration," said Senator Vandenberg. "Cheap politics," said Congressman Taber. "Never in the history of American politics has a Chief Executive stooped so low in his desperation to garner votes for his re-election," said Illinois Senator Wayland Brooks. "This petulant Ajax from the Ozarks," said Senator Bridges, "will be met by the maddest Congress you ever saw." Southern Democrats were likewise alarmed that the hated civil-rights measures might be jammed through. Senator Russell said it was an effort "to badger and harass the South with a misnamed civil-rights program," and Senator George said the South was "over the barrel."

The liberals greeted the nomination of Truman with resignation or disgust. Max Lerner wrote, ". . . This has been the convention of the vacuum. . . . They are the empty men, the unpossessed. . . . The only ruling passion of empty men is the feat of looking foolish." But the acceptance speech gave a different coloration to his viewpoint. Lerner wrote, "It was a great speech for a great occasion, and as I listened I found myself applauding. . . . I came away with a sense of respect for the vitality of the Democratic Party and the way in which the great tradition of progressivism defies the stifling forces of an era of fear."

It is a tribute to feminine insight that amid the lamentations there were two women reporters at the convention who saw that Truman, though average relative to Roosevelt, did have a chance. Anne O'Hare McCormick wrote in the New York *Times* that in the postwar period peoples abroad had shied away from Churchill and DeGaulle because they were too much "personalities"; Schuman and DeGasperi had been able to weather crises because they were "average." Rebecca West in the New York *Herald Tribune* said that it was Truman's misfortune to succeed a giant, but giants produce many ideas that must be digested. "It is not only that giants do not usually have giants in hand to succeed them. It is actually inadvisable for giants to be succeeded by giants. . . . Has he [Truman] not perhaps a perfect realization that a nongiant age has dawned and that he is as good as most nongiants likely to present themselves?"

Southern newspapers greeted the outcome of the convention with sorrow. The Chattanooga *Free Press* said, "This should be a day of mourning for Southern Democrats. Their only consolation is the grim satisfaction that President Truman and his unfaithful cohorts are going down in ignominious defeat." But there was little enthusiasm for political secession. The Atlanta *Journal* thought it was "pitiful" the party should be split "by an issue which could be easily adjusted." The moderate sentiment was voiced by Ralph McGill, editor of the Atlanta *Constitution*: "The party we have known in our time is dead. There is developing a new party. It will be based on strength in the cities. . . . The Democratic Party that eventually must develop . . . will be an urban party, one further to the left of Franklin D. Roosevelt." He saw Mississippi as the focal point of the movement to secede and said, "The general opinion is that they would not be satisfied with less than a repeal of Lincoln's Emancipation Proclamation." Again, "We have seen a curious and hypocritical effort by the tidelands oil interests to use good Southern people who feel a deep and personal sense of injustice and who are hurt by what they consider ingratitude by their party." He said that the South should save its powder for the FEPC fight since the rest of the civil-rights program was inevitable. "Those who love the South realize that the trend in the world is against the Southern idea as expressed in Philadelphia." The best hope of the South was a two-party system, since, if the Democratic Party could be certain at all times of a state's electoral vote, that state could hope for little in the way of office. Kentucky showed that; Barkley got the Vice-Presidential nomination because he came from a state which had a two-party system.

On July 17, two days after the nomination of Truman, a States' Rights ticket of Governor Thurmond of South Carolina for President and Governor Wright of Mississippi for Vice-President was launched by a convention at Birmingham with five hundred delegates representing not only Southern states but California, Indiana, and Maryland. Most of the delegates had not been at the Democratic Convention, and were self-appointed, representing only themselves. Some were college students.

However, Thurmond and Wright were not nominated in the technical sense but "recommended" to the various states so that they could instruct Democratic electors to vote for Thurmond. Senator Russell had been offered the nomination, but declined. He did not want to desert the party of his fathers, and as a matter of personal honor, he felt that since his name had been presented to the Democratic Convention, he was bound to remain in the party. He was a candidate for re-election as Senator from Georgia but since electors could exercise their independent choice, he might have run for President and United States Senator at the same time.

The platform said, "We stand for the segregation of the

races and the racial integrity of each race." There was no mention of "white supremacy" in the platform, which "stunned and amazed" Reverend Gerald K. Smith, who was present. The candidate was escorted to the rostrum under the American and Confederate flags. He said, "We believe that there

Thomas in The Detroit News

"Marching on Washington."

are not enough troops in the Army to force the Southern people to admit the Negroes into our theaters, swimming pools, and homes. . . . If the South should vote for Truman this year, we might as well petition the Government for colonial status. . . . We are going back to the real bosses of the Democratic Party, the people." There was a scrupulous insistence that this was not a "bolt." Governor Wright said,

"I say to you that we are the true Democrats of the Southland and these United States."

The auspices under which the new party was launched did not augur too well for it. Governor Laney, who had been so prominent in the movement, preferred to stay in a hotel room in Birmingham rather than be on the floor, and issued a statement saying, "Whatever is done must be done through and by the official Democratic organizations in each respective state." Southern leaders like Senator George, Senator Russell, and Senator Byrd did not attend. Recognizing the power of political patronage, one speaker scored "office holders of the South" for not attending.

The Southern revolt in 1948 is as perplexing as the secession of 1861. Lincoln did not have the Congressional support in 1861 to restrict slavery and obtained it only when the Southerners walked out of Congress. In 1948 the strong civil-rights plank in the platform was obviously opposed by Truman and the Southerners must have realized that. But tempers had been aroused and forces which had been in motion for several months remained in motion, as was the case in 1861.

Among the pieces of evidence as to Truman's position are these: Representative John Rankin of Mississippi leaving the White House shortly before the convention said that the 1944 plank would be satisfactory to the South. Senator Scott Lucas for the Administration led the fight in the Resolutions Committee for the weak civil-rights plank. At the convention Rhode Island, controlled by Chairman McGrath, voted for the majority plank and so did Missouri. Conclusive proof is in the Forrestal diary, for July 15. ". . . He [Truman] made the observation that he had not himself wanted to go as far as the Democratic platform went on the Civil Rights issue. He said he had no animus toward the delegates from the Southern states, who had voted against the Civil Rights plank and against his nomination. 'I would have done the same thing myself if I were in their place and came from their states.' "

On the surface the Truman record on civil rights was satisfactory to Negro leaders. As a Senator he had voted for cloture in behalf of civil-rights legislation; as President he had demanded that the House Rules Committee release the FEPC bill and then had purged Roger Slaughter in Kansas City for his vote against it; he had appointed William Hastie as Governor of the Virgin Islands and had appointed the first Negro judge in the Continental United States.

Yet the verdict of H. L. Moon in *The Balance of Power—The Negro Vote* (1948), covering events through the civil-rights message, was "Nevertheless, neither the actions nor the words of Mr. Truman carry the conviction that was inherent in Roosevelt's every word and move. There are great numbers of American citizens who remain unconvinced by anything the President says or does."

After the civil-rights message, despite the President's claim that he would not retreat, he was afflicted with what Lincoln called "the slows." In his *Memoirs,* Truman emphasizes his insistence that the program be carried out. "I would not stand for any double talk on this vital principle, however, and insisted on plain language being used. Members of the Cabinet and others warned me that I was riding to a defeat if I stuck to my FEPC orders and if I did not let up on the battle for civil-rights legislation."

But no legislative recommendations were made by the Administration to Congress in 1948 to carry out the civil-rights program. In his civil-rights message the President had proposed a law forbidding interference by public officials or private individuals with the right to vote. Bills to carry out these objectives were drafted with care by the Department of Justice but were not sent to Congress. In his message on civil rights the President said, "I shall shortly issue an Executive Order containing a comprehensive restatement of the

Federal nondiscrimination policy together with appropriate measures to insure compliance." At a press conference on May 13 Truman appeared puzzled when asked if the Executive Order was being prepared. Hours later the White House announced that spadework was being done. From the time of the civil-rights message till the near-end of the campaign in October, the President's only declaration on civil rights was the request to the special session to pass the legislation.

The Washington *Post* (July 21) said editorially, "The President must take the ultimate responsibility for smothering the work of the Department of Justice and for failure to supply the detailed recommendations that the Judiciary Committees of Congress had been led to expect. Nor can we forget that the President himself is ultimately responsible for perpetuating segregation in the Armed Forces which the Democratic Platform condemns."

In March a delegation of eight Negro leaders called on Truman to ask for immediate end of segregation in the Armed Forces. The spokesman was A. Philip Randolph, head of the Brotherhood of Sleeping Car Porters, who had influenced the establishment of FEPC in the war. He told Truman that the Negroes would refuse to bear arms in a future struggle unless the policy were changed, to which the President replied, "I wish you hadn't said that." For months there was no move in that direction. At the end of July, following the convention, the President issued an order setting up a commission to bring about fair employment practices in the Government and setting up an advisory committee to bring about "the equality of treatment and opportunity in the Armed Forces." The New York *Post* asked why an "advisory committee" and why not say "end segregation." Randolph said that the order was "misleading and confusing" and that "segregation would continue." He said that Negroes should refuse to register for the draft but then abandoned that position. It did seem, indeed, that nothing would change. The

President had allowed the Services to decide how quickly equality could be enforced "without impairing efficiency or morale." An assistant to Secretary Forrestal said, "As far as I know, there is no discrimination in the Armed Forces," and Chief of Staff Bradley said that the Army would continue "to put men of different races in different companies."

The Northern Liberals, who were more ardent than Truman on civil rights, did not believe that they were wrecking the party but rather that they were building a broader and stronger base. Marquis Childs, who was in close rapport with them, wrote that Southern conservatives were behind racial discrimination because it enabled them to maintain a low wage base. "Those who argue the Democratic Party should be refashioned point to the Roosevelt heritage. On that foundation they insist a new beginning can be made. They believe that in the South, as industrialization increases there, a new Democratic Party will evolve with genuine ties with the North." The Negro vote in the South itself entered into the calculations. At least 600,000 Negroes in the South were qualified to vote. Even in South Carolina, under the order of Federal Judge Waring which stirred up so much anger, 60,000 Negroes would vote.

At any rate the heavy electoral vote was in the North. Except in the election of 1944, Roosevelt could have done without the electoral votes of Southern and border states. In 1944 he needed only the vote of Maryland among them.

[VI]

THE WALLACE NOMINATION

THE BRITISH JOURNALIST Sir Wilmott Lewis, when a fellow Britisher commented that Henry Wallace was a "singular" man, answered, "No, no, the trouble is that he's plural." Certainly, no one who has talked with Wallace will dispute the fact that the man is complex and not of the common mold.

In his own mind the agonies of his 1948 campaign stemmed from the fact that "I am not a politician." Diffident, withdrawn, other-worldly, life had thrust him into the hurly-burly of handshaking, backslapping politics and almost into the Presidency, which demands the supreme master of the art of politics in the job.

Professionally, Wallace is a scientist and a gifted one. At an early age he made discoveries in cross-fertilization and built a fortune out of his successful development of hybrid corn. (It was certainly ungracious of Soviet Russia to claim during the campaign that his discoveries in biology were Russian contributions along with the radio, electric incandescent bulb, and other inventions.) At the present time on his South Salem farm in New York he has 12,000 chickens and is experimenting in the production of eggs; every twentieth egg on the market today is a Wallace-developed egg. Such explorations to unravel the mysteries of nature do not provide the training and equipment for the mundane task of handling human beings that the politician requires.

Fuzzy in his political thinking, but willing to talk off-the-cuff on many subjects, he could utter gems such as, "For the peace and prosperity of the world, it is more important for the public to know the liberal truth than the reactionary truth. Perhaps one day all of us will be strong enough to stand the real truth." When visiting Soviet-Asia in 1944, he likened Siberia with its huge slave camps to the American frontier of the nineteenth century, saying, "Men born in wide free spaces will not brook injustice." In May, 1948, at Salem, Oregon, he said in a speech, "If people insist on living on such [marginal] land then the Government should not let them have children. People who live on that kind of land have no right to have children." His staff was stunned and prevailed on him to explain in a later speech that day that he had no intent to interfere with procreation.

Another quality that distinguishes him from the ordinary practitioner of politics is that he is a devout Christian and has applied it in his public life. This was the soil for his idealism, embodied during the war in his "Century of the Common Man"; it gave him a sense of mission and fortified him from the abuse that he suffered during the 1948 episode. Discussing the difficulties he had in conveying his message in the campaign he recalls the long time it took for the teachings of Christ to be accepted.

Wallace has human passions and one important for the 1948 story was his abiding hatred of Harry Truman. Wallace regards Truman as a "politician," without principle or conviction and with an amazing capacity to be on all sides of a question not only at different times but at one and the same time. This mediocrity, this "politician" had won out by a hair with the votes of city bosses for the 1944 Vice-Presidential nomination—though Wallace was a renowned world figure. For that Wallace blames not Truman but Roosevelt. He would have been renominated "if Roosevelt had stayed out of it." Then on September 20, 1946, President Truman had fired him from his job as Secretary of Commerce, presumably because of a speech he had delivered in Madison Square Garden on September 12. Secretary of State James Byrnes, negotiating with the Russians in Paris, took violent exception to the speech, since it advocated a radical change in our foreign policy, attacking the "get-tough" policy toward Russia. When Wallace said, "I am neither anti-British nor pro-British, neither anti-Russian nor pro-Russian," he added, "Just two days ago when President Truman read these words he said that they represented the policy of his Administration."

Truman on the morning of the 12th told reporters he had approved the speech that Wallace was to make that night, but later when the storm broke he said he had approved only the making of a speech but did not approve its contents. Wallace says bluntly that that is as untrue as any fact can be. But he says that it was not Byrnes' threat to resign which caused his ouster—Byrnes was already on the way out. Truman in his *Memoirs* says that since his "I'm tired of babying the Soviets" letter to Byrnes, dated January 5, 1946 (which Byrnes denies seeing), "it was understood between him [Byrnes] and me that he would quit whenever I could designate his successor." This immediately precedes the Wallace incident in the Truman *Memoirs*.

The real reason for the ouster in Wallace's mind was the unauthorized release by Wallace of his July 23 letter to the President questioning our foreign policy. The size of our defense budget, the testing of atomic bombs, and our effort to obtain air bases, wrote Wallace, "make it appear either (1) that we are preparing ourselves to win the war which we regard as inevitable or (2) that we are trying hard to build up a preponderance of force to intimidate the rest of mankind." The letter referred also to a school of thought in the country which advocates a "preventive war" now. It was a distorted interpretation of our policy which understandably nettled Truman.

Wallace says that the compulsion for his 1948 campaign was his concern about the atomic bomb and the imperative need for an understanding with Russia to prevent a disaster to mankind. Everything else in his party's program was of minor importance to him except civil rights, about which he felt deeply since one of his forebears, a minister, had been a part of the pre-Civil-War underground railroad. Dr. Vannevar Bush, a fellow scientist, had told Wallace of the bomb in early 1940. Wallace had been aware of the Manhattan Project during the war and had given the implications deep thought.

During 1945 there was a concerted effort by many scientists who worked on the atomic bomb in the laboratories, particularly a group in the Metallurgical Laboratory at the University of Chicago, to dissuade military and civilian leaders from using the bomb against Japan. The full story is told by Alice Kimball Smith, "Behind the Decision to Use the Atomic Bomb: Chicago 1944-1945" (*Bulletin of the Atomic Scientists,* October, 1958). The Report of the Committee of Scientists headed by Dr. James Franck had said, "If the United States were to be the first to release this new means of indiscriminate destruction upon mankind, she would sacrifice public support throughout the world, precipitate the race for armament and prejudice the possibility of reaching an international agreement on the future control of such weapons." On May 28 at Spartanburg, South Carolina, Jimmy Byrnes, to whom Dr. Leo Szilard and Dr. Walter Bartky were referred by Truman, reportedly said that the Government had to go ahead because it had invested $2 billion in the bomb.

There is nothing in Mrs. Smith's account to indicate that Wallace took up the cudgels for the scientists in 1945. "Dr. Franck recalls that he and Dr. A. H. Compton had breakfast with Wallace at his hotel [April] and that he left a copy of the memorandum with him but Wallace had other engagements and the interview was brief." If Wallace's concern about the bomb was as intense as he claims it to be, he could have made his great contribution at that time.

In the *New Republic for* April 15, 1946, Wallace praised Roosevelt for "the highest sort of executive courage" for initiating the atom bomb project. In his history of the bomb, *Dawn Over Zero,* by William L. Laurence, Wallace is mentioned as one of a five-man General Policy Group which launched the Manhattan Project in 1942.

On September 22, 1945, the New York *Times* published a story that in a Cabinet meeting Wallace had proposed that Russia be given the secret of the atom bomb. The Wallace idea, according to the dispatch, was that it was a good time to make a real start toward a working world union through a demonstration of good faith to the Soviet Union. This kicked up something of a newspaper furor; Truman denied that Wallace took a more active part in the discussion than anyone else in the Cabinet. Wallace claims that the subject was brought up by Secretary of War Henry Stimson and that Stimson was the one who proposed the atom-sharing since it was only a matter of time before Russia would produce the bomb. Truman was furious about the leak. Wallace believes that the likely source who misrepresented his role was Matt Connelly, who alone of the President's staff sat in on Cabinet meetings. Wallace says he had only seconded Stimson's position; the *Times* soon afterward said that Abe Fortas, Under Secretary of the Interior, sitting in for Harold Ickes, approved the idea. Tending to corroborate Wallace's version is Mrs. Smith's statement that in April, 1945, Secretary Stimson "was by no means out of sympathy with . . . the two memoranda on the subject of communicating atomic energy developments to the Russians."

After leaving the Cabinet, Wallace became editor of the

liberal weekly the *New Republic,* and its circulation doubled. During 1947 he was acclaimed in Europe when he called for peace, attacking our foreign policy. He addressed at least a quarter million in a successful tour of the United States under the auspices of the radical Progressive Citizens of America. The adulation of the crowds undoubtedly affected him; he showed less interest in the *New Republic* and became more interested in his new political cronies. Communists were now moving in to take charge of the PCA. William Harlan Hale, an editor on the *New Republic,* notes that while in March 1947, Wallace wrote that Americans hesitated to risk an all-out peace effort with Russia because they "are convinced that both the Communist and Soviet Government are intent on dominating Europe and eventually the world," in the late spring he killed a proposed editorial spelling out our suspicions of Russia.

A close associate of Wallace was Dr. Rexford Guy Tugwell, a former member of the Roosevelt brain trust. Dr. Tugwell in 1955 published *A Chronicle of Jeopardy,* which relates his own thinking and mirrors that of Wallace during this period. The Greek-Turkish aid program was an open "affront" to Russia since it supported corrupt military dictatorships and continued the British policy of denying Russia warm-water ports. The Marshall Plan inviting European nations to submit their own plans for reconstruction was an improvement. "Mr. Wallace had the right to claim that he singlehandedly at least changed the Truman Doctrine into the Marshall Plan. He did not exercise the right but everyone knew that it was so." Truman had liquidated the New Deal. Tugwell has a unique explanation for his ouster of the New Dealers. "Though he [Truman] was now collecting honorary degrees voted by the trustees of great universities, he often made remarks indicating a feeling of inferiority because he had never earned one; on the other hand, the Roosevelt liberals all seemed to possess several."

"Big business and the military had taken over the Government," according to Tugwell. "A preventive war was now a fairly established activist objective. . . . Aggression from the combined free world forces was most feared in the Soviet Union." Unless some accord were reached on the atom bomb, "would we not have to become a military state, disperse our cities, go underground, become robots in the interest of an always oncoming struggle?"

Since the Marshall Plan, according to Tugwell, was "substantially what he had advocated," why did Wallace turn against it? He was as inconsistent in rejecting it as in heading a new party, which he had said he would never do. But if he had accepted the Marshall Plan, he would have lost the left-wing support which, as we have noted, wanted to use his candidacy to break labor's support for the Marshall Plan.

Aside from Tugwell and C. B. "Beanie" Baldwin, his former Agriculture Department aide, chairman of the new party, there was hardly a top aide who was not identified either with the Communist Party or a Communist-front organization. The *Daily Worker* gave Wallace reams of publicity and the Communist Party took credit for his candidacy. Why did he not repuditate that support? He was forced to do a continual bobbing and weaving on the subject. He had met only one or two card-carrying Communists; he did not keep up with the Communist press; if the Communists supported him they would have to do so on his own terms; he would have to look up the record and find out what Roosevelt did about Communist support (it was well known that Roosevelt had repudiated it), etc., etc.

Wallace today admits that he broke with the Progressive Party in 1949 because he saw Communists taking over. He expresses doubts, however, about the Communist ties of those in his party, not admitting the charges unless the individuals admitted it or it was proven. This doubt on his part extends even to the notorious pro-Red Vito Marcantonio, of whom

Wallace once said, "He has the best voting record I know of." At any rate, since the Communists had the same objectives in part, he does not know how he could have prevented those friendly to Russia from being for him. Obviously, it was a vexing problem. In New Hampshire, shortly before his party convention in July, he said that he wished that the Com-

Page in The Louisville Courier-Journal

"With a fringe on top."

munists would have a ticket of their own—in that way he might lose 100,000 votes but would gain 1,000,000—but at Philadelphia he changed his tune.

Wallace was certainly not "confused" in accepting Communist support. He was practical enough to have known the score on an issue as clear-cut as this. If he had cast himself free from the left-wingers, lacking labor and Rooseveltian liberal support, the Wallace movement would have disintegrated early. Tugwell had written to Leon Henderson in the spring of 1948 begging him as chairman of ADA to shift progressive strength to Wallace, but the non-Communist left would have none of Wallace. In his *Chronicle of Jeopardy,* Tugwell concludes, "If Mr. Wallace had had the support generally of American progressives, he might more quickly and more firmly have repudiated the support given him by the American Communists." Wallace's admission to me that foreign policy, and particularly the atom bomb, were almost his sole concern strikes at the heart of the matter. It vindicates the stand taken by the progressives against him in ignoring his domestic platform.

Through the early months of 1948 Wallace expended tremendous energy in leading what he called "Gideon's Army." To some extent it was a good analogy, since Gideon's Army of only three hundred had won by blowing horns, clanking pitchers, and sowing general confusion in the ranks of Midianites. But Gideon himself had done the winnowing down to three hundred men from ten thousand—he had not been deserted as Wallace was, and elections are won by counting of noses. Even the Townsendites on whom Wallace had counted and who had supported the Lemke candidacy in 1936 refused to give him support.

This Gideon's army was well heeled. Many of the publicized backers of the party, like Frederick Vanderbilt Field, Wallace cannot recall. The unpublicized angel who made the party possible was Mrs. Anita McCormick Blaine, the eighty-two-year-old daughter of Cyrus McCormick of farm-reaper wealth and widow of Emmons Blaine, son of the renowned Senator James Blaine. She had been a leader in Chicago society for fifty years. Tugwell estimates that she gave at least a million dollars, almost all to local PCA organizations. She ran unsuccessfully as Progressive candidate for trustee of the

University of Illinois. In September, 1948, she gave a million dollars to form the Foundation for World Government.

In many places Wallace met with hostile demonstrations. At Evansville a crowd of 2500 tried to block the entrance to the Coliseum, and "Beanie" Baldwin was roughed up. In Indianapolis the American Legion prevailed on local hotels to refuse rooms to the Wallace group. But this genuine hostility was mixed with a deliberate invitation to persecution, such as Glen Taylor's insistence on entering a meeting in Birmingham through an entrance reserved for Negroes in violation of the state segregation laws, for which he received a well-publicized fine.

Wallace's rally seemed to strike a messiah-like chord. Gardner Jackson saw it in "the single spotlight in the darkened auditorium focused on the lone speaker (the holy leader) . . . the organized chants through a loudspeaker system proclaiming the urgency of the need and the self-sacrificing courage of the saviour . . . the spotlight ceremony of lighting the path of the saviour when he threads his way among the multitude." Margaret Marshall in the *Nation* saw the "leader principle" in his attachment to Roosevelt fetishism and the fact that he offered no way of achieving his goal of peace except by elevating him to power. Wallace admits that he had no specific peace program except voting for him. He was practical enough to be a showman. Wallace rallies were unique because admission was usually charged and collections were made. The collection plate served, he says, to cement the crowd together in the same way as a church congregation.

In March, 1948, Westbrook Pegler published some remarkable letters Wallace had written during the early New Deal to one Nicholas Konstantinovich Roerich—an account of these letters was republished widely, notably by *Newsweek* (March 22).

Roerich, a Russian, was the head of a religious cult connected with theosophy. He had many admirers, including

Igor Stavinsky, some of whom regarded him as a god. Wallace supposedly became an admirer.

In 1934 Wallace sent Roerich on an expedition to Outer Mongolia, presumably on a quest for drought-resistant grasses, but according to Wallace's assistants actually to look for signs there of the second coming of Christ. Then Wallace soured on him, and he was fired in January, 1936. Letters purportedly written by Wallace were produced by Roerich followers in connection with a lawsuit concerning the building housing the Roerich Museum on Riverside Drive and 103rd Street in New York, the intent being to embarrass Wallace.

Photostats of the letters circulated through many hands in the 1940 campaign. There were rumors that Republicans would use these letters as ammunition against Wallace as Vice-Presidential candidate. This news caused consternation in Democratic ranks. Harry Hopkins fumed, "Why didn't I hear about this? Why didn't I hear about this sooner?" Only Roosevelt seemed unruffled. But Joe Martin, then head of the Republican National Committee, decided not to engage in a mud-slinging contest and so the letters were shelved.

Full of mystical mumbo-jumbo, they were known as the "Guru letters" since they addressed Roerich as "Dear Guru" (spiritual leader). Personalities were referred to by symbolic titles—Roosevelt was "The Flaming One," Churchill, "The Roaring Lion," and Cordell Hull, "The Sour One." Here is an excerpt from one letter. "I have been thinking of you holding the casket—the sacred, most precious casket. And I have thought of the new country going forth, to meet the seven stars under the sign of the three stars. And I have thought of the admonition 'Await the stones.' " The handwritten letters were pronounced by experts hired by three newspaper chains to be in Wallace's script. Some of the letters were signed "Wallace," others "Galahad."

Assuming that Wallace wrote the Guru letters, it would have been absurd to have attempted to explain his dabblings into the esoteric to the average American. Theosophy antedates Christianity, and one can understand how Wallace, with his unquenchable curiosity, his religious bent, and his absorption in the mysteries of nature, could take off on an excursion like this. If he had written them, Wallace would have been well advised to have admitted the authenticity of the letters and to have laughed them off. As his caustic critic H. L. Mencken wrote, "No one really cares what foolishness he fell for ten or twelve years ago."

Wallace's alleged influence by the occult and Roerich came up in connection with the Great Pyramid on the back of the dollar bill.

Former Treasury Secretary Henry Morgenthau in his *Diary* wrote that Wallace persuaded him to put it on the bill and only later "I learned that the pyramid . . . had some cabalistic significance for members of a small religious sect." Wallace has a bill framed in his home with a tribute for authorship from Morgenthau.

The fact is that the emblem is the reverse side of the Great Seal of the United States, adopted by the Continental Congress in 1782. Charles Thomson, Secretary of the Congress, said that the pyramid signified "strength and duration." The eye over it is the eye of providence. As Wallace tells it, he noted the reverse side of the Great Seal one day in the State Department and read the Latin legend, *Novus ordo seclorum,* which translates as "The new order for the ages." It struck him as a fine idea to put a permanent proclamation of the New Deal on the dollar bill; when he broached it to Roosevelt, the President was tickled by the idea and endorsed it to Morgenthau. The Wallace noncabalistic version sounds plausible.

The formal birth of the new party took place in Philadelphia in the same convention hall in which the major party nominations had taken place. Arriving at Philadelphia, Wallace reread an old statement that Communist support is a liability, but he wouldn't repudiate "any support which comes to me in the interest of peace. . . ." "No matter how hard you try, I am not going to engage in Red-baiting."

A mammoth press conference with two hundred newspaper representatives in the ballroom of the Bellevue-Stratford turned into a circus. First Wallace announced that he would not repudiate Communist support, "so you can save your breath." Then Wallace was obviously taken by surprise when Martin Hayden of the Detroit *News* asked, "Have you ever repudiated the authenticity of the Guru letters?" Wallace replied, "I never engage in any discussions about Westbrook Pegler." Pegler arose and Wallace repeated the answer. To a flurry of queries from others, Wallace said that he would not engage in discussions with a "stooge" of Pegler and that he would handle the question "in my own way and in my own time." H. L. Mencken, after getting Wallace to agree that he was no "stooge" of Pegler's, said, "Why not answer now, we are all here now. Say yes or no, it can't hurt you." But Wallace wouldn't say yes and wouldn't say no and was impervious to a plea from Doris Fleeson that those who defended him in 1940 and 1944 were entitled to an answer.

For the rest of the conference he was continuously harassed. On a question concerning Tito, he was challenged by Dorothy Thompson on his statement that Yugoslavia of pre-Tito days was feudal. Feudalism had been abolished there by the Turks in the fourteenth century and Wallace didn't seem to know what feudalism was. Reporters who had covered elections in Russian satellites asked him if he could defend Russian dominance of elections in Hungary, Roumania, and Czechoslovakia, and he answered amid general grumbling, "I'd like to have a free election in this country also."

Along the streets of Philadelphia there were Caravans for Wallace like the Peace Caravans which toured the United States against conscription during the period of the Nazi-Soviet pact. Indeed, the personalities in the Wallace camp were the same as in the American Peace Mobilization of 1940—Harry Bridges, Paul Robeson, Lillian Hellman, Donald Henderson, president of the United Food and Tobacco and Agricultural Workers of America, CIO, Grant Oakes, president of the United Farm Equipment and Machinery Workers of America, CIO. Lew Frank, the young scion of a wealthy Detroit family, who wrote many of Wallace's speeches, had been linked to pro-communist causes, including the APM. Choral leader of the convention was Earl Robinson, author of "Ballad for Americans" who also led the APM singers. Supporting the movement were Julius Emspak of the United Electrical Workers, CIO, reportedly "Comrade Juniper," and Ben Gold of the Fur Workers, an acknowledged Communist.

A few days before the convention opened a Federal grand jury in New York had indicted the twelve-man national board of the Communist Party for sedition under the Smith Act. Wallace, arriving at the convention, attacked the indictments as an attempt to silence the third party's opposition to the get-tough-with-Russia administration policy. "The defense of civil rights of the Communists is the first line of defense of the liberties of a democratic people." Baldwin said that the indictments had been timed to embarrass the Wallace party. Asked if he would clean the party up, he replied, "It is the cleanest political organization that ever existed in this country." This was no temporary election coalition, but the "birth of a new party soon to be the first party."

The platform committee deliberated under the chairmanship of Dr. Tugwell. Tugwell says that he was so heartsick about Communist infiltration of the party that he discussed earnestly with his wife his disaffiliating the night before the convention. In his *Chronicle of Jeopardy,* Tugwell says of the convention that the news reports from Philadelphia were sufficient to convince progressives that they were right in shunning Wallace, and then he gently draws the curtain on the unfortunate campaign.

The drafting of the platform was done by the secretary, Lee Pressman, former CIO general counsel who was fired for his leftism and who has admitted that he was a Communist. Appearing before the committee to testify on proposals were a cross-section of members of the party described by the Baltimore *Sun* as "poets, female chiropractors, a gentleman who sought the abolition of interest on mortgages, an artist of renown who wanted art socialized, Negro Elks, members of Greek letter fraternities." There was one witness who was kept waiting eight hours and then asked if he wouldn't forgo testifying since he had distributed his statement to the press. It was James Loeb, Jr., Secretary of the ADA, who accused the party as "a dangerous adventure undertaken by cynical men." Tugwell dismissed Loeb after his testimony without questions, merely saying that his comments were "insincere, hypocritical, and immaterial." He offered the gratuitous remark that the ADA was preparing to support Dewey.

Keynote speaker of the convention was a Negro (among the organized chants was "Jim Crow must go"), a lawyer from Des Moines, Charles Howard, who said that Russia wanted peace but had been thwarted by the United States. "What is at stake is the very survival of Western civilization." Permanent chairman was Albert Fitzgerald, head of the United Electrical Workers, CIO, notorious for its leftist leadership, assisted by leftist John Abt, formerly counsel to the Amalgamated Clothing Workers. Tugwell presented the platform and revealed that this was all in the design of Franklin D. Roosevelt, who had foreseen the new party. In the summer of

1932 on a porch, discussing the future, he said, "Rex, at the end of eight years there may not be a Democratic Party, but there will be a progressive one."

The platform in the domestic field called for the nationalization of utilities, railroads, merchant shipping, and big banks. As for civil rights, in view of the strong Democratic platform all it could say was that Wallace meant it and Truman didn't. It called for the abandonment of the draft, liquidation of our bases abroad, scrapping of our atomic stockpile, the abandonment of the Marshall Plan and the Truman Doctrine, and the end of aid to anti-Communist governments. Tugwell was personally for the Marshall Plan, and the contradiction in the platform he called "unimportant." He also had to swallow an independence-for-Puerto Rico plank to which, as a former governor, he was opposed.

There was no word of criticism about Russia for any action or inaction. A resolution was introduced by a delegate from Vermont that nothing in the platform should be construed as an approval of a foreign power, but this was squelched with the argument that this country had no control over the foreign policy of another country and therefore the resolution could accomplish nothing.

"Wallace or war," chanted the assemblage of true believers (compare "Togliatti or war," "Gottwald or Fascism," "Rakosi or Reaction"). To reporters it all looked like a ceremony, cleverly staged, using the techniques of mass hypnosis. The name of "Progressive Party" was adopted for the third party, now the fourth party in the field. Wallace was nominated as Mencken wrote, "to the tune of such frenzied rhetoric that strong men paled and shook."

Glen Taylor was nominated as his running mate—the problem of Communist support was a simple one to him. "Pink" Communists who believe in changing the Government by evolution would back the New Party, but "Red" Communists would support Governor Dewey because they believe that the best way to get another revolution is to have another Hoover Administration.

Rules proposed by Vito Marcantonio and adopted by the convention gave control to city members predominantly of the Communist Party. Unlike the major parties, representation on the national committee was weighted by population. There was no quorum provision and a majority present could pass resolutions. Forty additional members-at-large could be added to the committee from left-wing organizations.

Lest anyone should get the impression that the party was anticapitalist this would have been corrected at a side show called "National Businessmen for Wallace." Professor Frederick L. Schuman told the gathering that Wallace was "the only capitalist running for President. . . . The Presidential candidates of the old parties have never met a payroll, never run a successful business, and have never acquired capital through their own efforts."

Wallace accepted the nomination at Shibe Park where the faithful paid $30,000 in admissions and made $50,000 in contributions. In accepting the nomination, Wallace offered a solution for the Berlin blockade which pleased the multitude—withdrawal by us from Berlin. "The cold war has already brought death to millions of Americans," he said, adding up the mortality tables for heart disease, cancer, tuberculosis, pellagra, and infantile paralysis, and implying that without the cold war all of them would now be living. Mencken wrote that the "animal magnetism" radiated by the "orgies" in Shibe Park was so strong that the next day the Athletics walloped the Detroit Tigers and moved into first place in the American League.

The Communist Party endorsed the ticket shortly after, and its platform plank by plank was practically the same. Concerning the indictment of eleven Communists on conspiracy charges under the Smith Act, including the outstanding William Z. Foster, a statement of the Communist Party said, "Terrified of the growing support of the Wallace-Taylor ticket, the Democratic high command is seeking to brand the new party as criminal."

The Maryland delegation to the convention offered a resolution condemning Mencken's acid reporting of the activities, but it was not voted on. Mencken could see aside from the Communists, charlatans, and feeble-minded in the "paranoic confection," only a "few raisins," whom he described as "reasonably intelligent folk . . . grocery store economists, moony professors in one-building universities, editors of papers with no visible circulation, preachers of lost evangels, and customers of a hundred schemes to cure all sins of the world."

Wallace has been pilloried sufficiently for his 1948 adventure. He has admitted that he was deceived about Russia's peaceful intentions. In 1948 he says he did not accept the Czech coup as proof of Russian aggressive intentions but as part of the historic drive toward Pan-Slavism. Today he admits that he was "probably" wrong in attacking the Marshall Plan and that a lot of his statements were "campaign oratory." He points out that the press ignored a September statement that he would be in favor of going to war if Russia moved toward the Persian Gulf.

However misguided he was, he convinced himself by one rationalization or another in 1948 that he was a sincere man in a good cause. He seemed sincere in May 1948, when Stalin accepted his letter as an agenda for a peace discussion and Wallace gave thanks that he had been a humble instrument for peace. He seemed sincere when in the same month he boasted that he had more effect in advancing civil rights by getting Truman to act than "all the speeches of all the liberals in the old parties in years past." His deep concern seems genuine today when he says that the problem of reaching an accord on the atom with Russia is an imperative one. When he says that without our foreign aid and armament programs we would be plunged into a depression greater than that of the Thirties, this viewpoint has overtones of his 1948 attitude toward the Marshall Plan as a project put forward for profits. Aside from his professed disenchantment with Russia's intentions, Wallace's approach to our foreign policy is much the same as in 1948.

It is easier to understand Wallace by recalling that he was a product of the Midwest where there were examples of insurgency, like that of La Follette and Norris, who went through periods of martyrdom. Wallace himself by temperament and profession was an experimentalist and innovator. The Third Party was "new" as was his policy toward Russia—in his eyes the "old" policy resulted only in an exacerbation of the rivalry. As an example of trying something new, A. N. Spanel of International Latex tells of an episode in 1946. After a conference with Spanel, Wallace flew out to Detroit to persuade Henry Ford, Sr., that he could atone for his Dearborn *Independent* anti-Semitism by making a handsome gift to the Jews in Palestine. (Ford was too sick to see him.) A final factor to bear in mind is the incredible naïveté on the part of Wallace and his associates. It is staggering to hear from Tugwell that he hoped that the Wallace movement would persuade Truman to put Wallace back in a top spot in the Government, possibly as Secretary of State.

[VII]

THE EIGHTIETH CONGRESS

On July 27 the "worst Congress" confronted the "worst President" in a special session. Speaker Martin's introduction, "The Chair presents the President of the United States," was the shortest on record.

The President's message was not fire-eating in tone but asked for a program mammoth in its dimensions: Anti-inflation measures, low-cost housing, aid to education, increased social security, revision of the Displaced Persons Act, ratification of the International Wheat Agreement, civil-rights legislation, a higher minimum wage. Under anti-inflation powers he asked for price ceilings on goods that significantly effect the cost of living, rationing of products in short supply, and an excess-profits tax. In their spare time in the fifteen days (which Truman had said at the Democratic Convention was all that was necessary) the President suggested it might take up a health-insurance program, a new labor law, universal military training, a stronger Reciprocal Trade Act, and strengthening of the antitrust laws, among other issues. The proposition that Congress could enact this program at the special session was nonsense delivered deadpan.

The President had pulled a brilliant political coup. If Congress came through with any new legislation the President could use it to prove his indictment of what had remained undone; if Congress didn't come through with anything, then the indictment of a do-nothing Congress would be dramatically sharpened. Generally, members of the House and their leaders were in favor of immediate adjournment after hearing the President. The argument was that besides being transparently political, the special session had been pre-judged by Truman when he said, "They are going to try to dodge their responsibility."

Even accepting the bromide that politics is as inseparable from legislation as sex from creation, one is surprised at the frankness of Truman in his *Memoirs* in admitting that he called the special session for political reasons. "Of course I knew that the special session would produce no results in the way of legislation. But I felt justified in calling the Congress back to Washington to prove to the people whether the Republican platform really meant anything or not."

Walter Lippmann pointed out that the President had never threatened to recall Congress while it was in session or as it prepared to adjourn. In fact, he had been traipsing over the country for three weeks and returned only the day before Congress adjourned. It was certainly the feeling of Democrats as well as Republicans that Congress should not reconvene. Three weeks before adjournment Senator Barkley, now the running mate of Truman, had said, "If we sit here between conventions or after the two conventions the entire time of Congress will be taken up with political bickering and political legislation and political oratory and I do not want that to be brought about. I want to finish what we can finish and adjourn the Congress."

Who was responsible for the inspiration? It has been attributed to Bernard Baruch. His biographer, Margaret Coit, pictures Baruch giving the President advice to call the special session while Truman, pacing up and down, said, "You've got something there." This may be so—but it is more likely that the idea flowed so naturally from the President's artificial feud with Congress that he must be given credit as the author.

Dewey was in a dilemma. He had taken the position at the time of the Republican Convention that it would be a "frightful imposition" to call Congress back again. Yet, now he could no more condemn Truman's program than condemn a program to ban sin. The Dewey camp felt that it was unfair to call on the special session to enact housing and social-security planks in the Republican platform. Campaign Manager Brownell ruled out action at "a rump session called at a political convention for political purposes in the heat of a political campaign." Even though the session was legally speaking not "rump," certainly there is no question that the Republican platform contemplated the election of a Republican President. Jim Hagerty, Dewey's press chief, finally announced that "The Governor feels that Congress should stay in Washington and give careful consideration to whatever is proposed in the President's message."

Dewey had taken counsel of many people and got varying advice. Harold Stassen, whom Dewey regarded as a fellow liberal, gave him this advice, "Don't straddle. Either take charge of Congress at the special session or drop it. If you choose to take charge, a few things can be done quickly such as raising the minimum wage above forty cents. But don't straddle." What Dewey did was to straddle.

Republican Party leaders met at the Mayflower Hotel on July 26 to discuss a program for the special session. Brownell attended as Dewey's representative. Those at the meeting recall Dewey wanted two pieces of legislation passed as "must," and the rest of the program was up to Congressional leaders. First, he wanted the loan for the UN Building in New York; second, he wanted a revision of the Displaced Persons Act passed in June. That Act, though admitting 205,000 persons into this country, was labeled as discriminatory. By adopting December 22, 1945, instead of the House proposal of April 21, 1947, as the date when refugees had to be in the US zone of Germany, it barred up to 15,000 Jews who fled the Polish pogroms of 1946. Since thirty per cent of those admitted were required to be farmers and few Jews are farmers, it discriminated against them, and since forty per cent had to come from the primarily Protestant Baltic countries, it discriminated against Jews and Catholics.

Senator Revercomb as Chairman of the Immigration Subcommittee flatly refused to consider a liberalization of the Act. Senator Vandenberg in the Mayflower meeting pleaded for ratification of the International Wheat Agreement, saying "Truman really has us over a barrel." (That agreement would have provided an export market for 185,000,000 bushels of wheat annually.) Agreement was reached on a program for the UN loan, a mild housing bill, a mild anti-inflation bill, Senator Wherry's plan to highlight the South-North Democratic conflict by letting the Southern Senators filibuster to death the anti-poll-tax bill passed by the House, and then adjournment.

Hearings were next started on the Administration anti-inflation bills. The Administration's case was poorly organized. Paul Porter, former OPA Chief, summoned from private practice, defended the Administration bill for a price rollback for selected cost-of-living commodities to November 1947 levels. Senator Capehart, who favored an all-out price freeze if anything, told Porter, "The price of meat can't be controlled without controlling the price of everything that goes into it." Porter could make no convincing reply.

Federal Reserve Board Chief Thomas McCabe said he was not ready to testify. Treasury Secretary Snyder insisted that McCabe testify first. In the face of this "passing the buck" act, Senator Tobey called the President to make them appear.

Marriner Eccles, a member of the Federal Reserve Board, testified as a private citizen and did the Truman cause no good. He viewed the President's message to the special session of Congress as "more political than economic." He thought that the controls would do no good as long as other policies remained unchanged. "As long as you have easy housing credit, as long as you have a floor on farm prices, as long as you have a budget which has no surplus, then you have no chance of controlling inflation." Eccles claimed that Truman was responsible for Humpty Dumpty's fall, was now trying to put him together again. He read the list of controls that Truman had prematurely scrapped. Three days after V-J Day, he ordered controls on prices and production to be lifted as soon as possible. He had scrapped the excess-profits tax. "You know what happened to the wage controls." He said these were "harness controls," and after they were gone it was like a horse trying to pull a load with part of the harness gone.

Secretary Snyder, when he testified, said that price controls were like castor oil, to be taken in an emergency but would not say this was an emergency. The Chairman of the Federal Reserve, Thomas McCabe, conceded that "price controls should be a last resort."

While the price hearings were going on, a polite filibuster went on for days in the Senate against the anti-poll-tax bill passed by the House in the regular session. There were not sufficient votes to impose cloture so the filibuster won out. No civil-rights legislation had been passed in 1948.

While the Capehart price-freeze plan was beaten in the Senate Banking and Currency Committee, five to five, the Administration's plan for selective controls lost six to four. In the end both houses voted to give additional powers to the President to control inflation, to raise reserve requirements of member banks of the Federal Reserve, and to reinstate installment credit controls for consumers, requiring buyers to put up one-third down payments and requiring an eighteen-month limit on payments.

To get consent from the House for the credit controls, Senator Taft was forced to consent to postponement till the next session of the Wagner-Taft-Ellender bill for low-cost public housing. When Senator Tobey nonetheless got the bill reported favorably out of the Banking Committee, Taft was put in the peculiar position of opposing his own bill in the Senate. (Truman made much use of this reversal by Taft in the campaign.) "Damn the torpedoes," said Senator Tobey, and addressing the House members standing in the rear of the chamber, he said, "You have been denied by your leaders the right to vote on the bill." But the Senate went ahead and voted a different housing-assistance bill sponsored by Senator Joe McCarthy, giving substantial financial assistance to private builders, liberalizing Government loan and mortgage guarantees to low cost builders in the $6500 to $7500 bracket and to builders of apartment projects, and the House adopted it.

A notable piece of legislation passed as part of the compromise arranged by Taft was a $65 million loan to enable the UN to build its headquarters in New York on a $13 million site donated by John D. Rockefeller. With these accomplishments, the Eightieth Congress adjourned after an eleven-day special session as Truman denounced it for "feeble compromises" and "failure." The original plan of the President was to go on the air to denounce the Congress but he apparently felt that he had done enough.

The record of the Eightieth Congress played a vital part in the campaign. An astute political analyst, Arthur Krock of the New York *Times,* commented shortly after the 1946 election that it was bad fortune for the Republicans to have carried both Houses. "Long-headed GOP politicians hoped their gains would fall just short of the majorities in the House and Senate." Thus, along with the conservative Democrats they would be able to control legislation and "at the same time to be able to blame all consequences on the nominal majority." Again, in January 1948, he commented that it was "unlucky for the GOP to have carried the Senate as well as the House in the 1946 elections. That gave them responsibility for Congress at a time when foreign policy was about to be engaged in a cold war with Russia and the Constitution reserves to the President the conduct of foreign policy."

Republican control of both Houses did give Truman a winning issue in the campaign. But the label of the "do nothing" or "worst Congress" does not seem to be deserved. The 1952 platform of the GOP referring to the accomplishments of the Eightieth Congress said, "We have a record of accomplishments which was grossly defamed by the party in power."

The list is an impressive one. Aside from what was passed in the special session, here is a partial list of the legislation enacted:

> The Congress launched the program to stop Communism by enacting the Greek-Turkish Aid Plan.
>
> It enacted the Marshall Plan.
>
> It appropriated $9,579,657,129 in foreign aid.
>
> By the Vandenberg Resolution authorizing regional pacts among nations, it ended US isolation forever and gave the basis for NATO. Thus, by the Marshall Plan and the Vandenberg Resolution the program of economic assistance to Western Europe began and the foundation for military assistance was laid.
>
> It unified the armed services.
>
> It revived the draft on a peacetime basis.
>
> It enacted the Taft-Hartley law.
>
> It passed the first long-range agricultural bill enacting the flexible farm price support principle.
>
> It enacted a tax-reduction bill freeing 7,400,000 in the lower tax brackets from payments and enacting the community property principle of splitting taxes among husband and wife.
>
> It gave legal status to the "Voice of America."

It provided for American participation in the International Refugee Organization.

It permitted war veterans to cash terminal-leave bonds.

It extended rent controls.

It added $184,000,000 to Social Security payments increasing benefits to 3,500,000 needy dependent children, the aged, and the blind.

It passed a portal-to-portal pay bill.

It authorized a seventy-group Air Force.

It permitted 205,000 European refugees to enter the United States in two years.

It authorized the Hoover Commission study of government reorganization.

It enacted a Presidential Succession bill.

It submitted to the States the constitutional amendment limiting the President to two terms.

It granted States $450 millions for a two-year period for highway building, authorizing the greatest rural road-building program in history.

It ratified peace treaties with Italy, Bulgaria, Hungary, and Roumania. It approved the Rio de Janeiro Treaty for Western Hemisphere solidarity.

It conducted investigations into the steel industry, grain speculation, and finally the Communist-spy exposés which rocked the country for many years.

It established veterans preference for housing and set up a secondary market for GI mortgages to help private housing.

This is a formidable record and whatever the merits of the legislation, it refutes the indictment of "do-nothingism." In its issue of June 14, *Life* magazine expressed its awe of a hyperactive Congress which passed one thousand bills. If the

Congress had merely passed the Marshall Plan and the Taft-Hartley law, these would have marked it as a notable Congress in our history. In considering the sum total, can one recall a Congress except the first one of the New Deal, 1933 to 1935, which has left an equally living imprint on the life of the American people?

When Truman opened his sudden and unheralded attack in June, it did not occur to independent critics that the record of the Congress was a vulnerable one. Arthur Krock of the New York *Times* in surprise said that the Congress "accepted and in large measure sustained the foreign policy on which Mr. Truman expects, if nominated, to base his chief claim for election." The Washington *Evening Star* said, "Actually this first Republican Congress in sixteen years, handicapped by the need to accommodate itself to a President of another political faith, accomplished a great deal. One may not approve of all the things that were done and one may be justifiably critical because of some of the things that were left undone, but the record of achievement speaks for itself." The Washington *Post* said that in the foreign field Congress showed "statesmanship of high order" and summarized by saying, "The Eightieth Congress seems to be in little danger of falling to the level assigned to it by Mr. Truman in the ardor of his pre-convention campaign."

The Republicans, in fact, thought that the achievements of the Congress would be a major selling point. The *Wall Street Journal* said that Dewey's chief asset was "not a magnetic crowd-appealing personality but the enthusiasm of his followers for his party's record in the past two years." Speaker Martin said, "We are going to brag about it as the most constructive Congress in many years."

Dewey at the opening of the Republican Convention told the press, "the Congress in two years had made a remarkable record, and I am proud of it. For the first time in our peacetime history this Congress launched a great effort to unite and shore up the free nations of the world. It started to rebuild the nation's defenses that the Administration had permitted to collapse at the end of the war. It made good its pledge to bring about a better balance between management and labor and bring some freedom to individual members of labor organiza-

Berryman in the Washington Evening Star

tions." This was to be Dewey's most articulate and spirited defense of the Eightieth Congress.

After the special session, it was believed that Truman was beating a dead horse. A cartoon in the Washington *Evening Star* expressed that feeling.

The Washington *Post* said editorially about his repeated charge of do-nothingism, "Given the limitations of time it [the Congress] actually accomplished a good deal. . . . The charge will not stick for the Eightieth Congress can take credit for some highly important legislation in the field of foreign policy and domestic defense." The Washington *Evening Star* said, "It seems hardly probable that he will get far with attempts to plaster the 'do-nothing' label on the Eightieth Congress as a whole . . . in this instance if he keeps on resorting to it he will find the Republicans capable of reducing it to an absurdity. . . . The Eightieth Congress achieved bipartisan foreign policy accomplishments excelled by few if any earlier peacetime Congresses."

The record of the Eightieth Congress, like that of any Congress, any group or person, can be assessed in terms of what might have been done and was found lacking. At the time of the State-of-the-Union Message no one had believed that the President would hold the Congress to book if it did not enact the whole program into law in 1948. We have pointed out that Walter Lippmann called it a "program for his successors."

Throughout the New Deal and the war period Congress had been dominated by the Executive in the person of Roosevelt. But since 1944 the pendulum of control had shifted back to Congress. In the Seventy-ninth Congress, which Truman had also once labeled as "worst," Truman had been beaten on proposals for emergency housing, expansion of unemployment compensation, stockpiling of strategic materials, a central agency for public works, a fair-employment-practices commission, and a boost in minimum wages. He won only on the Full Employment Act.

Truman called attention constantly to the derelictions of a Republican Congress, overlooking the fact that it was Democratic votes which had defeated him. On public housing the record of the Democrats in the House was no better than the Republicans. Democrats voted 27 to 10 in the Senate to override the veto on tax relief. On the Taft-Hartley law the 20 Democratic votes in the Senate and 106 in the House made it possible to override the veto. Truman's veto of the Social Security bill excluding 750,000 persons but hiking benefits to many groups was overridden with bipartisan support, 297 to 75 in the House and 65 to 12 in the Senate. Truman's personal relations with Congressional leaders were not calculated to bring success to his program. For the first two months of the 1948 session, he had no consultations with his Democratic leader in the Senate, Barkley, and with Rayburn in the House. Barkley had protested to Clark Clifford that he had no advance notice of Truman's forty dollar a person tax-reduction plan. How could he "catch the ball in the dark?"

The Eightieth Congress was no doubt a conservative Congress, as were the Seventy-ninth and Eighty-first Congresses. Roosevelt as well as Truman found trouble on this score with a representative body made up of lawyers and middle-class businessmen. The Eightieth Congress extended the Reciprocal Trade Program for only a year and put in a provision for Tariff Commission peril points that the President could exceed only by reporting to Congress; it turned down money for a TVA steam plant; it allowed railroads to make rate agreements with the approval of the ICC. The failure to raise the minimum wage above forty cents an hour was a glaring omission. Chairman Jesse Wolcott of the House Banking and Currency Committee blocked the Taft-Ellender-Wagner public-housing bill and when a petition forced it out of his committee, Chairman Leo Allen of the Rules Committee prevented consideration. Wolcott says that he was deeply influenced in his opposition to the measure by John Flynn's *The Road Ahead* (proving what a book can do).

The course of legislation is slow and a backlog is always passed to the next Congress. Certain accomplishments in domestic legislation should be examined.

Vetoing the Taft-Hartley bill, Truman said, "I find the so-called emergency procedures would be ineffective. It would provide for clumsy and cumbersome Government intervention. It would result in inequitable injunctions and it would probably result in public confession of failure." The President was wrong in his prediction. He used the emergency provisions six times before the 1948 election to break strike threats, a seventh time unsuccessfully. In May, 1948, he halted an eighteen-day strike of coal miners which John L. Lewis had initiated, by wiring the miners that the contract was no longer in effect. When the Government got an injunction Lewis ran to cover. Then the President used the injunction to halt the threat of a railroad strike. After twelve years intact, the Taft-Hartley Act stands as a monumental achievement.

The tax-relief bill was not a "rich man's tax bill" as Truman charged. It gave seventy-one per cent of tax cuts to those with incomes under $5000 and freed 7,400,000 from paying taxes altogether.

Economy cuts made in the early part of the Congress, called "Taberizing" for Chairman John Taber of the House Appropriations Committee, were so well publicized that they blotted out restoration of the cuts made afterward. The Eightieth Congress appropriated $389 million for reclamation, which was $142 million more than any other Congress, and $800 million for Rural Electrification, which was $244 million more than any other Congress. The peacetime draft enacted by the Eightieth Congress remains and the "flexible support" principle was an important step forward in farm legislation and a basic principle today.

Whatever its conservatism the achievements of the Congress surmounted its failures. The highly liberal Republican New York *Herald Tribune* on May 25 said editorially, "The present session of Congress has been an extraordinarily fruitful one." On June 19 it said in reference to the omissions, "For a Congress under Republican leadership to adjourn with such a record in a presidential year would be political suicide." On June 21 it summed up by saying, "But the great issues were faced and the greatest of them were given in the end the answer which they demanded."

The focal problem was that of the inflation. The wholesale price index which had been 105.2 on V-J Day (1926 equals 100) had risen to 168.8 by July, 1948. The main domestic problem was how to check or control the inflation and to what extent the measures Truman proposed were in harmony or in conflict with that aim.

It did not require an economist to see that there was a patent contradiction between Truman's anti-inflation program and other parts of the Truman program. How could one complain of higher food prices and at the same time ask for high farm supports and more payments to farmers? The program to increase housing expenditures in 1948 when the number of new housing starts was 930,000 (compared to 849,000 in 1947 and 670,000 in 1946) was obviously inflationary, as Marriner Eccles pointed out. The Truman social-welfare program was a spending program in time of inflation. Again, how could one reconcile the proposal for the excess-profits tax with the Truman announcement in his State-of-the-Union Message that the economy needed another $50 billion of investment by industry to expand production and thus, by the law of supply and demand, check the inflation.

The predominant feeling in Congress in 1946 was that controls over prices should be lifted to increase production and Truman himself had taken the lead on that decision, scrapping meat controls before the November elections in 1946 and all controls immediately afterward. At that time he said, "The law of supply and demand operating in the market will, from now on, serve the people better than would continued regulation of prices."

What had frustrated the expectation that prices would go down were several factors—the huge increase in the money supply from $68 billion in 1939 to $173 billion by 1948, the unexpected strength of pent-up consumer and industrial demand, the monopoly power of unions to raise wages, price supports that resulted in a subsidization of our exports, credits given foreign governments through the Marshall Plan, International Bank, and Export-Import Bank, and an easy money policy.

As far as the imposition of wage and price controls were concerned, there was never even a remote chance that Congress would ever accept them. The President was engaged only in politics. In 1947 Truman himself had referred to them as "police-state" methods. When Truman asked for controls in an April, 1948, speech to a meeting of publishers, the Washington *Post* said, "This program, sound though it is in principle, would entail a degree of peacetime economic regimentation that the Congress has no intention of considering in an election year. Under the circumstances, the time and energy that the President has expended in a lost cause could have been devoted much more effectively to vigorous support of specific measures to cope with threatened inflation, such as proposals for giving Federal Reserve authorities additional authority to check inflationary expansion of bank credit."

Experience had shown that selective price controls now urged by Truman would not work. In 1946 Truman himself had said that "our economy is so interrelated that once we start on a program of regimentation we cannot stop short of regulating all major products and rationing many of them." Rationing controls would take months to work out. Most important of all, inflation controls could not work out without wage controls, and Truman as a sop to his labor supporters did not propose to check "noninflationary" wage increases, and he would therefore make price controls meaningless.

The New York *Times* said that the presentation of the background of inflation outlined by the President in the Special Session was "almost inexcusably slipshod and superficial." The attack on inflation was like a "man trying to hit a specific target by standing off and throwing a handful of birdshot at it." When Truman said that the rise in industrial prices was threatening to "destroy a fair balance between industry and agriculture," he was off base, since agricultural prices were 225 per cent above what they were before the war, while industrial prices were only 72 per cent higher. "While it [the message] may not have much to do with inflation, there is something in the document for everyone," said the *Times*.

The President was only going through the motions. When the Korean War started in 1950, there was no attempt on the part of the Administration to impose controls for six months while industrial and consumer prices soared. It was only in 1951, after the Chinese intervention, that the Administration yielded to Congress and re-established controls. In *The Future of American Politics,* Samuel Lubell asks the obvious question, "Why did he seek price control in 1948 but not in 1950? Could it have been that in 1948 he requested legislation that he knew would not be enacted so he could blame the Republican-controlled Congress for whatever happened, while in 1950 he feared that price-control powers *would* be given him, leaving him no alibi for failing to check the rise in living costs?"

The country fattened on the inflation and there was hesitancy on the part of the Administration to curb it for fear that it would be succeeded by deflation and depression. There was a bad commodity break in February and Agriculture Secretary Anderson announced the purchase of 50,000,000 bushels of grain. To the claim of Senator Taft that he was trying to hold up prices, Anderson answered that the purchase had been long in the works. But it was a relief to many when prices started up again. As Bernard Baruch sagely commented, "All I know is that people were wringing their hands when commodity prices got high and now that it looks like they might go down again, they are wringing them all over—or unwringing them, I don't know what." At the time of the special session, Taft in a radio address said, "But the truth is that the moment any agricultural price ever threatens to decrease, the Government rushes in to bolster it by purchase and propaganda. They are really more concerned about depression than inflation." This gave the chance for Chairman McGrath to throw in the harpoon, "It is true the Democrats do not share the traditional Republican indifference to depressions."

A major factor in the inflation was ignored by Truman, that is, the expansion of credit by the willingness of the Federal Reserve Bank to buy back Government securities at par. That was the biggest source of expanded credit since commercial banks could raise money for more credit whenever they needed it. The measures taken in the special session to restrict credit were a nullity for that reason. It was only in the closing months of the Truman Administration that by agreement of the Treasury and the Federal Reserve the "pegging" of Government securities at par was discontinued.

The inconsistency between Truman's spending proposals in his welfare-state programs and the fear of runaway inflation is highlighted by the unpublicized fight within the Administration over the size of the defense budget, the details of which are revealed by Forrestal in his diary. Congress over the wishes of the Administration had authorized a seventy-group Air Force and had appropriated $822 million for it—Air Force Secretary Stuart Symington had pushed for the bigger Air Force, defying Forrestal's wishes, and Congress wanted to make air power a substitute for the Universal Military Training bill. But there was a "hooker" in the $822 million appropriation, making it dependent on a Presidential finding of "necessity." Forrestal prepared a supplemental budget request of $3.5 billion to put the Army and Navy in balance with the bigger Air Force. This was cut by the Budget Bureau to $3.1 billion. Then, on May 13, 1948, Truman decided that he would request the supplemental budget only if the money was not spent and he would use the "hooker" to hold up the enlargement of the Air Force. This was due to the general fear within the Administration that the economy could stand for no more public spending.

There was a clear demarcation in Truman's mind between his foreign and domestic programs. Halleck recalls that in the former he summoned leaders of both parties to the White House; in the latter he summoned Democrats, if any were consulted at all. There is no dispute as to the glittering record of the Eightieth Congress in the foreign field. In February Walter Lippmann wrote, "The real issue, now as in Roosevelt's epoch, is the ability to grasp and master crises. Today it is the crisis of the unsettled peace and the threatened war and the obstructed recovery." In March the Alsops wrote, "The great overriding issue which will confront the country in the next few months will concern the American response to the Soviet expansion abroad." On that great overriding issue the performance of the Eightieth Congress in cooperation with a President of the opposite party who was bent on election left nothing to be desired. In June Senator Vandenberg said he "doubted whether a better record has been made by any Congress." During the campaign Vandenberg said in a speech, "When history is written the Eightieth Congress will be remembered for the record in foreign relations long after other relatively transient issues have been forgotten. I respectfully suggest that the record makes the Eightieth Congress in all that it relates to our foreign affairs not the 'second worst' in history as we sometimes hear in general attack, but the first best."

The standard bearers of the Republican Party in 1948 did not choose to defend the Congress in these terms. Charlie Halleck says today, "It always galls me to think that Harry Truman won in 1948 by attacking the Congress which gave him his place in history."

[VIII]

THE GREAT MISCALCULATION

IT IS GENERALLY accepted today that the Republican campaign strategy of 1948 was a mistake and cost the election. Dewey himself is candid in admitting the error: "The people want a blood and thunder campaign on the national level." Two weeks before the election, as we shall see, he realized that he was losing ground, but then, he says, it was too late to switch the strategy.

After the conventions there was every reason to believe that Dewey would carry on the same aggressive campaign that he had waged in the 1944 Presidential race. He had given the Administration no quarter during the preconvention campaign. In a message to the New York State legislature in January, he had put the blame squarely on the Administration for causing inflation by scuttling controls at too early a date. In February in endorsing the Marshall Plan, he had blasted the Democrats for their appeasement policies which delivered millions of people in Central Europe and China to the Communists. In April he had criticized foreign policy as being too often wrong before being right, and had taken the Administration to task for its careless endorsement of the Madison Square Garden Wallace speech in 1946, its belated stand against Communists in the US, and its muddling in China. In Oregon Dewey attacked this "incredible Administration of ours" for its course "of appeasement one day and bluster the next." In Oregon he had shown his mastery in debate when he tore Stassen limb from limb. Dewey and Warren had climbed to prominence as prosecutors and they had an inviting wide-open target for prosecution in the inept administration of Harry Truman.

It was in early September that inspired stories indicated the Republican strategy would call for other than fire-eating. The Alsops reported that Dewey would take the "high line." He would resist the temptation to engage in recrimination or play the prosecutor on the Red issue. On foreign policy he would stress the gravity of the crisis and our role in world affairs. Robert Albright reported in the Washington *Post* that Dewey would give Truman the silent treatment and would refuse to "rough" it—that he would leave to others the running of interference. He would do very little harking back to the past, because it was time to stop raking it over. He would act as if Truman were the candidate on the defensive. If he took time to answer every Truman sally, "it would let the President, not the Governor, determine the kind of campaign Dewey makes."

During July and August the fateful decision had been made to wage the "high-level" campaign which cost the victory.

The recollection which lingers in the popular mind today about 1948 is that because of smug overconfidence Dewey took the election result for granted, put no real effort into the campaign and thus lost a sure thing by default. Clarence Buddington Kelland, national committeeman from Arizona, put it that way after the defeat. "The Dewey campaign was smug, arrogant, stupid, and supercilious. . . . It was a contemptuous campaign, contemptuous alike to our enemies and our friends."

To make this judgment from the barren content of Dewey's speeches is as misleading as to say that Hamlet was "smug" and "supercilious" about his father's murder because he took no action. The election was not thrown away by indifference or lack of effort. Preparation and more preparation had always been the distinguishing characteristic of Dewey and his team throughout his career from the time he was a rackets prosecutor. Meticulousness and detail marked everything that was done to get Dewey the nomination. These habits of work were not suddenly jettisoned after he became the nominee. Dewey, in spite of a painful siege of bursitis, worked as hard as anyone could in a type of campaign innately distasteful to him. The truth is that the type of campaign was the result not of careless, but too careful and painstaking, calculation. The Dewey campaign line was frozen into inertia not because it had been underthought, but because it had been overthought.

Dewey had a two-platoon system, a team to get him the nomination and a team to win the election. The first team, Herb Brownell, Russ Sprague, and Ed Jaeckle, having done its work, was shunted off. Brownell as campaign manager and National Chairman in fact was put in charge of a housekeeping operation, maintaining liaison with the state candidates and organizations, arranging TV and radio time and the financial details. Sprague was given a fine office in Washington with not much to do, and he commuted with his Nassau bailiwick. In 1944 he had assembled a volunteer group of the highest-paid public-relations minds to meet regularly in New York City to create campaign ideas. The group included Carl Byoir, Steve Hannagan, Bruce Barton, and John Flynn. Ideas were sent to Albany, but when it became apparent that none would be used the meetings halted. Sprague was cured and did not try again in 1948. Jaeckle was on the campaign train, but he was along mainly to greet politicians.

The second team, "the Albany crowd," now took over. At the head of the brain trust was Elliott V. Bell, State Superintendent of Banking. If anyone can be tagged as the architect of the disaster, it is Bell. He had met Dewey years before when he was a financial writer for the New York *Times,* and they became close personal friends. Dewey imbibed his knowledge of economics and national affairs from Bell. Bell had worked out for Dewey the blueprints for his two successful gubernatorial campaigns and was his chief speech-writer in 1944. The relationship was so close that some have regarded the strong-minded, opinionated Bell in the role of Svengali to Dewey's Trilby. The influence could not have been as great as it was, if Dewey's thinking had not tended along the same lines as that of Bell, but the Trilby image has substance. Bell is scholarly and able to think along broad, philosophic lines, while Dewey, although he is superb in a delimited subject with a set of facts, is lost in the realm of abstract ideas.

Dewey needed and relied on Bell for facts, too. Senator Jenner, who headed the GOP Speakers Bureau in 1948, points out an obvious fact which is overlooked—that Dewey was ill-informed about national affairs at a time when they had become so complex that one needed to be a specialist in them. Dewey's background did not equip him with that knowledge. He had been a lawyer, racket-buster, district attorney, and state administrator. The Governorship of New York is not a good training ground today for the Presidency. He did not know national issues, except in a broad sense. It was to prove a fatal handicap in the campaign, particularly on the farm issue. He relied on Bell to fill the gap, but Bell himself had been immersed in state affairs for years.

Because of their background as New Yorkers and the fact that their reading was confined to the metropolitan press, the outlook of Dewey and Bell was "provincial"—which was an important element in their campaign conduct. It is significant that Dewey's two "must" items for the special session—the UN building and revision of the Displaced Persons Act—were those which he as a New Yorker would understand.

There were many visitors to see Dewey at the Executive Mansion in Albany in the summer months and after seeing him they conferred with the strategy board in a suite in the DeWitt Clinton Hotel. This inner-circle group was headed by Bell. It included Senator Henry Cabot Lodge, whose influence grew steadily in the campaign. It also included Representative Everett Dirksen, retiring from the House because of failing eyesight. He was supposed to have been the authority on the Midwest, but he fitted in quite well at the time with the Eastern "liberal" group. He was a different Dirksen from the Dirksen of today.

The group rubber-stamped Bell's ideas. The 1948 strategy emerged out of Dewey's traumatic 1944 experience in being beaten for the Presidency. It is reasonable to say that had it not been for 1944 the 1948 strategy would have been different.

With his great will to win, Dewey finds defeat hard to take. He did not take into account how well he had done in 1944 against the master politician of the age. There were only 3,600,000 votes between Roosevelt and Dewey—the closest race since 1916. Roosevelt had squeaked through in many states. In twelve states with 211 electoral votes, he had fifty-three per cent of the votes, or less. But as far as Dewey was concerned, he knew only the sting of defeat.

The first lesson in 1948 was the danger of a slam-bang attack. Dewey and Bell believed that a change in strategy beginning with the Oklahoma City speech was a major contributing factor to the defeat in 1944. In his celebrated "Little Fala" speech before the Teamsters Union, Roosevelt poured ridicule on Dewey. This infuriated Dewey and in Oklahoma City he made a fighting speech in which he accused Roosevelt of "fraud and falsehood" and of "maligning, ridicule, and wisecracks." Roosevelt was "indispensable" only to Harry Hopkins, Madame Perkins, and Harold Ickes. He accused the President of not preparing the country for war, a charge previously leveled by the war investigator, Senator Truman. "The simple truth is that Mr. Roosevelt's record is desperately bad. It is not one on which any man should seek the confidence of the American people." Republicans were delighted with the invective approach, wires poured in and also contributions. "More, more," they cried. Dewey was under pressure to use the Oklahoma City sizzling tone for the rest of the campaign.

Elliott Bell felt that party rallies, although they gloated over the Oklahoma-City-type barbecue, were deliberately sacrificing the national candidate to local passions, that the statesman was losing out to the politician and that the applauding audiences were solidly Republican anyway. The dissatisfaction of liberal columnists (who were not for Dewey anyway, but whom Dewey and Bell read avidly) with the Oklahoma City speech impressed them. A passage from Robert Sherwood's *Roosevelt and Hopkins,* published in 1948, carried commanding weight, purporting to give Roosevelt's inside view of the campaign. The Teamsters speech

> ". . . disrupted Dewey's carefully cultivated self-assurance and caused him to start swinging wildly against the most artful dodger of them all. More and more Dewey felt impelled to appeal to the prejudices of his immediate audiences in order to get applause. He had been given a well-rehearsed performance as a liberal crusader, albeit a soundly practical one; but now his speeches began to sound more and more like those of his running mate, John W. Bricker. . . . Dewey seemed to forget that these audiences were recruited by the local Republican machine and were therefore composed largely of people who would still have been grimly and irrevocably determined to vote against Roosevelt even if the Republican candidate had been named Tommy Manville instead of Tom Dewey. Such audiences greeted in stony silence the advocacy of any policy, such as minimum wages or social security, which smacked of the despised New Deal. In bidding for their cheers and for their hoots and catcalls whenever Hopkins or Ickes or Frances Perkins was mentioned, Dewey ignored the great mass of undecided voters who were listening over the radio. . . ."

Reinforcing this viewpoint as to the Oklahoma City speech, was a capsule summary in Dewey's mind as to his experience. Dewey says, "I waged an all-out fight [against Governor Lehman] in 1938 and lost. I waged an all-out fight in 1944 and lost. In 1942 and 1946 I waged a different kind of campaign for the Governorship, not even mentioning my opponents, and won by large majorities." This seems to be a fallacious *post hoc, ergo propter hoc* type of reasoning. In 1938, for example, the very narrow margin by which Dewey lost to Lehman was in itself a sensational upset and put him into the national limelight.

Fulton Lewis, Jr., says he talked with Dewey in August at his office in Albany about a radio broadcast. "This campaign will be different from 1944," said Dewey. "That Oklahoma City speech—," Lewis began.

"Exactly," Dewey replied, "it was all wrong. I was attacking the dignity of the office I was seeking."

"I didn't think so," Lewis replied, "I thought it was great. I thought you were attacking the dignity of the man who was seeking the office."

A second lesson of 1944 was the danger of emphasizing local issues. The Los Angeles Coliseum rally with 90,000 present, the second biggest rally in history, had been entertained and thrilled for hours by Hollywood celebrities introduced by Adolph Menjou. Dewey arrived dramatically and doused out all enthusiam with a dull discourse on social security. "This is wrong, all wrong," said Bell to speech-writer Arthur Barnett, as soon as he surveyed the mob. The idea behind the choice of subject was that people in the Los Angeles area were Townsendites. In reference to this experience Raymond Moley, to whom Dewey had turned for advice since 1940, wrote to Dewey on March 26, 1948: "As I look back to 1944, it seems to me that you have weighed too heavily in each speech the appropriateness of what you say to the specific section or audience that you are addressing. People are not essentially different as you move from one part of the country to another. . . . The Social Security speech in Los Angeles you know and I know was a turkey for the simple reason that people there do not want to be identified with one idea." Moley advised Dewey to work out some basic concepts for his campaign on which his speeches could be built. This was sound advice which Dewey did not carry out. The "high-level" campaign was an attempt on Dewey's part to rise to a higher level above local, parochial appeals but the one basic concept Dewey worked out was the bloodless one of "unity."

The third hangover of 1944 played perhaps the greatest part. In 1940 Dewey was considered a conservative—he had written that year a book, *The Case Against the New Deal.* He was considered to have isolationist tendencies. In January, 1941, he attacked Roosevelt's Lend-Lease proposal. Not until the Mackinac Island conference in 1943 did he blossom out as an internationalist. In 1944 he was a full-fledged liberal on the lines of Wendell Willkie. In the 1944 campaign his program was labeled as "me too." In Seattle he endorsed the Wagner Act. In San Francisco he advocated a Government guarantee of full employment for all, protection of farmers against excessive price fluctuations, and maintenance of unemployment insurance, minimum-wage laws, and old-age pensions. In Los Angeles he urged that old-age pensions and survivors insurance should be extended to twenty million not covered by existing laws. The New York *Times* commented, "Mr. Dewey has just about completed the process of running for President on the domestic platform of the New Deal." Dorothy Thompson wrote, "Dewey seems to think he is applying for an office manager's job."

Dewey was well aware of the fact that his liberal position in 1944 had cost him votes of old-line Republicans. Yet, Bell had sold him on the idea that this was the "realistic" approach, that a Republican could not win without votes of

Roosevelt independents and therefore the regular Republican votes must be taken for granted. This "schizophrenia" in the Republican Party as Bell calls it weighed heavily on Bell's mind as well as that of Dewey.

Facing the campaign of 1948 Dewey saw the "schizophrenia" in the party in an even more aggravated form than in 1944, since the contest between the liberal and conservative wings, isolationist and internationalist, had been waged in the Eightieth Congress. The record of the Eightieth Congress, moreover, was more heavily slanted on the conservative side than Dewey's own personal philosophy. Whatever position Dewey took, as he saw it, he was sure to be caught in the cross fire between the two wings and exposed to attack by Truman, who would single out features of the legislative record for which Dewey would be held responsible.

In an article in September's *Harper's,* Elmer Davis referred to the "antediluvian troglodytes" in Congress whom he called "Dewey's strange bedfellows." He did not find them in the Senate but in the House. They included Halleck, Martin, Knutson, Taber, Arends, and Wolcott. He said the GOP "must run on the total record of the 80th Congress and the Democrats immediately realized that the record of the House of Representatives is the glass jaw of the Republican Party. They will be poking away at the glass jaw through the campaign; they may not be able to hit hard enough for a knockout but they may cause Dewey a good deal of embarrassment by compelling him to keep covering up." Dewey shared that feeling about Republicans in the House.

There was a conflict of impulses—to speak out boldly on New Deal lines and thus risk antagonizing the conservative wing or make concessions to the conservatives and thus risk the loss of the "independents." What better escape then from the dilemma than to soar to empyrean heights, disassociating himself from the more mundane issues of the day?

The lofty position Dewey assumed gave some collateral

advantages, which people around Dewey say were considerations in the strategy. During the campaign Dewey felt that he was laying the groundwork for his term as President. He wanted to be able to say as in his acceptance speech that he had made no commitments and that he therefore enjoyed freedom of action in framing policy. Moreover, on his Olympian heights he could act the part of a statesman and not a politician and thus gain the confidence of the electorate as a person to whom the affairs of Government could be entrusted. The unusual success of Dewey's stand in his Stassen debate fortified the belief that moderation, statesmanship, and non-divisiveness would appeal to the voters.

People say Dewey was so overconfident because of the polls, and therefore said nothing in the campaign. This is a complete misconstruction of what happened. Actually, because of overconcentrated thinking, Dewey saw the dangers in an outspoken campaign. Then the question arose, can we get away with silence. The role of the polls was only to assure the Dewey people that such a strategy would be safe. The three big national polls, the Gallup Poll, the Crossley Poll and the Roper Poll, showed Dewey far ahead. Elmo Roper announced in July that he had stopped polling, that it was silly to continue to take polls since the result was forgone and he could spend his time profitably otherwise. "I can think of nothing duller or more intellectually barren than acting like a sports announcer who feels that he must pretend that he is witnessing a neck-and-neck race that will end in a photo-finish or a dramatic upset of the favorite and then finally have to announce that the horse which is eight lengths ahead at the turn is still eight lengths ahead at the end."

Then there was the opinion of political experts that Dewey was sure to win. Never had there been such a unanimity of feeling. *Fortune* magazine in August asked, "Is the country again entering into an 'era of good feeling'? . . . The prospects of Republican victory are now so overwhelming that an era of what will amount to one-party rule may well impend." Of course, Dewey was infected with this rosy prospect. Stassen says that when visiting Dewey at his farm in Pawling

Justus in The Minneapolis Star

"There's many a slip."

in July he warned Dewey that he faced a formidable foe. Dewey, smiling, pulled out an advance release of Elmo Roper's announcement and said, "My job is to prevent anything from rocking the boat."

Then there was the hallucination called Farley's Law

which read that people had made up their minds by summer how they would vote and campaigns were necessitated by custom and the need to pep up party workers. Why voters' minds were not pepped up and changed as much as party workers' and why events occurring between September and November could not have at least as much effect on people's minds as events before September nobody bothered to explain. Actually Farley's Law meant only that in Roosevelt's time F.D.R. was sure of victory by summer, and even that was doubtful in the Willkie campaign.

Then there was the traditional idea that the radiation of confidence by a candidate was an automatic vote-getter because of the "band-wagon tropism" of the voters.

Dewey was the first Presidential candidate who was born in this century and prided himself on being "a child of the twentieth century." He was an exponent and exemplar of efficiency. When he ran for the Republican nomination in 1940 he had his own pollsters who tested every stand he took. The 1948 plan of action (if it can be called action) must be viewed as a reflection of a twentieth-century modern-management approach. You must study not only the present but the past. You must profit by the experience of past errors. You must have a plan which is worked out by collective thinking of the best brains. That plan must set the fixed pattern for execution. (This is dangerous if the plan in operation shows flaws.) The great weight assigned to the polls in the framing of the plan is typical of the importance that pseudo science assigns today to statistics.

The results of the election showed the flaws in the modern technique—an a priori plan could not provide for the vagaries of human psychology, a fixed plan of action robbed the Dewey camp of the spontaneity, originality, and mobility which Truman enjoyed by playing the game by ear. Raymond Moley, boarding the Dewey train at Albuquerque, was astonished to find so many speech-writers headed by Bell together in the "squirrel cage," the next to the last car of the train. The last was Dewey's private car. It occurred to Moley that writing speeches by the collective-thinking method would only result in reducing the content to the lowest common denominator and would squeeze all the juice out. When he was Roosevelt's chief brain-truster in 1932, he alone had worked with Roosevelt on the final drafts. Speaking of the group method, William H. Whyte, Jr., in *The Organization Man,* says, "Vital they are to executing ideas but not to creating them. Agreement? To concentrate on agreement is to intensify that which inhibits creativity."

Warren had no hand in the strategy decision. The Dewey inner circle found Warren a "strange duck," a viewpoint which they continue to hold. Warren said that he was interested in only two issues, socialized medicine and Government building of transmission lines from dam sites to compete with private utilities. Dewey said "no" and Warren retorted that he had no more to talk about. He was, however, a "good soldier" in the campaign and followed the Dewey line religiously. His net contribution to the Dewey vote was viewed as zero—he had been expected to lend weight to the ticket in California and Minnesota.

Just as Dewey sidetracked details of domestic issues, he foreclosed himself on foreign issues. Tension was at a high point after the political conventions. From June 24, the day that Dewey was nominated, the Soviets had blockaded Berlin so that the Western sector had to be supplied by air. The foreign-policy plank of the Democratic platform was enough to make the Republicans foam at the mouth. It claimed sole credit for the United Nations charter and the European Recovery Plan, ignoring Republican votes and the active labors of Republicans like Senator Vandenberg and John Foster Dulles. On a dog-eat-dog basis, as David Lawrence pointed out, the GOP could have made political hay by pointing out that if the Democrats took credit for the ERP by the same token they should take credit for the inflation that it was aggravating. Lippmann said that the Democratic platform was a "scandal of ingratitude, ungenerosity, and untruth."

Immediately after the convention it was believed that Dewey would soon take the wraps off the foreign-policy issue. In his first press conference he said he would attack the Administration for "bungling" and "vacillation" on policies on which no bipartisan collaboration had been asked—China, Greek-Turkish aid, Palestine, and the Potsdam Conference. He put great emphasis on China. But on July 24 Dewey issued a statement whose importance was overlooked at the time. Referring to the Berlin crisis he said that Americans would not be "divided by past lapses" in foreign policy in the interest of the country. We must "unite to surmount present dangers. We shall not allow domestic partisan irritations to divert us from the indispensable unity."

Dewey at the time felt quite strongly that the Berlin blockade was due to the mistaken decision made at the London conferences preceding the Potsdam Conference: that it was unnecessary to get specific corridor rights to Berlin. But after conferring with John Foster Dulles and Senator Vandenberg, Dewey decided not to make this a political issue. Dewey let it be known in early August that in the 1944 campaign he had not made a political issue of the fact that Pearl Harbor happened, even though the United States had previously broken the Japanese Naval Code. Some of the messages decoded had tipped off the attack. Dewey was silent because General Marshall asked him to refrain from using this issue since we were still decoding Japanese messages in 1944. Now he was forgoing another issue for patriotic reasons. But in 1944 we were at war, in 1948 we were not.

From this decision about Berlin, it was an easy step to be persuaded to forgo the entire foreign policy issue, including how Democratic Administrations had lost the peace. Allen Dulles was the foreign-policy specialist on the Dewey campaign train. Forrestal recorded in his diary on November 7 after the election, "Allen Dulles said he thought the greatest mistake in Mr. Dewey's campaign strategy was the failure to attack the Democratic record more vigorously. . . . Among other areas in which they [his advisers] restrained Mr. Dewey was the sequence of diplomatic decisions at Tehran, Cairo and Yalta. They did not do so [sic] because they felt that injecting these issues into the campaign would have been destructive of the effort toward bipartisan foreign policy."

There was one tentative stab by Dewey into the foreign-policy field. On August 17 Dewey said that the former Italian colonies should be returned to the administrative control of Italy under a UN trusteeship. Of course, this would have a great appeal to Italian voters and the Democratic National Committee was upset. Truman replied that Dewey was playing politics, to which Dewey answered that he "had a solemn obligation to lay fully and frankly before the American people his views on world affairs." The Administration took the position that if the US by treaty or compact associated itself with other nations in solving problems or was in process of negotiation with other nations in the United Nations, then the problems should not be brought into the campaign with new or unilateral proposals for solution. Since every international question was in multilateral conference or in dispute, under this interpretation Dewey would have been barred from discussing Palestine, China, the Pan American Conference, Germany, Western Europe, Berlin, or colonial questions. Nevertheless the subject of Italian colonies was poorly chosen for an excursion into foreign policy. The colonies had been a drain on Italy and Premier deGasperi, replying to the Dewey wire, said he was not interested in the proposal. Although Dewey was not expected to acquiesce to the Administration viewpoint, he not only dropped the subject of the Italian colonies but never criticized another foreign problem during the campaign.

The research staff of the Republican National Committee, on the basis of the memoirs and papers of thirteen officials in the Roosevelt and Truman regimes such as Morgenthau,

Bullitt, and Hopkins, prepared a monumental document, "Democratic Duplicity and Appeasement in Foreign Policy," a compilation of all the alleged blunders which lost the peace. It was submitted to Albany for clearance. The reply was that although it had "appetizing" material its proper use was to make it "available" to members of Congress who were interested. So it was shelved.

There was one area of foreign policy in which Dewey's election might have made a difference. Dewey and his advisers, notably John Foster Dulles, were China-minded, while the eyes of the Administration were glued to Western Europe. The Nationalist position in China in the fall of 1948 was rapidly deteriorating. Congress had voted $125,000,000 in aid in early April but six months later not a rifle or bullet had reached Nationalist China. As President, Dewey might have sponsored a massive aid program and avoided what may turn out to be our most costly mistake in foreign policy.

At the end of July during the special session of Congress the Communist-spy issue exploded with an intensity which put all other issues temporarily in the background. A self-confessed Communist, Elizabeth Bentley, testified before the House Un-American Activities Committee that as a Communist spy she was intimately acquainted with two spy rings operating in Washington during the war, one headed by Nathan Gregory Silvermaster, formerly of the Board of Economic Warfare, and another by Victor Perlo, formerly of the War Production Board and now an economic adviser to Henry Wallace. She said the rings had a pipeline into the White House through Laughlin Currie, formerly an assistant to Presidents Roosevelt and Truman. She testified that Harry Dexter White, formerly Assistant Secretary of the Treasury and father of the International Bank and International Monetary Fund, was connected with the ring, and got them "top secrets." Currie and White, she claimed, had intervened to prevent Silvermaster from being kicked out of his job on the Board of Economic Warfare in 1942 after the Office of

Naval Intelligence had protested because of allegations of disloyalty. Secrets had been so freely given out that one member of the ring won a pool by correctly "guessing" the date of D-Day. He got the information from Currie, Miss Bentley said. And when the United States was on the verge of breaking the Russian code, that news also came from Currie. She said thirty-two Government employees gave her information which she took to her lover, spy-chief Jacob Golos, who in turn passed it on to Russia.

She was followed to the stand by Whittaker Chambers, then an editor of *Time* magazine, a self-confessed ex-Communist, who said he had been connected with a ring which sought to infiltrate Government agencies. He gave sensational testimony about spy charges that he had brought to the attention of President Roosevelt at the outset of the war through Assistant Secretary of State Adolf Berle. He said that Communist rings had included prominent names like former high State Department official Alger Hiss, Donald Hiss, Nathan Witt, who was former secretary of the National Labor Relations Board, Lee Pressman, John Abt, and others. Harry White had worked with the rings. To these charges Pressman, Witt and Abt pleaded the Fifth Amendment. Hiss, Currie and White denied them outright. White and Currie admitted friendships with members of the alleged ring and intervening with Under Secretary of War Patterson to keep Silvermaster's job, but disavowed any meaningful connection with Communism. Both admitted that they had visited the basement in which Miss Bentley said Silvermaster had equipment for photostating Government documents.

John Abt, of the Wallace movement, had called the charges a "red herring" during the Bentley testimony. In a press conference Truman a few days later characterized the hearings as a "red herring" designed to distract public attention from the failures of the Eightieth Congress. He said, "The public hearings now underway are serving no useful purpose. On the contrary, they are doing irreparable harm to certain persons, seriously impairing the morale of Federal employees and undermining public confidence in the Government." Truman adopted the unusual procedure of allowing himself to be quoted. A few days later the President again attacked the hearings as a violation of the Bill of Rights and said that the "red herring" was the strongest type you could smell. Truman was genuinely annoyed that the spy hearings were taking the spotlight from his pet issue, the Eightieth Congress.

Although public interest was centered on the issue of veracity of Hiss or Chambers, the more significant figure from the standpoint of public administration was a thirty-two-year-old economist, William Remington, named by Elizabeth Bentley as an espionage source. She said he had given her information on airplane production and how to make synthetic rubber out of garbage. Remington took the Bentley charges with a good deal of *sang-froid*. In fact, he hailed her for her public contribution. Remington admitted that he "was definitely associated with individuals who were Communistic in their sympathies." He testified that he met Miss Bentley in such surreptitious places as street corners and park benches and in a manner which he characterized as "unusual." He admitted that he received and paid Miss Bentley for copies of the *Daily Worker* and gave her money, which she said was for Communist Party dues. He admitted that all her testimony was true—but that the information was not secret and she had misunderstood his motives.

The Ferguson Senate Investigations Subcommittee, whose counsel was William P. Rogers (now Attorney General), made a report on the Remington case on September 4. It was not concerned with the truth of the charges against Remington (who later came to a tragic death), but rather with the attitude within the Administration to an employee who was suspect of disloyalty. Elizabeth Bentley told her story completely between August and September 1945 at the New Haven office of the FBI. But Remington was able to hold sensitive positions in the Government up to the end of June 1948 when he was suspended and his case referred to a loyalty board. He himself characterized his ability to hold high posts as "fantastic" in the light of the information the FBI had from which he had not been cleared.

In 1944, applying for a Navy commission, Remington had stated on his application blank that he was familiar with the Manhattan (atom bomb) project, which was so confidential that the facts about it were kept from the Truman Investigating Committee. Yet after the Bentley charges in 1945 he worked with the Harriman committee which framed the Marshall Plan, during which time he was being investigated by a New York grand jury; he became chairman of the *ad hoc* committee in the Commerce Department's Office of International Trade which screened exports to Russia and her satellites; he was even offered a position on the Atomic Energy Commission but refused it because he said he would be put in an "uncomfortable" position. The Ferguson Committee asked for the employment file on Remington, not the security file. "The subcommittee wants to know (1) whether the interested Government agencies were notified of Remington's alleged espionage activities; (2) the manner in which and to whom and when such notice was given; and (3) what action, if any, was taken by Remington's superiors upon receipt of the information."

In other words, the committee wanted to know how the loyalty program was working, what the Administration was doing about persons *suspected* of Communism, a proper and legitimate concern of Congress. The Administration refused the information. The Bentley and Chambers charges were not proven, but the Remington case did show that the Administration's loyalty mechanism was most ineffective. The Silvermaster case also raised the question as to how a man could hold important government jobs for years after the Civil Service Commission had impugned his loyalty. A Civil

Service report said that Silvermaster "was and is now probably a Communist and an agent of the OGPU." Silvermaster invoked the Fifth Amendment on his being a Communist.

The Ferguson Committee attacked the whole loyalty administration for a lackadaisical approach. Executive Order 9835 governing the loyalty program was issued March 1947 but not until December, 1947, was the Loyalty Review Board which implemented the program established. Seventeen months after Executive Order 9835 the organization of agency loyalty boards had not been completed, no attempt was being made to give priority to investigation of employees in particularly sensitive posts and applicants were being appointed without any investigation whatsoever.

It seemed certain that Dewey would pursue the issue which providentially had been thrown into his lap. *Newsweek* reported that Speaker Martin had advised that Communism be made the number-one issue of the campaign. House Leader Halleck issued a statement saying that coddling and bungling abroad in Yalta, Quebec, Teheran, and Potsdam had resulted in the need to ship $30 billion abroad. "Congressional disclosure of Communist spy rings running through the Truman Administration, like water through a sieve, shock the American people and leave them resentful against the Administration for failure to rid the Government of subversive rascals." Campaign Manager Herbert Brownell said that the people were "shocked" at what he called the President's attitude in "seeming to cover up" information as to Communist Party activities.

The country seemed more emotionally stirred by the spy allegations than it had been by any other issue of the Truman Administration. The great debate as to whether Hiss or Chambers was lying occupied the headlines. On top of this came a real life drama which would have seemed bizarre if filmed by Alfred Hitchcock. A Russian schoolteacher, Mrs. Oksana Kasenkina, while on a White Russian farm in Rockland County, New York, run by the Tolstoy Foundation, was kidnapped and taken to the Russian consulate in New York City, allegedly because she did not want to return to Russia. The Russians claimed that they were rescuing her since she had been kidnapped in Central Park by the White Russians. Mrs. Kasenkina solved the argument as to who did the kidnapping by jumping to freedom from the sixth story of the Russian consulate, and the Russian consul was sent home on our demand.

All this was high drama against which Dewey could have painted a picture of the Russian menace in the United States and the inertia of the Administration. He could have made the same kind of vivid presentation that he had made of gangster domination in one of his New York campaigns. Dewey gave the issue only cursory treatment during the campaign. Why didn't he take hold of it? While the whole Washington apparatus including Brownell favored its strong use, Albany said no. Dewey says today, "The charges were not proven. If I had done so, I would have been attacked for Know-Nothingism by the liberal press and columnists, and I would have lost five million votes." But Dewey did not have to indulge in any smear of the accused. He could have presented a case against the Administration on the ground of negligence in its loyalty program along the lines of the Ferguson report. Again, apart from the truth of the charges, as Congressman Mundt pointed out, the fact that so many high officials in the Democratic Administration chose to take the Fifth Amendment was highly significant. Even in the Administration there was doubt that it was all a "red herring." Thus, Commerce Secretary Sawyer said, "Only the uninformed will believe that we have no spies among us. The current investigation indicates that they were operating during the war."

The fact is that Dewey was genuinely concerned and had a group of ten experts on Communism meet with him without publicity in Albany in August on the problem of Communist infiltration in Government. There are two theories explaining why he did not pound it as a campaign issue, both related to his "provincial outlook." One is that he was influenced by the New York press which was condemnatory of the investigation as a "witch hunt" particularly when Harrry White died of a heart attack soon after he testified. The New York *Herald Tribune* said, "The injury to the reputation of certain individuals named in the proceedings was a flagrant violation of elementary rights and a frightening example of what an unfettered inquisition into matters of public opinion can produce." The attitude of the metropolitan press was not typical of the nation as a whole. As Senator Mundt says, "Dewey didn't realize how much old-fashioned July Fourth patriotism there is in the country."

The second theory is that Dewey's entire political outlook was controlled by his experience in New York politics. One of his fixations was the Jewish vote. Since some of the names were Jewish, though not the principals, his automatic reflex was that if he took up the issue he might be accused of being anti-Semitic.

It was during this period that Representative Richard Nixon of the Un-American Activities Committee came to the fore. It was due to him that the Chambers version of the Hiss case was explored. William S. White of the New York *Times* said of him, "He is at pains to try to keep the Committee on a legally sound basis and he has considerable reputation for fairness to witnesses," and the New York *Herald Tribune* said editorially that Nixon "has shown himself one of the committee's ablest and most thoughtful members." Nixon pressed the Administration hard on the issue, asking why J. Edgar Hoover was not allowed to testify from FBI reports on the charges. He did not see that the hearings were an "inquisition" or "witch hunt" as they were characterized; they were necessary Congressional investigations in which witnesses were protected by their privilege against self-incrimination. The Royal Commission of Canada was praised because it held hearings *in camera,* but witnesses before it could not escape testifying.

National Chairman Hugh Scott made a twenty-eight-state tour during August and reported that everybody was asking, "What about the Communists and fellow travelers in the Federal Government?" Scott often said that after Election Day the country would see "the greatest housecleaning since St. Patrick drove the snakes out of Ireland." Scott campaigned hard on the Communist issue. He made use of a letter which was printed in the *Daily Worker* on August 20, 1944, in which Truman congratulated its Washington correspondent Adam Lapin for a laudatory article on Truman's record in the Senate. When it was pointed out to Scott that Roosevelt had disavowed Communist support in 1944, Scott replied that Truman had never done so. (Dewey in 1944 had attacked Roosevelt for his "soft" disavowal of Communist support.) Scott also claimed that a leak in the State Department had enabled Tito to learn within a week of a report from our economic attaché in Belgrade of waste of our relief funds and sale of relief food. Scott had an aristocratic background, was a member of the Union League Club and Philadelphia Cricket Club, and McGrath referred to his charges not as a "red herring" but as a "blue-blooded herring."

When Scott got together with Dewey in Albany in early September he found he was on the wrong track and was advised of the "high-level" line. "All you would have to do to win this election would be to make two Oklahoma City speeches," he said. Dewey recoiled from the idea. "What, that terrible speech, that terrible speech!" So Scott, like the others, was now reformed. On Warren's campaign train in October, Scott said, "Governor Warren's style fits this particular year like a glove. He isn't mad at anybody. The people aren't mad at anybody either."

[IX]

OPENING THE CAMPAIGN

TRUMAN seemed so hopelessly behind that his strategy was carved out for him. Truman's close adviser Clark Clifford said of the situation in summer, "At that time we were on the twenty-yard line. We had to be bold. If we had kept on plugging away in moderate terms we might have reached mid-field when the gun went off, so we had to throw long passes." There was nothing to do but to go razzle-dazzle. The motto would be, *"L'audace, plus l'audace et encore l'audace."*

A Truman crony, Leslie Biffle, on August 1 set out by truck on a trip through West Virginia, Kentucky, southern Ohio, and Illinois disguised as a chicken farmer to sound out grass-roots sentiment. When he returned three weeks later he reported to Truman that from his soundings he thought he could win. "Do you think so, do you really think so?" the President said in surprise and delight, and suggested that Biffle hold a press conference with the White House reporters as to his findings.

As in Dewey's campaign, the real authority now shifted from the National Committee to an inner strategy board around the candidate, composed of Clark Clifford, William M. Boyle, Jr., who had been his aide when Truman was a Senator, and Donald Dawson, formerly personnel director of the RFC. All were from Missouri. Also in the inner circle were Matt Connelly and the press chief, Charlie Ross. The picture brightened as political bosses, disaffected during the convention, now gathered about the ticket. These included Mayor O'Dwyer, Boss Hague, and Jake Arvey.

The party treasury was empty due to the pall of defeatism. After a number of persons including Bernard Baruch and Assistant Air Secretary Cornelius Whitney had turned down the post, Louis Johnson became chairman of the Finance Committee. Thousands of dollars were needed to get the campaign started and arrange for the campaign trips. Johnson advanced sums out of his own pocket. Without his efforts there would have been disaster. He raised money with great acumen, contacting businessmen who had given money to the GOP, reminding them that they should take out an insurance policy on the risk of Democratic victory, a risk that seemed as remote at the time as death. Johnson called it "the two-party system" of raising funds. Of the first $300,000 raised, Johnson says that $200,000 was raised by the "two-party approach." Baruch got a scorching letter from Truman for not taking a post on the Finance Committee, in which he was reminded that friendship is a two-way street, but Johnson recalls that Baruch did help to raise funds and contributed to Congressional campaigns. The Southern defection caused several states to withhold badly-needed funds, but that was solved in part by charging to those states money that would otherwise have gone to them.

Contributions from officeholders were spotty. Secretary Snyder's family gave $8000, the largest outlay by any family. Averell Harriman gave to the legal limit, Secretary Symington and Cornelius Whitney gave generously. The wealthy Secretary Sawyer, who ducked out of a Finance Committee meeting because of a date on the golf links, gave $1000. Interior Secretary Krug would not take the phone calls from the Finance Committee, and Forrestal would not contribute.

Under Secretary of State Robert Lovett was a Republican and was not asked, and Ambassador to Britain Lewis Douglas, though a Democrat, would not contribute. Harold Ickes gave nothing.

Clark Clifford says that the Democratic campaign was consciously pitched to four distinct interest groups—labor, the farmer, the Negro, and the consumer. Every move had these four interest groups in mind.

Of the four groups, Truman was most responsive to the strength of labor because of his personal background. He reminisced to others that his 1940 Senatorial campaign was made possible by a loan of $8000 from the Brotherhood of Railroad Trainmen. He felt that he owed his 1944 nomination as Vice-President to labor. In Truman's *Memoirs* he records what he did when he came to Chicago for the 1944 convention. "When I arrived in Chicago I had breakfast with Sidney Hillman, who was a power in the labor faction of the convention. . . . Then I had a meeting with Phil Murray, head of the CIO, and one with A. F. Whitney, head of the Railroad Trainmen. . . . The next morning, William Green, head of the AFL, asked me to breakfast at the Palmer House." Truman says that he was campaigning for Jimmy Byrnes and told the labor leaders so, but records that all told him they were for him, Senator Truman. According to Truman's own record, these were the only men he saw prior to being told by Democratic Chairman Robert E. Hannegan that he was Roosevelt's choice for Vice-President.

Since 1947 labor had become more politically conscious due to the passage of the Taft-Hartley law. Among other restrictions, the Act made it illegal for "any labor organization to make a contribution or expenditure" for political purposes. Unions get around this by setting up separate organizations with "voluntary" contributions. The Supreme Court helped out with a ruling that union newspapers, even though financed by union funds, could support political candidates. In San Francisco in 1947 the AFL set up Labor's Educational and Political League to conduct its political activities. In this the AFL was following in the path of the CIO's Political Action Committee set up in 1943 by Phil Murray, R. J. Thomas, and Sidney Hillman, who was chairman. In 1944 besides helping Roosevelt to be re-elected, the CIO-PAC took some credit for purging Congress of such figures as Joe Starnes of Alabama, Cotton Ed Smith of South Carolina, Martin Dies of Texas, and Hamilton Fish of New York, regarded as reactionaries. Although the Labor League and the PAC were presumably independent organizations, the Labor League was headed by AFL President William Green and the PAC was governed by an executive board run by Phil Murray, UAW President Walter Reuther, and CIO Secretary-Treasurer Jim Carey.

Truman had predicted that the liberals and labor leaders would troop back to the Democratic colors after the convention, and he was right. They had no other place to go. Harold Ickes made an analysis showing that while the Republican platform was muddled and confused, the Democratic platform was "pellucid." Gerald W. Johnson wrote in the New York *Post* that "The great argument for the President has no reference at all to Truman. It is simply this: Take a look at the others. Stacked up against the Archangel Gabriel Truman doesn't look so good, but stacked up against the array opposing him he begins to look like the Archangel Gabriel. After all, Gabriel is not a candidate."

The Americans for Democratic Action now endorsed Truman as did the Liberal Party in New York, carrying along the International Ladies Garment Union, which pledged $100,000 for his campaign. Truman was endorsed by the CIO by a vote of thirty-five to twelve, about the same vote by which it turned down the third party a year earlier. The dissenters were for Wallace.

On August 8 Victor Riesel reported that in the last ten

days the CIO Political Action Committee had organized a bigger-scale campaign than it had against Dewey in 1944 when the emphasis was more on publicity than on precinct work. Jack Kroll, head of the PAC, had an army of block-workers enrolled in a five-prong campaign: (1) A big election turnout mechanism employing baby sitters and transport for voters; (2) mass communications, including newspapers and radio; (3) a breakdown of voters in each district with all potential labor votes listed; (4) organization of campaigners in each shop and ward; (5) advanced techniques for canvassing and registration of voters. In early September Marquis Childs warned that the Democrats should not be counted out. "Organized labor could conceivably wreck what appears today to be the virtual certainty of a Republican victory."

The President was visited by CIO head Phil Murray, Jack Kroll, Jim Carey, Emil Rieve, head of the Textile Workers, Emil Mazey, secretary-treasurer of the UAW and George Harrison, head of the Railway Brotherhood Clerks (AFL), who advised him of their support. He was told that only 1,000,000 of the 6,500,000 in the CIO could not be counted with him. Harrison became head of the Labor Division of the Democratic National Committee. The President was told that the AFL Labor League for Political Education under Joseph Keenan was mobilized, and that at least seven million out of eight million workers in the AFL would be for him. Dan Tobin of the Teamsters Union (AFL) stayed on the sidelines in this election because it was believed that Dave Beck on the West Coast would throw his support to the GOP. The Carpenters Union (AFL) stayed on the fence; in 1944 its boss, Bill Hutcheson, was all out for Dewey. The little remaining support for Wallace among the unions was wilting as the United Electric Workers in convention refused to vote him outright endorsement because of fear of a split in the union; the right wing behind Jim Carey supported

Truman, even though President Albert Fitzgerald and the majority of the leadership were for Wallace.

Compared to this massive and militant labor support, what could Dewey muster? He pointed with pride to the fact that he had gotten the support of 175,000 Building Service Employees—or at least their leaders. John L. Lewis in the wings indicated that he might come out for Dewey.

The President opened the campaign with a Labor Day speech in Detroit. The crowds were astounding. He addressed half a million people in his tour of Michigan. In Cadillac Square in Detroit there were 175,000 people. Even his most enthusiastic supporters expressed surprise as at the city of Hamtramck where the entire population turned out. His themes were the fear of labor legislation even worse than the Taft-Hartley law and fear of a bust. If the GOP were elected, "I would fear not only for wages and the living standards of the working man but even for the domestic institutions of free labor and free enterprise." "You and I know that the Taft-Hartley law is only a foretaste of what you will get if the Republican reaction is allowed to continue to grow. . . . You men of labor can expect to be hit by a steady barrage of body blows." A reactionary Republican Administration could bring "another boom and bust cycle similar to that which struck us during the last Republican Administration. . . . The boom is on for them and the bust is on for you." The issue was "Do you want to carry the Taft-Hartley law to its full implications and totally enslave the workingman, the white collar and union man alike? . . ." The President described his reactionary opposition as "a man with a calculating machine where his heart ought to be" and "those who hate labor."

The union heads kept up a steady drumbeat against the Taft-Hartley labor law. Phil Murray orated that "labor is threatened with shackles that threaten its eventual destruction." William Green charged that the policies of Congress "have robbed many millions of workers of the means to provide what they need for themselves and their families." Administration officials chimed in. Agriculture Secretary Brannan said in a speech that the members of the Eightieth Congress "seem to have adopted the reverse of the old saying and are out to soak the poor." Federal Security Administrator Oscar Ewing in a speech to the National Urban League in Richmond said that any Negro who voted against Truman would be "betraying his race," and victory for the GOP "would wipe out every vestige of social and economic progress which the American Negro has made during the past decade and a half."

To all of this there was only Harold Stassen's rejoinder in Detroit before an audience of 3000 in the Masonic Temple, which seated 5000. His speech had logic, but no fire. While Truman said that Taft-Hartley had put a "dangerous weapon in the hands of the corporations," he had used it himself many times to halt strikes. Stassen pointed out that under the Taft-Hartley law the man hours lost in strikes had been cut by one third between 1946 and 1948. Later, explaining the almost half-empty hall, Stassen charged that workers had been coerced into attending the Truman rallies, that James Hoffa, head of the Teamsters in Detroit, had ordered union members to attend or be fined.

Why was Stassen chosen to make the reply to Truman's attack on the Taft-Hartley law? Taft would have been the logical person. Stassen had no standing in the labor field. As a matter of fact, his only substantial declaration had been for something tougher than anything that emerged in the Taft-Hartley law. In his testimony before the Senate Labor Committee in 1947, which was hammering out a new labor law, he advocated that, along the lines of his Minnesota law, a secret strike vote should be required before a strike is called. Taft rejected Stassen's premise that workers would be less likely to be in favor of strikes than their leaders and thought the whole proposal was "trivial."

Stassen was called from Albany and asked to answer Truman. "Why doesn't Dewey answer Truman?" he said. "The Governor doesn't want to start his campaign for another two weeks," was the reply. Dewey sought Stassen's assistance since

Fitzpatrick in the St. Louis Post-Dispatch

Gulliver's Travels, 1948

he was mesmerized by Stassen's supposed appeal to "liberal" Republicans. While he took no steps to win over Taft's organization, he did try to weld Stassen's strength to his own. He invited to Albany, Vic Johnston, Stassen's aide, who was head of Neighbors for Stassen, and after giving him some dazzling VIP treatment asked him to head the Dewey-Warren Volunteers. "But I'm the man who beat you in Wisconsin," said Johnston. "That's exactly why I want you," replied Dewey in his most gracious manner.

The farm vote turned out to be the key to the election result. The unusual prosperity of the farmer first deserves note. Since 1940 farm purchasing power had increased by seventy per cent as compared with the average of fifty per cent for all groups. The excess of farm assets over liabilities had soared from $44 billion in 1940 to $113 billion in 1947. Bank deposits and currency had increased from $4 billion to $16 billion, holdings of US Savings Bonds had increased by $4.5 billion, while mortgage debts had decreased from $6.6 billion to $4.9 billion.

The concept of gearing farm prices to parity, defined as farm purchasing power during the years 1909-14, had been invented during the depression crisis period to keep farm prices up. It was extended during the war period on the theory that it would stimulate production. The plan had been to discard it two years after the war.

The parity principle was an obvious anachronism in a period of inflation when the problem was to get farm prices down, not to keep them up. But the farmer was not willing to risk losing a prosperity to which he had been unaccustomed previously. Price supports were scheduled to expire on January 1, 1949. The House passed a bill to extend the fixed farm supports at 90 per cent of parity for a year and a half after the expiration date of January 1, 1949. The President on May 14 sent a message to Congress, asking for the adoption of flexible farm support prices instead of fixed supports. Because of increased mechanization and better soil techniques, production per acre had greatly increased in recent years. Under flexible farm supports the price would be lowered below 90 per cent parity where there was a bumper crop and the same return to the farmer would be maintained. Flexible supports were sponsored by Agriculture Secretary Anderson and defended before Congressional committees by Assistant Secretary (later Secretary) Charles Brannan.

The Senate passed the flexible farm support bill by 79 to 3 on June 17. In the closing hours of Congress a compromise was worked out with the House, the Hope-Aiken Act. Fixed farm supports would be continued for one additional year only, 1949, and then, beginning in 1950, the Secretary of Agriculture could inaugurate flexible farm supports at 60 to 90 per cent of parity for basic crops. When the supply of a crop was 130 per cent of normal, the support price could drop to 60 per cent. Actually, there was a gimmick in the law which would have prevented them from going under 72 per cent, but the 60 per cent was there to shoot at in the campaign.

The passage of the Hope-Aiken bill turned out to be a major factor in Dewey's defeat. Not only did the President advocate the flexible support principle (it was not new—Henry Wallace had put it into a farm bill in 1938) but it was also supported by farm organizations, including the National Grange, the American Farm Bureau, and the National Council of Farm Co-operatives. They feared that high retail prices might ultimately bring about an attack on the whole support principle. But ardent farm Congressmen were against any modification of 90 per cent supports and protested against the compromise in the closing hours of Congress. The House leadership had to make a substitution in the House conferees to get House agreement on the bill. One member charged on the floor that the House conferees had been "raped." The important fact for the campaign is that it was a Republican Congress which had enacted the switch from fixed supports to flexible supports.

On September 2, Harold Stassen made a sortie on the farm issue that was to recoil on the Republicans. He charged that the Administration was deliberately trying to keep food prices up, pointing to a statement by Brannan of his intent to make big food purchases for export. "I believe that it was a deliberate step to stop the downward trend of food prices that followed the report of large crops." Stassen charged food prices would drop in a few months were it not for actions contemplated by the Administration.

This gave the Administration the chance to brand the GOP as the enemy of the farmer. Agriculture Secretary Brannan replied that the GOP was opening "a very sinister attack on the support system"—"it has become apparent that [the GOP] intends to destroy the farmers' price supports by falsely attributing to that legislation the exorbitantly high prices of certain foods." Brannan seized on the occasion to charge that Dewey sold milk from his Pawling estate at a price higher than agreed on by the Agriculture Department and the Milk Commission of New York. Truman joined in the attack in a press conference, saying that supports did not contribute to high prices (which is true in a time of high demand). Stassen replied that he was not attacking the support principle, but Brannan answered that one would have to deduce that. "Otherwise his statement would be more characteristic of a Sophomore at the University of Pennsylvania than a prospective college president [of that University]." (Stassen had been chosen for that post.)

The Stassen charge was as disastrous to the Dewey cause as any single incident in the 1948 campaign. The Democrats plastered the Midwest with reprints of his statement. The *Wall Street Journal* commented that Stassen was "proposing a far-reaching reform of the price-support policy or he doesn't make sense." Actually, when Stassen spoke of the "deliberate step to stop the downward trend of food prices," he was not referring to supports. He had in mind the disclosure of huge food purchases by the Agriculture Department in the grain-speculation probe in the early part of 1948 in which he had been a prime accuser. That is why he said food prices would drop "unless the Democrats pull another Pauley." He was referring to the profits in commodity speculation made by Edwin W. Pauley.

Dewey says that Stassen made this statement without clearing it with him. Although Stassen spoke at a press conference in the Executive Mansion in Albany where he was preparing his labor speech, this is quite possible. Stassen says that he made no statement during the campaign that was not cleared by Dewey's brain trust. But as Vic Johnston says, "If Dewey disagreed with Stassen's statement, why didn't he repudiate it? He knew of the furor it created. He must have thought the issue of lower food prices was valuable in the East." Again, we encounter the Eastern big-city orientation of Dewey.

It was not until September 17, over two weeks later, when the implications of the Stassen statement had been hammered home in the farm belt, that Dewey, after a conference with Republican Senator George Aiken and Representative Clifford Hope, authors of the Hope-Aiken Act, said that he was all in favor of the support system. The charge against him was "created out of thin air and intentionally fabricated in a design to deceive the producers of foods." He said he was for the flexible-support legislation "both for the present and future," which, of course, many farmers did not want.

It was in his answer to Stassen that Secretary Brannan brought forth for the first time an issue that was to play an important part in the final result—that the Republican Eightieth Congress had refused to appropriate money to the Commodity Credit Corporation for grain storage bins and therefore there would be a shortage of space for storing grains. As a result, farmers could not get loans at 90 per cent of parity.

The CCC had been liquidating bin space from the end of the war, when it had a total of 292,000,000 bushels. By the summer of 1948 it had less than 50,000,000 bushels of bin space left. The CCC required a new charter in 1948 because it was a Delaware corporation and under the Government Corporation Control Act no wholly-owned corporation could continue beyond June 30, 1948, unless it was a Government corporation.

Now fate or accident pushed a button. In the House the bill renewing the CCC might have been referred to the Agriculture Committee which was in charge of bills "for agriculture generally." But the House parliamentarian decided that it should go to the Banking and Currency Committee which was in charge of bills for "farm loan" programs. The Agriculture Committee might have been more farm-minded; the Chairman of the Banking and Currency Committee, Jesse Wolcott, under the influence of banker Randolph Burgess, was economy-minded. Wolcott says that the bill could have gone to either committee. As he saw it, the new charter might as well take cognizance of the fact that the CCC was liquidating, not buying, storage space. The new charter, as his committee reported it, provided that the CCC "shall have no power to acquire or lease any such plant or facility or acquire or lease real property except office space."

The bill came up on June 18, the next to the last day of the session under a suspension of the rules prohibiting amendments. Representative Hope saw "serious defects" in the bill and he and Representative Carl Anderson, both Republicans, might have reframed the bill if it had been open for amendments. No Democrat voiced any objection whatsoever to the bill. The National Grange and American Farm Bureau in their comments did not object to the limitation; the National Council of Farm Co-operatives did. It slid through with no debate on the limitation and the Senate in its closing minutes accepted it without change.

Fate or accident pushed another button. This was a year of bumper crops. The corn crop of 3,681,000,000 bushels was the greatest in history—fifty-five per cent greater than in 1947.

The wheat crop of 1,313,000,000 bushels was the second greatest. Farm prices were falling. Corn, which was $2.46 a bushel in January, was down to $1.78 by September 15. Wheat had fallen from $2.81 a bushel in January to $1.97 a bushel by September. There was a need for farmers to store grains to get farm loans at 90 per cent of parity. But there was now a shortage of bin space and the CCC could not add to it.

According to Arthur Krock of the New York *Times,* newspaper publisher James M. Cox (Democratic Presidential candidate in 1920) was advised in August 1948, by his agricultural editor in Dayton that the CCC had said that it was prevented by law from adding to its bins in Ohio. Cox asked his Washington correspondent, W. McNeil Lowry, how come, and was told about the new law. Cox then got in touch with Secretary Brannan and Chairman McGrath and told them to look into it. And thus it started. Republican farm leaders, however, doubt that the Democratic National Committee was unaware of the issue and believe that the issue was always held in reserve as a campaign maneuver. They point to the fact that the CCC had prepared a complete study of the storage problem which was a splendid background for the political issue.

On September 17 Truman set off on a nationwide trip. "I'm going to give them hell," he said. "Mow them down," said Vice-Presidential candidate Alben Barkley in encouragement. With that the President retreated into his private car, the "Ferdinand Magellan," so heavily armor plated that bridges had to be reinforced as insurance against the great weight. The President had said he would be visiting "every whistle stop in the United States," forgetting that only a few months before the Democratic National Committee had ridiculed Taft's use of the term "whistle stop." When someone said that some places would object to the term, he answered, "Only San Francisco and Seattle." The President compared the campaign to the Lincoln-Douglas debate. No comparison could have been less apt in view of the campaign that developed.

There has been a good deal of comment that the "give 'em hell" technique of Truman was synthetic in view of his personal geniality, that it was like a member of Rotary using the bloodthirsty words of a French Revolutionist. Senator Wheeler, out of his intimate knowledge of Truman, says this is not true, that when he campaigned he did what came naturally. The important element in his behavior as a politician was the many years he had spent in the wards of Kansas City. "Did you ever hear a ward leader when someone has crossed him? Have you seen him clench his fist and say 'I'll get that so-and-so?' Well, that's Harry Truman."

His first speech was at Dexter, Iowa, the national plowing contest, where 75,000 were present to hear him. "The Wall Street reactionaries are not satisfied regardless of what happens to the other fellow. They are gluttons of privilege. These gluttons of privilege are putting up fabulous sums of money to elect a Republican President. . . . These Republican gluttons of privilege are cold men, they are cunning men and it is their constant aim to put the control of the Government of the United States under the control of men like themselves. They want a return of the Wall Street economic dictatorship. . . . Wall Street expects its money this year to elect a Republican Administration that will listen to the gluttons of privilege first and the people second. . . . The GOP Congress has already stuck a pitchfork in the farmer's back. When the Republicans rewrote the charter of the Commodity Credit Corporation this year, there were certain lobbyists in Washington representing the speculative grain trade. These big-business lobbyists and speculators persuaded the Congress not to provide storage bins for the farmer. . . . They don't want the farmer to be prosperous. . . . What they have taken away from you thus far will be only an appetizer for the economic tapeworm of big business." Truman reminded the farmers of the drop in wheat and the Stassen statement. "Republican spokesmen are now complaining that my Administration is trying to keep food prices up. They have given themselves away. . . . They are ready to let the bottom drop out of farm prices."

"The support price has nothing to do with the price the common man is paying for his bread. When wheat prices went up the price of bread went up steadily, from ten cents to fourteen cents. Now wheat prices have fallen a dollar a bushel but the price of bread has not come down. There you have the policy of reactionary big business. Pay as little as you can to the farmer and charge the consumer all he can bear." This was the only stab Truman ever made at reconciling high prices for farmers and low prices for consumers—the middleman was the villain.

Since farm prices had gone up far more than wages or stock prices, was the farmer not a "glutton of privilege" more than any other group? At least sixty farmers came to Dexter in their personal planes. Joseph Alsop pointed out that since the farmers were so prosperous, if Truman did "the authentic dance of death from the platform, he would still fail to raise a single goose-pimple," but he missed the point that the farmers might genuinely fear a loss of the prosperity they were now enjoying.

On September 19 Dewey boarded the *Victory Special* for his transcontinental trip. To diffuse the aura of victory, the badges and baggage checks of the entire entourage—including the press—bore the inscription, "Dewey Victory Special." All were enlisted as bearers of the victory tidings. The President's train was named only *The Trip of the President*.

On August 30 Governor Dewey had promised a "rugged and intensive campaign" and in his Labor Day message he said that he was looking forward to discussing the price of meat and how it got there, and the issue of decent housing.

Confidence pervaded the Republican campaign train. There had been warnings of overconfidence from Dewey and National Chairman Scott, but when more closely examined it was overconfidence about the Senate which was then Republican by fifty-one to forty-five. The word was that the trip was mainly SOS, "Save Our Senate," and the first stop was Iowa, where Senator George Wilson was having trouble with former Senator Guy Gillette.

Certainly, Republican Iowa was in the bag. Dewey had carried it in 1944 over Roosevelt. It had not elected a Democratic congressman since 1940. At Des Moines Dewey made the first of what were to be typical Dewey speeches. He discussed no farm issues. "Tonight we enter on a campaign to unite America. We propose to install in Washington an Administration which has faith in the American people, a warm understanding of their needs and the competence to meet them." He promised "a government of teamwork," in which "every act of mine will be determined by one principle above all others: Is this good for the country?" Our foreign policy would be "based on the firm belief that we can have peace." He promised to unite us as "we have never been united before to meet maladjustments at home and to resist aggression abroad." His magnanimity was widely praised in the press. "I will not contend that all our difficulties have been brought about by the present national administration. Some of them are the result of circumstances beyond the control of any Government." His modesty was also praised. "I have no trick answers and no easy solutions."

Dewey's charitable statement about the Democratic Administration followed a few days after Warren's opening speech in Salt Lake City: "Good Americans are to be found in both parties . . . there are progressives and conservatives in the ranks of both . . . party affiliation does not change human instincts or affect loyalty to country." This brings to mind the famous remark of the French General Bosquet watching the charge of the Light Brigade, *"C'est magnifique mais cè n'est pas la guerre."*

Joseph Alsop summarized the two opposing speeches, "There was something rather sad about the contrast between the respective campaign debuts here in Iowa. The Truman show was threadbare and visibly unsuccessful—the Dewey show was opulent. It was organized down to the last noise-making device. It exuded confidence. The contest was really too uneven. After it was all over one felt a certain sympathy for the obstinately laboring President." This is typical of the Procrustean reasoning of commentators during the campaign. As a matter of fact, Truman had scored a hit. His rally of 75,000 contrasted with the small crowd of 8000 in the Drake University Field House which heard Dewey. After his formal speech Truman returned to the platform for an informal, folksy talk. He said that he had been asked if he could plow a straight furrow. "A prejudiced witness said so—my mother." He told how he used to seed a 160-acre wheat field "without leaving a skip" and how he plowed with four Missouri mules and a gang plow while now they used a tractor. Farmers who heard Truman at Dexter talked him up all over the farm belt. Truman had given the farmer something to think about. The farmer remembered nothing of what Dewey had said precisely because Dewey had said nothing.

[X]

CAMPAIGN—MIDDLE STAGES

IT IS TRADITIONAL in American political campaigns to view the possibility of victory for the opposite party as akin to the triumph of Satan. Thus, Timothy Dwight of Yale University said that the victory of Thomas Jefferson would make "our wives and daughters the victims of legalized prostitution." Colonel Robert Ingersoll in the campaign of 1888 said that the Democrats were "the friend of an early frost and believers in the Colorado beetle and the weevil." Overstatements are accepted by the public as part of the game. But where there is a ring of plausibility to a charge, and it is repeated over and over again and never denied, there is a chance that it may sink in. Certainly something of that occurred in 1948 as Truman hammered away at the derelictions of the Eightieth Congress.

The Iowa speeches launched the transcontinental tours by Truman and Dewey which terminated about the same time, in early October. The two men adopted entirely different approaches. Reversing the usual competitive styles of an election campaign, the President, the incumbent, was on the offensive with specifics—the challenger was on the defensive merely seeking to hold his lead with generalities. The incumbent told the people they were being abused—the challenger asked them to be satisfied. The day before the startling result Lowell Mellett wrote, "It has been a strange campaign. Take it all in all, we shall not look upon its like again."

At Denver, Truman said that a GOP victory would make the West an "economic colony of Wall Street." He recited the achievements of Democratic Administrations in soil conservation, hydroelectric power, irrigation developments, and industrialization of the West. But as soon as the Republican Party took over Congress, he said, "it began to tear down the whole Western development programs—they cut back projects to bring water to the land and electric power to industry." In Salt Lake City, Truman charged that the West had been "cruelly and wickedly cheated" by a Republican-backed power lobby. When the House Appropriations Committee cut back Truman's reclamation request by $90 million, Chairman Taber defended the cut by saying, "The West is squealing like a stuck pig." The President said, "There you have the Republican attitude toward the West summed up in a single phrase." Under the GOP, he said, you get "strangulation," and it is the party "whose money at election time comes from Wall Street." At Reno, Truman said that chairmen of Republican committees were "a bunch of old mossbacks living in the 1890's," naming Wolcott, Taber, and Allen. At Roseville, California, he pleaded for a crusade to "keep the country from going to the dogs." Coming to Oakland, he pointed out that due to a power shortage California must retain daylight saving time through the fall and winter and said that it was "a brown-out to gratify the greed of corporate monopoly."

In Los Angeles, Truman attacked the Wallace campaign saying that it would result in wasting votes and throwing them to the Republican reactionaries. Of Dewey he said, "This is a championship fight, and I am convinced of one thing. The American people are sold on the idea that nobody deserves to win a championship fight running away. . . . In our system the American people have the right to know exactly what our two major parties stand for on specific issues. . . . If the country falls into the hands of the leaders of the Republican Party, everything is likely to be all wrong within a very short time." The next day, of the record of the Eightieth Congress, he said, "When I called them back into session in July what did they do. Nothing. Nothing. That Congress never did anything the whole time it was in session." If the Republicans win "they'll tear you apart."

Heading East, the slashing attacks continued. Taking cognizance of the Dixiecrat threat he made twenty-four trainside speeches in Texas, the first time a Democratic candidate had campaigned in the state. He was met at El Paso by Governor Jester (who had earlier in the year accused him of "stabbing the South in the back") and by Sam Rayburn. He charged that the GOP doesn't like cheap public power because it means "that the big power monopolists can't get the rake-off at the expense of the public." He was joined on the train by Lyndon Johnson, who had just nosed out Coke Stevenson by eighty-seven votes in a contested Texas primary for the Democratic Senatorial nomination—Johnson had been Truman-approved. In Dallas, he mocked Dewey for high-level "talk about home and mother" and "unity." He said, "They don't want unity, they want surrender." Dewey was singing a "lullaby" to put voters to sleep. He added to his prepared speech that the Republicans dare not tell their aims, since "They [the people] would take them out and hang them if they did—and that would be disastrous—or would it?" At Bonham, he said the GOP wanted "unity in giving tax relief to the rich at the expense of the poor." Dewey was indebted to Joe Grundy and so "they want to kill" the reciprocal trade agreements program.

There was no reference to civil rights in Texas although the issue was on everybody's mind and Governor Thurmond had defied Truman to discuss it in a Southern state. He was mildly booed when he shook hands with a Negro woman at Waco, and he did say that every child was entitled to education, regardless of color. No embarrassment arose at the meetings, although no segregation was imposed; Negroes and whites segregated themselves voluntarily. In Dallas, he made a graceful gesture to a Negro idol when he was introduced by Attorney General Clark as the man who had stopped Joe Louis—"No," said Truman, "that was John [L. Lewis]. I don't have enough muscle to have stopped Joe."

In Oklahoma City, Truman made an all-out attack on the Communist issue. He said that the Communists hated the Democrats because of their strong foreign policy. The Communists supported Wallace because they wanted the GOP to win, "which would produce another economic crash which would play into the hands of Communism." He pointed out that the biggest advance of Communism had come under Hoover when they polled 100,000 votes in 1932 (but, of course, this was during the depression). In a series of Zola-like "I charge" statements he accused the GOP of trampling on individual freedoms, hindering the atomic-energy program, hindering the FBI, and "They have not hurt the Communist Party one bit, they have helped it."

At Ardmore, Oklahoma, he said, the GOP are "predatory animals who don't care if you people are thrown into a depression. . . . They like runaway prices." As for unity, "We have got to fight the special-interest lobbies instead of being unified with them. We must fight isolationists and reactionaries, the profiteers and the privileged." On national health insurance he said, "A well-organized medical lobby" had turned down his program. At Shawnee, Oklahoma, he quoted Chairman Taber as saying "to hell with the farmers out West," and called him one of the "worst old mossbacks in Congress." (Taber replied that he had been completely misquoted.) Taber's committee voted "to put an ax to your program of rural electrification, school lunches, and soil conservation."

At Lexington, Kentucky, nearing home, the President prophetically compared his race to that of the great race horse of 1948, Citation. "It's the horse that comes ahead at the finish which wins." At Charleston, West Virginia, he said, "I can tell you how you can achieve unity in a headlong race for depression. Just elect a Republican President to go along with a Republican Congress."

Let us now see how Dewey responded to these stinging, searing attacks.

After Des Moines, in a speech at Denver, Dewey talked in generalities, but he did state that the Eightieth Congress had voted far more funds for reclamation than any previous Congress. He said our foreign policy had "wobbled" and that it had showed us to be "lily-livered" and later told reporters that he would develop how it could be put on a "straight line," which he never did. In Albuquerque, Dewey charged that inflation had been "aggravated by the mistaken policies, bad management, and poor judgment of the Federal Government." He called for cuts in the "bloated and top-heavy bureaucracy" as an important attack on inflation. It was going a bit far for Dewey to call on individuals to "spend as little as possible to pay our debts as much as possible." There were lots of generalities about bringing competent people to Washington and "good management into the business of our Federal Government." He said, "National income is now at such high levels that we can build up our national strength, reduce our debt, and still see to it that taxes are less of a burden on our people." That would be fine, but no one had yet discovered the formula, and Dewey did not suggest one.

At Phoenix, Dewey eschewed politics to discuss atomic energy, saying that as soon as the Red threat eased, development of the atom should be turned over to private enterprise—"free peacetime atomic-energy research will solve the mysteries of the scourge of cancer, find a way to end the earth's food shortages, learn how to convert coal into oil, and make the Arctic and vast frigid regions livable." The Dewey brain trust was proud of this speech, but as the St. Louis *Post-*

Dispatch said editorially, the Manhattan project could have been carried out only by the Government, and firms like Monsanto and General Electric already had private contracts. As a matter of fact, three hundred firms had contracts, and of 70,000 workers on atomic energy projects, only 5000 were Government workers.

In Los Angeles at the Hollywood Bowl, Dewey proposed a vast counteroffensive of propaganda against Reds. In view of the "Voice of America" program there was not much novelty in his approach. He mentioned the "red herring" statement. "If they or anyone else break our law against treason, they'll get traitor's treatment." He accused the Administration of "giving aid and comfort to the enemies of our system" by the way it had "bungled and quarreled"—but there was nothing concrete by way of example. As usual, the solution was to bring to Washington "men and women who are able to make our Government once more measure up to America."

In San Francisco, Dewey discussing inflation said that it was not a political problem. "I don't place the whole blame on the Government in Washington." It was the result of war, foreign-aid programs, and Administration policies which restricted production. He advocated cutting the cost of Government, reducing the national debt, revising taxes to promote production, bringing "men and women of integrity" to Washington, and having a Government with faith in our American system. He took Truman to task for indicating that inflation could be cured by some "painless, patented panacea."

At this time the crisis over the Berlin blockade had become more critical as talks of the Western powers with Molotov and Stalin had broken down. Dewey now acted more and more like the President than a candidate. As one newspaperman put it, "How long is Dewey going to tolerate Truman's interference with running the Government?" He was in communication with UN delegate John Foster Dulles at Paris and discussed the teletype messages with Allen Dulles on his train. Touring the Northwest, Dewey asked for all to pray for a peaceful solution of the crisis. Again, he appealed to the Russian people over the head of Stalin for peace. In Missoula, Montana, he warned the Soviet leaders they could not brow-

Justus in The Minneapolis Star

"Little man, big drum."

beat America. "We will not compromise on principle." At Great Falls, Montana, he said that "peace may depend on making clear to every foreign nation that we are united," and that the United States would insist on "peace with honor."

Even though he was President, Truman was so busy getting votes that he was apparently taking no part in declarations and bargaining on the Berlin issue in Paris; he made no reference to the foreign crisis.

In Salt Lake City, Dewey's speech pivoted on the tenth anniversary of the Munich conference. "There must not be another Munich," said Dewey. "There's no longer any such thing in the world as isolation." He pledged to use the European Recovery Plan as a means "for pushing and if I may say so prodding and encouraging the nations of Western Europe toward the goal of European union." He wanted to bring an end to the "tragic neglect" of China. For the most part he dealt in generalities such as extending the hand of help to freedom-loving peoples and strengthening the UN. He refused to criticize Truman for past errors. "It wouldn't serve any useful purpose to recall how the Soviet has conquered millions of people as a result of the failures of statesmanship. . . . These things are done. The question is: What lies ahead?" Dewey was taking seriously his responsibilities as the incoming President. Marquis Childs reported from talking to Dewey that he did not call for the re-arming of Europe in his Salt Lake speech because of his belief that the Politburo was only two votes away from war and he could not take the risk.

The Democratic National Committee compiled a list of sentences from his speeches and out of context they did seem the sorriest of bromides. "You know that your future lies ahead of you," "Our streams should abound with fish," "Everyone that rides in a car or bus uses gasoline or oil," "The miners of our country are vital to our welfare." His speeches were full of glittering platitudes. One can glean from the speeches on his first cross-country swing that he pledged to cut Federal expenditures, cut the Federal debt, houseclean the bureaucracy, expunge the Reds, expand the support programs, strengthen soil conservation, go forward with public power projects, reclamation and irrigation programs, and end the Government monopoly of the atom. But there were never any specifics.

Truman in every speech had a chapter and verse indictment of the Eightieth Congress. There was no meat in

Dewey's speeches, no facts to hang one's hat on, nothing to arouse the emotions. It seemed enough to Dewey to say as at Oklahoma City, "I pledge to you that your next Administration will cooperate with the farmers of the country to protect all people from the tragedy of another dust bowl." On oil, "I propose to you that we get an Administration that will devote itself seriously to a wise and intelligent use of oil reserves." On forests, "I propose that we develop a national policy that will really save our forests through Federal, state, and local cooperation."

At Des Moines, Dewey had said that he would make "specific proposals" and would discuss "every aspect of the grave problems at home and abroad and the steps by which I propose to meet them." He never did. A firm decision had been made previously to avoid anything concrete that might engender controversy or friction. The problem facing Elliott Bell and his stable of speech-writers, including Arthur Barnett, Merlyn Pitzele, Stanley High, Stewart Beach, Robert Ray, and Allen Dulles, was how to write a speech saying nothing. This is far more difficult, Bell felt, than writing a speech saying something.

Eventually, he wrapped around himself an impenetrable blanket of words. What does this mean? It is from his speech at the Alfred E. Smith Memorial Dinner on October 21. "By a simple rediscovery of our devotion to human rights and the protection of others from the abuse of those rights, we can draw a line through every conflict and draw it straight and true. It can be drawn so that both civil liberty and social responsibility complement and fortify each other." From the same speech. "The highest purpose to which we could dedicate ourselves is to rediscover the everlasting variety among us." Indeed!

The two main issues in the forefront of public consciousness which should have been given vitality, the record of the Eightieth Congress and Communists in Government, were treated almost parenthetically by Dewey. In Spokane, he called Truman's attack on the Eightieth Congress "frenzied" and "frantic" and said that "the Eightieth Congress delivered as no Congress ever did for the future of our country." In Fresno, Truman had attacked Congressman Gearhart as "one of the worst . . . he has done everything he possibly could to cut the throat of the farmer and workingman." Dewey at Fresno said he was proud to be introduced by Gearhart and "I am very proud of the Eightieth Congress." In Missouri he adopted Taft's phrase and accused Truman of "blackguarding" Congress. "That Eightieth Congress you've been hearing about passed the first long-range farm price-support program in the history of our country." He made stray references to appropriations by the Congress for rural electrification, reclamation, and power projects. But this was about all in defense of the record of the Eightieth Congress.

Dewey must have known that the "Communists in Government" issue struck fire with his audiences. The interest of the people in the issue was evident from the applause whenever he mentioned it. His Los Angeles speech on Communism was better received than any speech in his campaign. He always got a big hand when he said, "This incredible Administration asked Congress for $25 million to clean Communists out of Government. I have a better idea and cheaper. We elect a Republican Administration that won't put in Communists in the first place." This missed the point—the issue was not one of economy but the sinister and damaging effects of alleged Communist infiltration. Another theme repeated was the pledge that after the election there would be the "fanciest housecleaning," or words that seemed to fascinate Dewey, "the biggest unraveling, unsnarling, untangling operation in our history." Again, there was a failure to stir the emotions of the audience or to state facts as to why that was necessary. At Cheyenne, he said that he would bring traitors before the grand jury. "I assure you witnesses will not be kept out of the grand jury in a Republican Administration." This was a reference to the fact that not all the witnesses before the House Un-American Activities Committee, notably Whittaker Chambers, had testified before the grand jury in New York, which had brought no indictments. Did Dewey actually assume that his audience understood these facts? It was another instance not only of a failure to dramatize but to document. There was never any defense of the House Un-American Activities Committee. Except for passing references to it Dewey ignored the chance to rip Truman apart for his "red herring" statement and his classic boner in May when he said of the Soviet dictator, "I like Joe."

"The great issue of this campaign is whether or not America in this critical hour of world history is going to be a united nation." "Unity" was the one broad issue that Dewey set forth in the campaign. In trying to sell Eisenhower as a candidate, Max Lerner had said that Truman was "divisive" in his approach to questions and that Ike would bring unity. In *The American President* in 1954 Sidney Hyman, a highly perceptive analyst, wrote that an opposition candidate "can parade himself as the source of a new and transcendant unity—this is in contrast to the divisive activities of the man in the White House."

But Dewey was oversold on an issue which had no visceral appeal to the average American. It was hard to understand exactly what Dewey was driving at. Sometimes it seemed that he was asking Americans to achieve unity by being united behind him. To Samuel Grafton writing in the New York *Post* this sounded "a trifle odd because real unity shouldn't even appear to bargain; it should be offered unconditionally like a mother's smile or a lover's kiss."

"Unity" might have plausibly referred to the bipartisan foreign policy. At other times the "unity" theme seemed to refer to Dewey's campaign ethics—that unlike Truman he would not split up Americans into different groups in a time of crisis. Thus, Brownell accused Truman of splitting the East from the West, the farmer from the businessman, the labor-union employee from the employer.

But the whole genius of our political system has been the interplay, compromise, and conciliation of diverse and conflicting interest groups in our economy. To call for an end to these conflicts is empty rhetoric. Bitter campaigns took place in 1940 and 1944 when the world was at war; in 1948 we were, in fact, united in our anti-Soviet foreign policy, and it would not have impaired national solidarity to have inquired in a partisan spirit how we had reached that unfavorable posture in the cold war only three years after World War II. When Dewey said, "We must get rid of sectionalism, of attempts to divide one group from another, to set group against group," he was promising not only what was visionary under the American system but something alien to it.

We get closer to the reason why "unity" was on Dewey's mind by looking at his acceptance speech. In contrast to the Democratic Party, which was split into three factions, "We are a united party. Our nation stands tragically in need of that same unity." Since both parties have deep splits, either party has the privilege of citing the argument. In 1952 at Baltimore, Adlai Stevenson said, "The GOP elephant has two heads nowadays, and I can't tell from day to day who's driving the poor beast, whether Senator Taft or the General. I doubt that America will entrust its future, its hopes, to the master of a house divided against itself."

Dewey got around to the same idea in his Madison Square Garden speech on October 30. The Democratic Party is "splintered" and "divided." "Its right wing doesn't know what its left wing is doing. . . . In this grave hour a party that cannot keep the peace within itself cannot be entrusted with the solemn task of uniting our country."

The most ironic feature of this statement is that Dewey at the time could not have believed it himself. He was, in fact, obsessed with a guilt-feeling that the GOP was not united, that it suffered from a "schizophrenia." At the Lincoln Day Dinner speech in February 1949, three months after the election, his main theme was that the GOP is "split wide open. It has been split wide open for years, but we have tried to gloss it over."

It seems probable that Dewey talked of "unity" paradoxically because the "disunity" of his party was uppermost in his mind, and the "unity" he was pleading for was unity within the Republican Party after he took office.

Brownell says, "Dewey did a good job on the unity issue during the campaign," which he explains as keeping the rifts within the party from public view. This required that the Congressional leaders, and particularly Senator Taft, be kept in the background. That Taft and Dewey did not see eye to eye is an understatement. After the election Taft said of Dewey to a close associate, Gordon Scherer, now a Congressman from Cincinnati, "A little man, and I don't mean physically." When Dewey disclosed his campaign strategy to Taft at Albany in August, Taft replied that he couldn't see how the issue of the record of the Eightieth Congress could be ducked. "They didn't want Taft in the campaign," says Senator Jenner, who was head of the Republican Speakers Bureau. Jenner arranged a Southern tour for Taft, based presumably on Taft's popularity in the South, as well as that of his father, President Howard Taft. But Dewey and Brownell admit that they never entertained serious hopes of winning any state in the Solid South. This means that they were willing to have Taft shunted off into a useless waste of his time, energy, and splendid talents.

When greeting Governor Warren in Columbus, Taft said to a reporter of Warren's Salt Lake City speech in which he belittled the differences between the parties, "I read with great interest what Governor Warren had to say. You know that is exactly contrary to everything I stood for." In his campaign speeches Taft saw the issue between the parties as a conflict of philosophies, as to whether or not prosperity was to be achieved by totalitarian controls. Going into the South, Taft appealed to Southern conservatives not to waste their votes by voting for Thurmond but to realize that on the issues of economic freedom they were closer to the Republicans. What was Dewey's reaction to this? To the liberal Democratic columnist, Marquis Childs, Dewey, in a revealing moment, said, "His [Dewey's] formidable task was to persuade a sufficient number to switch to the Republican side. He had to do so against the dead weight of his own party. With Senator Taft telling Southern Bourbons they were just like the Republicans, and under the forbidding stare of reactionaries and covetous spoilsmen, he could not have taken a clear and positive line even if he had been so minded."

Dewey explains that he did not defend the Eightieth Congress because "I have never fought on a battleground of another's choosing in a campaign." But it would appear that Dewey did not defend the Eightieth Congress because he felt in his own heart that Truman was right, that it was a nest of reactionaries. Brownell and Bell admit as much. Dewey says, "The issue was not the Eightieth Congress. It was the liberal platform adopted by the party."

Although the platform had accepted Government responsibility for social-welfare measures, such as housing and social security, it had emphasized that first reliance must be put on the states, that there should be "minimum" controls and maximum reliance on competitive enterprise. *Time* magazine said of it (June 28), "The domestic planks were cut pretty much to the policies of Robert Taft."

There was no need for ideological cleavage to be a factor in his campaign speeches, when his opponent was murdering the facts. For example, he could have answered instead Truman's charge that the Republicans were "gluttons of privilege," "bloodsuckers with offices in Wall Street," or "princes of privilege." The salient characteristic of the Truman Administration was that it was stocked with leaders of the financial and business community. Truman had recalled the same men who had run World War II to run the cold war, businessmen as well as military leaders like General Marshall. Max Lerner attributed the style of men in the top echelon to the fact that as an unsuccessful small-business haberdasher, Truman had an awe of Wall Street, just as an ex-Army captain he had an awe of Generals. In September Ickes ruminated as to whether he could endorse Truman in view of all the Wall Street people around him. A sample—James Forrestal was from the investment banking firm of Dillon, Read and Company, as was William H. Draper, Jr., Under Secretary of the Army. Under Secretary of State Robert Lovett was from the investment firm of Brown Brothers. Chairman of the Munitions Board Thomas J. Hargrave was president of Eastman Kodak; John J. McCloy, president of the World Bank, was a prominent Wall Street lawyer, Paul Hoffman, Administrator of the ECA, was president of Studebaker. One could go down a long list including Cornelius Whitney, Sidney Souers, Stuart Symington, Lewis Strauss, and Averell Harriman. If ever there was a case of the pot calling the kettle black, this was it.

It did not appear in the early weeks of the campaign tours that the Dewey technique was not working. Richard Rovere, who was on both trains, reported, "Dewey's effect on his audiences is unquestionably greater than Truman's." Robert Albright of the Washington *Post* wrote, "The crowds [for Dewey] eat it up. What impresses the newsmen is this—the audiences are friendly, intensely interested and almost as certain he will be the next president as he is." Doris Fleeson though characterizing the Dewey swing as a "terrible bore" and "operation precision" said, "It must be said that his audiences seem satisfied." Bert Andrews of the New York *Herald Tribune* wrote, "Reporters mingling with the crowds after the speeches find that the unity appeal goes over big, it makes a deep impression." One wonders how much of this was self-delusion in view of the accepted assumptions. Thus,

Robert Albright, after his return home from the first cross-country swing, wrote in the Washington *Post,* "One's lasting impression of the trip is the lack of genuine interest and real campaign enthusiasm. Western politicians have a phrase for it, 'The critter's eyes are sot,' the voters know how they will vote."

There were seventy-five newspaper and radio people on the Dewey train, a greater number than on the Truman train. The *Victory Special* gave Richard Rovere the impression that we are in for years of "cool, sleek efficiency in Government." The difference between the two trains was the difference between "horsehair and foam rubber, between the coal stove griddle and the pop-up toaster." Tom Stokes wrote "To transfer from President Truman's campaign train to Governor Dewey's is like leaving a casual free-and-easy stock company on tour to join up with a slick New York musical." As Rovere described it, Dewey's speeches were ready twelve to twenty-four hours before delivery "smooth and glossy as chromium" —often, as in Salt Lake City, Dewey's speeches were printed in the local newspaper hours before they were made. Correspondents on Truman's trains had to miss deadline after deadline waiting for Truman's speeches, which sounded "gritty" when they were produced shortly before the rally. Dewey's train was wired for sound—on Truman's train the correspondents had to scurry to the rear to mingle with the crowds which often late at night were precariously assembled on roadbeds. During night stopovers on Truman's train correspondents often had to fend for themselves, getting to hotels and washing their laundry in washbasins. On Dewey's train laundries were alerted a thousand miles ahead, luggage was carried to the hotels and coffee and sandwiches served at the hotels. The ultraefficiency of the Dewey train was such that when some tomatoes were thrown at the train, Jim Hagerty, Dewey's press chief, rushed to the press car to report how many were thrown. No detail was too small to be overlooked. When it was found that Mrs. Dewey's hat, red felt with black feathers, did not photograph well, it had to be taken off at the whistle stops.

As a campaigner Dewey had relaxed somewhat over previous years, but he was still pretty stiff. Richard Wilson wrote, "It is true that there is a 'new Dewey.' He is a far better campaigner than ever before. But it must be said that he has never yet put on an Indian war bonnet or a Western Stetson hat. Once he told an admiring audience that he 'just wouldn't look right.' " He first-named more and kidded photographers. He might open his rear-platform speeches with the same joke–as he had descended the steps of the state capitol in Salem, Oregon, an elderly man approached him and said, "Hello, Dewey, I'm glad to see you. I've been wanting to vote for Dewey for President ever since you licked the Spaniards at Manila Bay." He would quip at the size of the crowd. "There can't be this many Republicans in town, can there?" He bought tickets for a benefit dance and admired a portrait of himself held up by a local artist. Seeing children he repeatedly said that they had to thank him for getting out of school. At Tacoma he recalled that his uncle had been superintendent of schools and then asked how many had diplomas signed by him. His geniality, on the whole, however, was reserved and deliberate.

His appearance before audiences at rallies was a project in itself. Truman, as Rovere described it, was "a slender and almost pathetic figure" on the platform, surrounded by broad-shouldered politicians until his turn came to speak. As for Dewey, "He remains in the wings until all the invocations and endorsements are over. Sometimes he stays away from the meeting hall until the last moment. Then with a great whining of motorcycle escort sirens to hush the crowds and build up the suspense, he arrives. The instant his name is spoken he comes onstage seemingly from nowhere, arms outstretched to embrace the crowds and gather in the applause that breaks the hush." Tom Stokes said that "the offstage whirr of the sirens [was] like an overture to denote that the curtain figuratively is about to go up. Hollywood never did it better." Joseph Alsop found the whole Dewey style "too ostentatiously noble" with a "faint touch of Batten, Barton, Durstine and Osborne." It had, in fact, been planned by Ben Duffy of BBD&O.

Dewey and Bell were fundamentally unsympathetic to the campaign rally and regretted that television, then in early life, had not yet reached the stage where a candidate could make the speeches of a statesman reaching the people from a studio.

Dewey failed to realize that the national Presidential contest is superimposed over the kinetic action of thousands of local elections and that local people may be far more interested in the election of a sheriff than the Presidential candidate. There was a good deal of obtuseness in dealing with local politicians, who never got the red-carpet treatment from Dewey's aide, Paul Lockwood, that they got from Truman's aide, Matt Connelly. Kansas City is an example. When the Dewey crowd arrived at the hotel, the local reception committee phoned and asked if they could pay their respects. They were told that Dewey was too tired. Paul Lockwood visited the rally hall and insisted that the height of the rostrum be changed to suit Dewey's height. Dewey was asked to arrive early enough to say a word for the local candidates, but instead appeared a few moments before he went on the air. The feeling of the local politicos was to let the national ticket go hang.

The Truman rear-platform talk was a minor masterpiece of corn and the common touch. Richard Rovere saw it as a carnival re-enactment—the "beater" or advance man was Oscar Chapman; the "shills" in the audience, to clap at the right time and "help to build a good tip," were General Graham and Clark Clifford. Princess Bright Cloud who steps from behind the curtain was Margaret.

After "Hail to the Chief" played by the local high-school band, the President was presented with a bag of peaches, a mess of celery, a miner's hat, or the like. He then made a reference to the local area, on which he had been well briefed.

Thus, he might congratulate the community on its new salami factory near by. He worked himself up to the motif of the slam at the good-for-nothing Congress for which his audiences in time waited expectantly. "How would you like to meet my family?" he asked, cocking his head to catch the response. Then he introduced the "Boss," Mrs. Truman, winking at the audience, and then Margaret. In the border states he would say, "I would like for you to meet Miss Margaret." Margaret would throw a rose from her bouquet to a photographer as the train started to move. It was all very effective.

The Truman off-the-cuff talks were homely and delightful, and covered a wide range of topics. As Joseph Driscoll of the St. Louis *Post-Dispatch* wrote, he talked "of cabbages and kings, of horses, mules and tractors, of boarding houses and baseball teams, of alfalfa and lespedza." To the despair of the secret-service men he got off the train and mingled freely with the crowds. At Ardmore, Oklahoma, he got off the train to examine a horse and tell its age from its teeth. There was plenty of humor—in Iowa he told of the man who was informed at his wife's funeral that his mother-in-law would ride with him and protested that it would spoil his whole day. He explained why he wanted to be re-elected. "So if you do what I'm asking you to do on election day I won't have to be hunting around in the housing shortage for a house after January 20th."

He told of his troubles farming under the Republicans and of his failure in the haberdashery business. Most ubiquitous were his many relatives. There was his grandfather Solomon Young, who had crisscrossed the West, judging from the many places he had been; there was his uncle under the Republicans who had shipped cattle from a ranch in New Mexico to Kansas City and got bilked; there was the grandfather who owned a house on the county line and dodged from room to room to escape jury duty.

A notable difference between Dewey and Truman was that Truman worked a good deal harder at campaigning, starting early in the morning and concluding late at night. On his transcontinental trip Dewey made 47 platform and 13 formal speeches—Truman made a total of 140 speeches. Truman was an early riser—Dewey a late riser. By 10:00 AM when Dewey started in, Truman had already been at it for several hours. A campaign contretemps grew out of this in October. The Dewey campaign train arrived at Terre Haute, Indiana, at 7:00 AM. It was believed that Dewey would appear and a crowd gathered, including farmers from miles around. Dewey was too tired, snatching some sleep. In indignation, farmers pelted the train with produce.

Immediately after Truman's return to Washington an incident occurred which occupies more space in the Truman *Memoirs* than any other phase of the campaign—the abortive Truman plan to send Chief Justice Vinson on a mission to Moscow. As Truman tells it he broached the idea to Vinson on Sunday, October 3, and overcame his reluctance with the request, "in the interest of the country and the peace of the world, I am compelled to request you to go." As Truman states it Vinson was to explain to Stalin the dangers of war and "our nation's peaceful aspirations for the whole world." The one substantive issue Truman mentions is the dispute about inspection in the peacetime control of atomic energy. He does not mention what was on everybody's mind at the time, the crisis about the Berlin blockade which had become more acute with the breakdown of talks between the three western powers and Soviet leaders and the reference of the matter to the UN Security Council. Truman had sounded out Secretary Marshall in Paris about a mission such as Vinson's and had received a negative answer. The President decided to go ahead anyway. According to *Time* he paced the White House floor saying, "I've got to do something dramatic."

The idea of the Vinson mission was attributed at the time to Clark Clifford. Clifford emphatically denies that he was the source and says that the idea came to the President from someone in the advertising world. But Clifford got a stream of letters denouncing him. Apparently the idea came to Truman through his aide, Matt Connelly.

At 10:30 AM on Tuesday, October 5, representatives of the four networks were summoned to the White House and asked to arrange a half-hour network time for a nonpolitical speech by the President. The radio men wanted to know the nature of the talk and Ross told them, but cautioned silence. "I've rushed a bit to give you ample notice . . . a premature disclosure might do much harm. For Lord's sake let's have no leaks."

But a half-hour later all plans were called off. In a room down the hall, Truman was in contact with Secretary Marshall by telecon and Under Secretary Robert Lovett was by his side. Marshall did not threaten to resign, as reported, but did argue strongly. Truman's great respect for Marshall won him over. Both Foreign Minister Bevin for Britain and Foreign Minister Schuman for France were concerned about the consistency of our foreign policy. The negotiations on the Berlin blockade were in a crucial stage. A direct approach to Stalin would seem to undercut the UN and the concert of three powers. Truman said the mission was canceled and asked Marshall to return the following Sunday.

The President embarked on an Eastern tour and continued to "pour it on." At Philadelphia he said, "They're using the farmer as the whipping boy in the cities and labor as the whipping boy on the farms. Apparently, they figure that if they can get the city folk good and mad at the farmer, and the farmer good and mad at the city folk, they will have unity." He said the GOP slogan for housing was "two families in every garage." Dewey's unity is "company-union unity." At Jersey City Boss Hague pulled out all the stops with a 300,000 reception. Fireworks turned into blazing portraits of Truman. "Do you want even stronger antilabor legislation than the Taft-Hartley law? A return to sweat shop wages, your social-security benefits endangered?" Truman asked.

He then cut short his Eastern tour and returned to Washington to greet Marshall on his return. The news had already leaked out. James Reston of the New York *Times* and Walter Trohan of the Chicago *Tribune* were bird-dogging it and Trohan was the first to get it into print, sending the story to his paper on Friday, October 8. The networks then admitted the truth. In his *Memoirs* Truman says that "an unfortunate

Russell in the Los Angeles Times

"Politics in Uncle Sam's clothing."

leak to an unfriendly newspaper" forced the cancellation of the mission, but he is in error in reading the calendar.

The abandoned mission to Moscow was the subject of universal comment by the time of Marshall's return. Truman issued a statement in explanation—that the purpose of the mission was to create a better atmosphere and to dispel Soviet fears. "I was wondering whether this attitude did not reflect a misunderstanding in the minds of the Soviet leaders so serious from the standpoint of world peace that we should be remiss if we left undone anything that might conceivably serve to dispel it."

There was hardly a word of approbation in the nation's press about the discarded plan. Henry Wallace praised it, saying that Marshall should have been fired for his opposition to the mission. All saw in the timing a political move; in May the Administration had flatly refused bilateral talks with Russia. The Washington *Post* termed it "fantastic," and the New York *Times* "amazing." It is true that there had been precedents for missions, such as Harry Hopkins' mission in 1945 to Moscow to clear the impasse for the San Francisco Conference which set up the United Nations. But the discarded plan would have short-circuited the groundwork laboriously constructed with our allies, by-passed the UN and created confusion in our foreign policy. How could the mission be confined to the control of atomic energy when the Berlin blockade was the critical issue?

This was a windfall for the Republicans. If Dewey wanted an example of disunity, here was proof of disunity within the Administration and with our allies. If he wanted to prove incompetence and lack of judgment, here was a case study. As a monumental blunder it was almost a carbon copy of Truman's endorsement of Wallace's speech in 1946 which undercut Secretary Byrnes in Paris.

What would Dewey do about it? There was now some feeling among his advisers that the high-level approach would not do. Dewey discussed the situation with his staff and his foreign policy advisers, John Foster Dulles and Senator Vandenberg. What was Dewey's decision? Thomas O'Neill in the Baltimore *Sun* on October 11 wrote, "After a day's conference on the Vinson incident, Dewey said, 'No, I won't do it. I'd rather lose the election than add to the damage this country has already suffered from this unhappy incident.' " He issued a seventy-four-word statement assuring the world that the United States was "united" in its foreign policy and behind our representatives in Paris demanding the lifting of the Berlin blockade. There was no specific reference to the bungled mission. Dewey dispatched Dulles to Vienna, Frankfort, and Berlin to carry his message of unity and our determination to stand behind the airlift. He attempted to undo the damage in keeping with his duty as the President-designate.

Dewey did not attack Truman frontally on the issue but only by innuendo. In his next speech at Pittsburgh he added a paragraph, that the Republicans would "unfailingly back up the work of their representatives in the UN." In Oklahoma City he said there would be no "undercutting." Was this enough? At a train-side stop in Pennsylvania, while the story was in the headlines, Dewey said that the Administration "should let its right hand know what its left hand is doing." Again, he said that foreign policy "should not be conducted on a happy-thought basis." Members of Dewey's staff wondered if these brief flicks conveyed any message to the audience.

And so the Vinson mission episode passed into the annals of a lost campaign. What might have been a liability for Truman in the end became an asset. After the election, Walter Lippmann said that he gained by the move, pleasing "many discontented Democrats who shared his dissatisfaction with the way things were being handled in the State Department and Pentagon." There was a strong will for peace and Truman had made a bid for peace. Columnist Tom Stokes stated the viewpoint of many that the plan was "sound in conception" since "it represented an attempt to have people speak to people over the heads of diplomats and Generals. . . . Try again, Mr. President." It is worth recalling that Dewey himself had the same viewpoint back in May. Campaigning in Oregon, he was told of Stalin's bid for bilateral talks and, not being apprized of the intricacies of our foreign policy, said, "If they mean it, it's the best news since V-J Day."

[XI]

WALLACE DECLINE—DIXIECRAT FIZZLE

THE COMMUNIST *Daily Worker* had warned before the Wallace candidacy that a third party would be futile without labor support and events were to bear out its prophecy. At best, one million organized workers were nominally in the Wallace camp, including electrical workers, longshoremen, farm-equipment workers, and fur workers. The refusal of the United Electrical Workers (CIO) to give an outright endorsement was a severe blow. Max Lerner said that Wallace was guilty of the "failure to base his campaign on the liberal American labor party movement or even to consult the major labor party leaders on their plans." There was no support among farm leaders, unless one were to count Elmer Benson, former governor of Minnesota.

At the end of August Frank Kent called the candidacy a "bust," and things were to go from bad to worse. Wallace was isolated in the blind alley about which he had been abundantly warned before he launched his candidacy.

Wallace's only prominent New Deal supporter, Dr. Rexford Guy Tugwell, was now uneasy and said he would take a walk if the wrong people controlled the Progressive Party. "I certainly don't know if they are Communists, but they act as though they were," he said publicly. Privately, he called Wallace from Chicago and told him of his misgivings. Wallace promised to purge him of doubts. Wallace took cognizance of the issue in a public statement which played both sides—his party was not controlled by Communists, but his objectives might command their support; he did not tolerate those who wanted to destroy the Government by force; there is as much difference within the ranks of Communists as within the ranks of Democrats and Republicans. If Wallace was sincere in believing all this, he was naïve. "Deviationism" is a cardinal sin among Communists, who do believe in overthrowing the Government by force. Tugwell was not reassured and stayed on the sidelines except for a couple of appearances with Wallace in the closing weeks.

In September Wallace embarked on a Southern trip which he admits today was probably a mistake. He would insist on addressing unsegregated meetings. He was obviously going to have a hot time. The Birmingham chief of police said, "I ain't going to allow darkies and white people to segregate together." Frederick Sullens, editor of the Jackson, Mississippi, *Daily News* wrote, "To say that he would be as welcome as a common prostitute at a family reunion or a skunk under the church at prayer meeting night is putting it too mildly."

In Virginia there was no trouble—the state called the meetings "private parties" to which no segregation laws applied; the meetings were so quiet that they resembled, as one observer put it, old-fashioned silent movies in a theater without a piano player. In North Carolina things were different. Wallace was splattered with eggs at various places including Durham and Burlington. Far outstripping Willkie's record, Wallace was to be pelted with at least twenty-seven eggs, thirty-seven tomatoes, six peaches and two lemons. The governor of North Carolina and the newspapers in this southern state, which was progressive on the Negro issue, deplored the attacks, approving Truman's characterization of them as "un-American."

All this Wallace apparently relished as shedding on him the light of martyrdom. He said as much, that he knew what it must have felt like to have been an early Christian martyr. He left North Carolina with these words, "As Jesus Christ said, if at any time they will not listen to you willingly, then shake the dust from off your feet and go elsewhere." His aide, Clark Foreman, candidly said, "This is what we want." Wallace saw an economic motivation in the attacks—he charged that he was prevented from speaking in mill towns which were owned by Northern industrial corporations. In Greensboro he said that he had "profound compassion" for his attackers "because most of them have not had enough to eat."

Whether it was designed that way or not the Wallace scheme of campaigning incited Southern sensibilities. His Negro secretary was always at his side. He dined only in unsegregated restaurants (eating a box lunch on a train where that was impossible) and slept in the homes of Negroes. In Little Rock, Arkansas, he could have gotten permission to speak in ten places, but chose four where he knew that he would not be allowed. In departing from the South he made his most provocative statement, that state laws in the South should be changed to permit intermarriage.

As Wallace went farther into the deep South, state governors gave him ironclad police protection. In Mississippi he was whisked through and out of the state by a police escort at ninety miles an hour, making only one speech at Vicksburg to a hundred people. It was noticeable that in the deep South where authorities prevented any outbreaks, Wallace's speechmaking ardor visibly subsided. He left the South after addressing only 25,000 people. But returning North, Wallace viewed himself in the role of a conquering hero. He was greeted by a supporter in New York with "we will hatch a bright new world," and he answered that he would return to the South ten million eggs a year for every one thrown, as a result of new chicken-breeding methods he had developed. In a speech at Yankee Stadium he told 50,000 frenzied listeners that he had seen "how hate and propaganda can turn Christian gentlemen into raving beasts, turn good wives and mothers into Jezebels."

Pro-Truman liberals went to work on Wallace's reputation as a liberal. The main target was his reputation as a friend of the Negro, which was largely based on his declaration in the 1944 Democratic convention that "the poll tax must go." Jim Carey related how he and a Negro, George Weaver, were at Washington National Airport and service was denied to Weaver; they appealed to Wallace, who replied that he was bound by Virginia law; however, Averell Harriman, a successor as Secretary of Commerce, had stopped the discrimination. It was charged that when he was Vice-President, Wallace refused to get a Negro into the press gallery, but the Negro attained entry through the good offices of Senator Vandenberg. Walter White of the NAACP claimed that Wallace had dodged speaking before the NAACP for years, that he said to Dr. Will Alexander, after he had resigned as head of the Farm Security Administration, "Don't you think the New Deal has undertaken to do too much for Negroes?" Gardner Jackson claimed that while Vice-President, Wallace ran away from a delegation asking him to intervene for a Negro sharecropper, Odell Walker, who was to be executed for murder under an allegedly unjust sentence. Harold Ickes had his own charge to make. The great Negro soprano, Marian Anderson, after she was denied the use of Constitution Hall in Washington by the Daughters of the American Revolution, sang before 80,000 gathered before the Lincoln Memorial in a memorable recital. Ickes said that Wallace refused an invitation to attend the affair.

Dwight Macdonald's conclusion in his book on Wallace published in 1948 was, "There is no recorded instance of Henry Wallace separating himself on an issue of principle from power or those who dispense it." In truth, there are perplexing facets of Wallace's career in Government which his enemies could dig into, such as his wholesale purge in the early days of the New Deal of the "liberal" faction in the Agriculture Department, including Jerome Frank, Alger Hiss, and Gardner Jackson. The faction was fighting the large profit margins of the milk industry. Wallace recalls the incident well. "There was no choice—I had to do it. Congress wouldn't stand for them."

The most severe indictment against Wallace was that his candidacy made the election of Truman virtually impossible and that his local candidates would split the anti-Republican vote and thus would elect a reactionary Congress. At a dinner of the National Businessmen for Wallace at the end of September at the Hotel Commodore, "Beanie" Baldwin announced that the party would withdraw its candidates against Chester Bowles for Governor in Connecticut and Helen Gahagan Douglas for Congress in California. Wallace, apparently taken by surprise, was grieved, "When guys go in two directions at one time, I just wonder where you're going to end up. . . . We've got to build a party, Beanie, we've got to build a party. . . . How can you get on with people like Helen Gahagan Dulles [sic]?"

But the next day Wallace retracted to the press, "I agreed that Baldwin's was a proper approach." He claimed that he had been misunderstood and that he had only referred to the "undertones" of the Baldwin statement. This retraction was as hard for reporters to take as his statement that he was misunderstood the previous December when he said that Taft's election had much to commend it.

Thus, the New Party (as Wallace continued to call it) retreated from its stand of fighting all candidates who had voted for the Marshall Plan. This was a blow to the Communist element. The party withdrew thirteen candidates initially and more later for House seats in California, Connecticut, New Jersey, and Massachusetts, including candidates against Mrs. Douglas and Chet Holifield in California. Tom Emerson would not run against Chester Bowles for Governor of Connecticut, and Elmer Benson would not run against Hubert Humphrey in Minnesota. By this time, the movement was so clearly on the downgrade that neither Mrs. Douglas nor Holifield wanted the endorsements they would have welcomed months before. Mrs. Douglas said, "I did not seek the endorsement of the Progressive Party and do not desire it." Wallace, in California at the time of the statement, said that while he would "support" her he would not "endorse" her, a distinction which left reporters gasping. Some of the candidacies left standing were perplexing. In New York Paul O'Dwyer, brother of Mayor O'Dwyer, was running for Congress against Republican Jacob Javits with American-Labor Party as well as Democratic endorsement, even though Javits had been an outstanding liberal in Congress. In Brooklyn, Lee Pressman ran for Congress with Wallace's endorsement against Abe Multer, whose record was also a liberal one.

Wallace denies that he wanted to be an instrument of defeat for Chester Bowles or Mrs. Douglas. But broadly speaking, he says, "What was the difference between Republicans and Democrats? What did it matter?" As far as the Presidential contest was concerned, he felt that Dewey was the more competent individual.

Wallace himself appeared on the ballot in forty-four States, a tremendous feat. He was not on the ballot in Illinois, Oklahoma, Nebraska, and Georgia. There was a good deal of political maneuvering between Republicans and Democrats since it was to the interest of the GOP that Wallace appear on the ballot and take votes from Truman. In Ohio the Secretary of State sought to bar Wallace on the ground that the party was guilty of un-American activities, rather than on technical grounds which would have been more effective. The move was upset by the Supreme Court of the State, which, of course, pleased Republicans, including the Secretary of State. The weirdest situation appeared in Illinois. It was claimed that Wallace should be barred from the ballot because he did not have the requisite two hundred signatures on petitions in the fifty required counties. The Attorney General of the State of Illinois, which was under Republican administration, appeared before the United States Supreme Court to contest the constitutionality of its own law and lost out when its own law was upheld, and Wallace was barred.

It was no longer Springtime For Henry, as one newspaper wag put it. The polls showed what all could sense and see, that the party was in a decline. At a Chicago rally, an aide proclaimed, "Give Gallup enough Roper and we'll hang them both." Wallace was fading in the stretch partly because he had made his bid too soon—it had been necessary to whip up enthusiasm early to get on as many state ballots as possible. That had been largely accomplished but now the steam could not be kept up.

At the end of September Wallace, at a luncheon in Dallas, got a lugubrious introduction from a Rev. Charles E. Wilson, "I see a lot of faces that aren't here, faces of good, sincere people who were with us a year ago." In answer Wallace said, "I don't know why they hate me. I'm still holding the door open for them. I used to say that they'd come after Truman was nominated. But they didn't come flocking to me the way I hoped."

The crowds thinned out. In Gilmore Stadium in Los Angeles where he had drawn 32,000 a few months before, he drew only 19,000; in Bakersfield he drew 330 in a stadium seating 3000—this in a state which Baldwin had once claimed for Wallace. After a Milwaukee rally, when only 2000 turned out in contrast to 8000 the winter before, a decision was reached to concentrate most of Wallace's energy on radio broadcasts.

His campaign continued to the end to be one of preaching appeasement or accord with Russia. He accused Truman and Dewey of manufacturing the Berlin crisis to promote their program of turning America into a war economy. In Dallas he said, "I charge that the two bipartisans, Truman and Dewey, cannot bring peace because their program is based on a war economy and not on production for peace. They must heap crisis on crisis to justify the draft, huge military appropriations, and the other devices they use to keep the economy going." At Houston he suggested an impartial commission to investigate the Berlin blockade, but when asked if he would accept its findings if it sustained the US position, he answered, "I can't answer that now." In Minneapolis he branded Churchill as a "racist" and an "imperialist" and a "scuttler of the century of the common man." Wallace branded the Marshall Plan as the "biggest steal" and "run by corporations for the benefit of corporations. . . . America's policy was born of a fear of peace and a dream of world conquest." Our crusade was as "cynical" and "deceitful" as Hitler's. "Will less people die under a false slogan if it is spoken in English rather than in German?"

His running mate, Glen Taylor, really went off the deep end. "Nazis are running the US Government. So why should Russia make peace with them? If I were a Russian at the Moscow conference, I would not agree to anything." He said, "Vishinsky's statement that we are aggressively preparing for war is truthful on the very face of it."

From city to city as Wallace traveled he was met by reporters with the same two questions, and gave the same two stock answers. About Communist support, he was against Communists who want to use force to overthrow the Government—there are two kinds of Communists, those who are real Bolsheviks and those who advocate peace. As for the Guru letters, "I am not engaging in any effort to reduce the publicity given me by Westbrook Pegler." He became bitter about the lack of labor support. In Detroit he read back past statements of labor leaders—Phil Murray had said of Truman that he had shown "abject cowardice" in the face of big industry; William Green had castigated him for proposing "slave labor under Fascism";

Al Whitney said, "Truman has attacked loyal American workers with more ferocity than had been displayed against the Japanese at Pearl Harbor." In a speech at the Allis Chalmers plant Wallace attacked the present leadership of the UAW and defended the ousted leaders, including Harold Christoffel, who was convicted of perjury for denying that he was a Communist.

Even the Soviet Union showed in the closing months a measure of disillusionment with Wallace. The Soviet *New Times* attacked him for believing in the possibility of establishing progressive capitalism in the United States.

Was Wallace crushed by the evident failure of his party to get popular support? On the contrary, the New York *Post,* which followed his campaign carefully, stated at the close, "The hesitant humility which once characterized his speeches is now usually replaced by stern insistence that he is answering the call of conscience. His demeanor is exuberant. He speaks of Mr. Truman's impending defeat in joyous tones, as if convinced the political punishment neatly fits the crime." At the end of October in a speech at Wilkes-Barre, Wallace said of Truman, "He is going to take the worst licking any Democrat candidate has ever taken."

Triumphantly, he closed his campaign in a rally of his followers at Madison Square Garden. "The cold war has been stopped," he announced, "there will be no war." He listed among his accomplishments besides stopping the cold war the following: The Greek fighters for liberty, the Chinese peasants, and the Haganah troops had gained new hope; Spanish anti-Fascists had learned they have friends in the United States; the Mundt-Nixon bill had been stopped; big brass had been stopped in its drive to impose military training; and the attempted betrayal of Israel had been stopped.

There were all sorts of explanations given by its opponents for the States' Rights campaign headed by Governor Strom

Thurmond in 1948—that it was a futile or insane gesture, that it was an attempt to intimidate the Democratic Party or control it after its defeat, that it was a deal with Dewey to split the Democratic vote, or as William Primm of the Democratic National Committee put it, it was "nothing more than a wing of the Republican Party financed by oil and public utilities interests." All miss the truth—that Thurmond expected to be elected President and believes to this day that he might have been.

His reasoning was this, as he explains it, "If the States' Rights candidates had carried only two or more of the larger States, or if the Republicans had not lost two of the three they were expected to carry but lost, to wit, California, Ohio, and Illinois, the Democrats would not have had a majority and the election would have gone into the House of Representatives. . . . If the election had gone to Congress, the States' Rights candidates might have been elected since it is very dubious that the Democratic states would have gone over to the Republicans or vice versa." His reasoning, moreover, is that if the election had been thrown into the House, where each state would have one vote, then all the Southern delegations, even from states which had given their electoral votes to Truman, could and would have cast their votes for Thurmond.

There were several flaws in the theory which he does not recognize. First, if the House in the Eighty-first Congress turned out to be Republican, as in the Eightieth Congress, then by votes of states Dewey would have been chosen. The Thurmond candidacy would thus have elected a Republican. Second, Thurmond, by splitting the anti-Truman vote, might have given Dewey a plurality in some Southern states and instead of throwing the election into the House, Dewey might have been elected. Third, Senator Russell, who is the acknowledged leader of the Southern bloc, says that he doubts that the Southern delegations, even from those states which cast their electoral vote for Thurmond, would have stuck with him if the election had gone to the House; there would have been a deal on civil rights with the Democrats, and they would have gone over to Truman.

Whatever the fallacies of the reasoning, Thurmond's candidacy is one which he personally and the South can look back on with pride. He was no extremist. He said, "We do not need the support of Gerald K. Smith and other rabble rousers who use race prejudice and class hatred to inflame the emotions of the people." There is no proof that he was a tool of oil or business interests, a slur repeatedly broadcast by Northern commentators. This allegation was built on the most tenuous reasoning, such as the fact that Birmingham, where the States' Rights convention was held, was the home of the Tennessee Coal and Iron Company and the Alabama Power Company. Every large city has some big industry connected with it. Thurmond declared in August, "I know nothing of any attempt by oil interests to make any contribution whatsoever to the States' Rights Democrats." Today he says firmly of the charge, "It is untrue." If they did finance Thurmond, the low gear in which the States' Rights campaign was conducted (it consisted of about thirty-five major speeches made by him alone) would testify, if anything, to the meager resources of the oil interests. Thurmond was often strapped for funds and for his final radio-hookup speech on the eve of his election, the money was raised by ten-dollar-a-plate dinners in South Carolina. The return of the tidelands to the states was mentioned only casually in the States Rights platform. The "conspiracy" idea, that Thurmond was used as a tool by big business to help elect Dewey, is the stuff that dreams are made of.

Thurmond regarded himself as a moderate on the race question. He had asked for repeal of the poll tax in South Carolina. While Governor he had enlarged educational facilities for Negroes saying, "If we provide better educational facilities for them not only will much be accomplished in human values but we shall raise our per capita income as well as the educational standing of our state." During the campaign he said, "All thinking Southerners know that the solution of the South's economic problems will depend to a large degree on the educational and economic gains by the Negro population." While he was Governor there was a lynching in Greenville—he imprisoned a host of suspects within forty-eight hours. Although they were acquitted, his dispatch in apprehending them was widely applauded in the North.

Thurmond was an impassioned believer in the justice of the South's cause. The general lines of his thinking emerged in his speeches before his nomination. In a radio speech on March 17 he charged that the President's Commission had insulted the South when it said, "It is a sound policy to use the idealism and prestige of our whole people to check the wayward tendency of a part of them." To this Thurmond said, "*They* have the idealism, and prestige, *we* in the South are the wayward." The close friendship of Thurmond with South Carolina's Jimmy Byrnes crops out in the next statement, "What makes the stab more humiliating is the fact that the hand that held the dagger [Truman] received its power not from an election by the people but from a minority which through pressure applied at the 1944 Democratic convention blocked the nomination of a Southerner for Vice-President. We know this from the recent book of Ed Flynn, the Bronx politicial boss who makes no bones about his part in the political intrigue." (In his *Memoirs* Truman lists Byrnes as one of the chief conspirators in the plan to dump him.)

In his May 10 speech keynoting the States' Rights conference at Jackson, Mississippi, Thurmond made an address which made him the logical nominee. He protested that in the civil-rights report there was "not a word of recognition of the progress which the Negro has made as a result of the efforts of the Southern people." He blocked out the different approach of Roosevelt. "Franklin Roosevelt was in the White House longer than any other President in history. Yet I challenge Harry Truman or anyone else to cite a single public utterance where the late President ever advocated the enactment by Congress of any of the proposals" made by Truman. He called attention to the debt the party owed to the South. "I hope the Democrats everywhere will not forget that the South has kept the fires of Democracy burning when other sections deserted the party. . . . Without the South the Democratic party long ago would have ceased to function as a major political party."

Thurmond and Governor Fielding Wright of Mississippi were "recommended" as candidates at Birmingham; they were officially nominated by the state Democratic parties of Alabama, Mississippi, and South Carolina. The voters were not asked to bolt the party but to vote for electors who would recognize Thurmond and Wright as the only real Democrats. Then Louisiana went into line, and Thurmond accepted the nominations of the four states in Houston on August 11.

When the Louisiana State Committee in a sudden move made Thurmond the choice of the Democratic Party in that State, making it mandatory for Truman electors to vote for him, William Primm, assistant to Democratic Chairman McGrath, branded this an act of larceny. Shortly afterward, Peyton Ford of the Justice Department visited New Orleans and according to *Newsweek* his conversations might have concerned insinuations in Congress about Governor Earl Long's income-tax returns. At any rate Senator-designate Russell Long announced that he "would not be surprised" if his uncle reconvened the legislature in special session and that did happen. The legislature put Truman electors back on the ballot though reserving the name "Democratic" for Thurmond. Thus, in four states, Louisiana, South Carolina, Mississippi, and Alabama, Democratic voters would have no choice but to vote for Thurmond, if they voted Democratic.

The traditional Democratic emblem, the rooster, was over the names of Thurmond and Wright. In Alabama, Truman was not even on the ticket. Two Truman electors in Tennessee and three in Florida announced they would vote for Thurmond if Truman carried their states. Only one from Tennessee carried through his threat.

Thurmond's experience in 1948 is a case study in the difficulties of political secession by the South today. For one thing, he recognizes the force of the almost unanimous newspaper sentiment against him. The Charleston *News and Courier,* the oldest paper in the South, supported him, as did the Augusta *Chronicle,* fourth largest in Georgia. Aside from that, he had only a sprinkling of help. Here is a sampling of expressions from newspapers. From the Raleigh *News and Observer,* "The music was Dixie but the plan of march was that first proposed for 1948 by Henry A. Wallace. . . . Dixie and the Internationale make strange music when played together." Douglas Southall Freeman, the famous historian, wrote in the Richmond *News Leader* concerning Birmingham, "When those enemies of the Truman regime unfurled the Confederate flag and held up an engraving of General Lee as if it had been an ikon, they went too far. General Lee was not in Birmingham in spirit. He had no part before or after the war of 1861-65 in sowing the seeds of hate between races and sections."

The *Columbia Record* said, "It was not the time for any spur-of-the-moment flare-up. The Southern politicians needed to give themselves a cooling-off period. They needed to think before they leaped." The Atlanta *Journal* said, "They proved again how natural it is to feel, how difficult it is to think." The Birmingham *Age-Herald* said that the idea of throwing the election into the House was a "wild dream." The Andersonville *Independent,* considered one of the best papers in South Carolina, recalled the tragic results of secession in 1860 and also the Republican depression. "Do we not remember the last Republican Administration with its five-cent cotton, forty-cent wheat and $7 a week part-time wages." Ralph McGill in the Atlanta *Constitution* wrote, "We will pay through the nose for the Dixiecrats as we still pay for the leadership which took us into the war between the States to 'save us.' Is Harry Truman immortal? Is he going to be the issue every four years?"

Thurmond's political support melted away. While Truman is fond of recalling himself as "the man alone," Thurmond really fits the description. Governor Laney of Arkansas, an ertswhile leader of the movement, defected to Truman, as did the other February hotheads, Governor Jester of Texas, Governor Cherry of North Carolina, and Governor Caldwell of Florida. Senator Eastland of Mississippi was openly for Thurmond at least to the extent of a speech or two, and Senators Hill and Sparkman had to be for him *pro forma* since Alabama's electors were instructed for Thurmond. "I will abide by my oath," said Sparkman. Except for a handful of Congressmen, vocal support was nonexistent even in the four states where Thurmond was the official Democratic nominee. Senator Johnston in South Carolina would say only, "I am a Democrat." Thurmond had the help of Boss Ed Crump in Memphis, former Governor Moody in Texas, and former Governor "Happy" Chandler in Kentucky.

Everywhere, says Thurmond, he had to fight the feeling of futility about the movement—"Why throw away your vote?"—and the fear of political reprisals—"Remember what happened to the bolters in 1928." Then, too, there was the feeling that on the race question Truman was definitely preferable to Dewey, who had set up a strong FEPC in New York. Senator Russell, who came out for Truman a few days before the election, felt that the South was safer with Truman. The chairman of the North Carolina Democratic Committee said, "What can we accomplish? . . . The Republicans are committed to a more determined [civil-rights] program than our party is and Governor Dewey has already put into effect in the New York government many of the proposals to which we in the South most vigorously object." They were definitely correct. Dewey had a complex about the Negro vote, which he had always courted in New York but never got.

There were a few minor victories outside the four reasonably sure Thurmond states. In North Carolina the Supreme Court reversed the lower courts to put Thurmond on the ballot, and in Florida the legislature passed a special law to put him on the ballot. But the major battles were lost. In Virginia the Democratic State Committee refused to use the provisions of a law proposed by Governor Tuck and passed that year to put on the ballot its own endorsed electors. As the *Times-Dispatch* of Richmond put it, the Tuck law turned out to be a "dismal and dolorous fiasco." Senator Byrd had attended strategy sessions for Thurmond—now he said nothing, while his colleague, Senator Robertson, was out for Truman. Attorney General J. Lindsay Almond said that Democrats should "stay in the house of their fathers even though there are bats in the belfry, rats in the pantry, a cockroach waltz in the kitchen, and skunks in the parlor." In Georgia the disappointment was more acute. Herman Talmadge won the Democratic nomination for Governor on a strong racist platform. He himself attributed his victory to Truman's civil-rights program. He was expected to throw his influence behind an instruction to the Georgia electors to cast their votes for Thurmond. The Thurmond people were supremely confident, and a Thurmond leader at a rally in Birmingham said that Georgia's State Chairman "told us in Atlanta not to worry." But Talmadge did not go through with what was regarded as a commitment, and the Democratic Executive Committee instructed the electors to vote for Truman. The Thurmond supporters had to scurry to get the requisite number of signatures to get on the ballot—five per cent of the registered voters—but lost the state by a wide margin.

Thurmond was undaunted—an ex-Brigadier General who was carried off wounded from the beaches of Normandy, he was a fighter. He did not bother to campaign in the four sure states. He had hopes in Virginia, Florida, and Georgia; he soon gave up on North Carolina. He campaigned in Maryland, hoping for write-in votes. He spoke in New York in order to get wider publicity for the crusade. He got on the ballot in North Dakota to demonstrate that the issue of States Rights was not a sectional one.

Alone among the four candidates, Thurmond discussed issues on a rational plane. His appeal was dignified and intelligent. The term "Dixiecrat" had been invented by the telegraph editor of the Charlotte *News* to fill a headline, and it caught on. Thurmond objected to the term. As he saw it, his was a crusade against centralization. "May God forbid that your state and my state, your county and my county, your city and my city, your farm and my farm shall ever be subjected to Washington bureacratic rule. . . ." "This is no sectional or regional matter. It is as important to the people of Arizona as it is to the people of Alabama. . . ."

Here were his views on the Truman program. The poll tax—he was personally opposed to it but the anti-poll-tax bill would invade the right of states to elect their own officials. The antilynching law—"Congress would seize the power to punish for crimes committed within a state," thus taking away the police power of a state. He pointed out that there had been only one lynching in the South in the past year and asked, "Would you want an antigangster law in New York, didn't you resent prohibition laws?" The FEPC—it "calls for an army of Federal police empowered to spy into the affairs of each business enterprise, to control the hiring and firing of employees"; the Communists would use the FEPC to suit their purposes; by claiming their rights under the law they could force their agents and saboteurs into every industrial plant. Segregation must be maintained. "We in the South know that the laws dealing with the separation of the races are necessary to maintain the public peace and order when the races lives side by side in great numbers." And, "Even in states where there are antisegregation laws the people voluntarily establish segregation—otherwise, there would be no Harlem in New York City, no Chinatown in San Francisco, no South Side in Chicago."

H. L. Mencken, who had no use for politicians, praised Thurmond after his appearance in Baltimore. The movement "looks from across the Potomac and Ohio like nothing more than a fresh pestilence of Longs, Bilbos, Tillmans, Bleases, Talmadges and Pappy O'Daniels. It is, in fact, nothing of the sort. It is fundamentally quite as serious in purpose and quite as rational as any other regional movement that has appeared in recent years. Certainly, it would be absurd to dismiss such men as Governor Thurmond as windbags of the common sort. They are men of intelligence and men of honor and when they take to the bush it is safe to assume that they have a genuine grievance." In his last pronouncement on politics, Mencken reached this conclusion. "It is my firm conviction, reached after long experience, profound pondering, and incessant prayer, that no man who is worth a hoot will ever be President of the United States hereafter—until, that is, the Republic itself blows up."

Thurmond was disappointed in the result, blaming Dewey as much as the Republicans, feeling that he could have carried more states if Dewey had waged a stronger campaign. He nonetheless feels that he left his imprint, paving the way for Eisenhower victories in the South in 1952. Taft and Republican Chairman Hugh Scott both campaigned in the South, claiming that the Republican Party was the party of States' Rights, and they made an impression. The Charleston *Evening Post* said editorially in the campaign, "If the Republicans should capture the White House and retain control of Congress and show a friendly attitude toward the South, much of the section's dislike of the GOP will fade. Already on many issues except that of civil rights Southern sentiment accords more with Republican views than with the Democratic Party's position." Many Southern newspapers, Jesse Jones' Houston *Chronicle,* the Savannah *Morning News,* the Dallas *News,* the Roanoke *Times,* the Charlotte *News,* the Norfolk *Virginian-Pilot,* and the *Delta Democrat-Times* of Greenville, Mississippi, of which the well-known Hodding Carter was editor, supported Dewey. A poll of 150 Southern editors taken a week before the election found that fifty-five per cent believed that the election of Dewey would be better for the country than the election of Truman.

In the latter part of the nineteenth century the critic of the New South on the race question, George Washington Cable, concluded that the South readily accepted the compact imposed by the Civil War because the doctrine of States' Rights was only so much window dressing to justify slavery. The vulnerability of the doctrine was recognized in 1948. Ralph McGill, editor of the Atlanta *Constitution,* called the States' Rights ticket a fraud. "Every Kentucky farmer is praying for the United States to invade his rights and hold up the price of tobacco. Others want Uncle Sam to invade States' Rights and help cotton, peanuts, roads, health, education and libraries." The Charleston *Evening Post* said, "Can we in good conscience oppose such a program [civil rights] and yet demand Federal funds and other assistance in meeting problems which were intended to be affairs of the states themselves? If the states and the people are to be wards of the Federal Government they must accept all that goes with such dependent status." The Greenville *News* said, "We stopped talking about states' rights and state sovereignty when we saw the national gravy train headed our way." The Baltimore *Sun* said editorially, "In the most outrageous invasion of civil rights which the Federal Government has ever attempted—and we mean prohibition—the South was a violent supporter of the Volsteadian tyranny."

[XII]

CONCLUDING THE CAMPAIGN

IN HIS *Memoirs* Truman describes the campaign. "In all I traveled 31,700 miles and delivered more than 300 speeches—356 to be exact. . . . Twelve to fifteen million people gathered in big crowds and small groups along the railroad junctions and stops from one end of the country to the other. . . . My one man crusade took effect."

Although credit for the victory belongs principally to one man, it was far more than a one-man effort. The massive efforts of many private groups and of Government itself were mobilized to back up the "one man crusade."

The thesis of a "one man crusade," would overlook the contribution that organized labor made in the election. The CIO-PAC and the AFL's Labor League each spent over $1,000,000. A PAC pamphlet proclaimed, "PAC needs a dollar from every worker." The Labor League used the union organization right down to the shop stewards who handled on-the-spot grievances, who were urged to become fund collectors.

Although some leaders thought that labor should concentrate on the Congressional elections, the more acute minds saw labor's cause bound with Truman. Jack Kroll, head of the PAC, was with Truman on his train in mid-October; when asked by Truman how he was faring, he replied, "Just as well as you are." It is significant that only those close to the labor movement saw the possibility of Truman's winning. Jack Kroll predicted publicly that Truman would win and privately that the election would be thrown into the House. Labor columnist Victor Riesel gave the lowest estimate of Wallace's strength, saying that Wallace would poll less than 1,400,000 votes but would run ahead of the Prohibition and Vegetarian parties.

The Democratic Labor Committee offered $2000 in prizes with $1000 as the top prize to the local labor committee which showed the greatest improvement over the 1944 vote. The UAW persuaded the city of Detroit to establish thirty-two additional registration places and distributed leaflets naming registration places at the plants. Phil Hannah, head of the AFL in Ohio, made 150 speeches for Truman in two months. In Massachusetts the AFL and CIO banded together to glamorize their campaign with stars like Vaughn Monroe. Settlement houses were recruited to take care of children on election day. Great ingenuity was used in registration drives. In Cleveland, with a hot pennant race, unions persuaded the sports announcer between innings when all the town was listening to say, "Go out and register"; a plane flying over the stadium had a streamer, "Go Out and Register"; leaflets peppered the fans, "Don't strike out on election day." In one Ohio town no member of the Building and Contractors Union could get a job unless he had registered.

One thousand radio speeches and spot announcements were paid for by the PAC. It hired fleets of cars to greet Truman with whistles at the whistle stops. In San Diego eight hundred cars were lined up to take voters to the polls. Ten million pieces of literature were published by the PAC. They often showed Truman in informal dress with a friendly smile; Dewey glowering in a top hat with white tie and tails. There were many independent labor groups for Truman such as the Railway Labor Political League, the Machinists Non-Partisan Political League, and the Boilermakers Non-Partisan

League. Dewey comments that in California when he saw all the streamers, "I wondered whether I was running against labor or the Democratic Party."

Truman continued to pour it on regarding the labor issue. At Hartford he said the GOP favors "labor-baiting, union-hurting, yellow-dog open-shop contracts." At Akron he said that the GOP had "tasted blood" when it passed the Taft-Hartley law, and that it wanted a GOP President to do a "real hatchet job." Jack Kroll called the Dewey program "Uncle Tom's Doghouse for Labor." Kroll said that there had been only two Republican Presidents who were for labor, Theodore Roosevelt and Lincoln, and the latter was "shot by a Dixiecrat."

On October 12 Dewey uttered a few words which many believe made the difference in the result, at least in Ohio and Illinois. At Beaucoup, Illinois, the campaign train suddenly started to back up into the crowd and there were some screams from people in the rear. It backed only a few feet and no damage was done. Dewey said, "Well, that's the first lunatic I've had for an engineer. He probably should be shot at sunrise, but we'll let him off this time since no one was hurt."

As soon as the remark was made the Dewey people realized that it was a serious error—newspapermen told them that. In order not to make matters worse, they never commented on the incident. If they had commented, they might have said that that engineer had given them a rough ride even before Beaucoup. Twice before the train had lurched back into small crowds at water stops. The engineer's sympathies were evident when he was told what Dewey said. He replied, "That doesn't change my opinion of him. I didn't think much of him in the first place."

The Truman people were not slow to capitalize on Dewey's asperity as proof that Dewey had no regard for human beings and laboring people in particular. In Logansport, Indiana,

Truman said, "The train crews on this train are all Democrats. We've had wonderful train crews all over the country." Then Truman made a radio speech from Washington sponsored by the International Ladies Garment Workers Union and was introduced by Tallulah Bankhead, who said that Dewey was a "mechanical man with a synthetic smile on his face. . . . Better leave him in his cellophane wrapper unspoiled by contact with the likes of you and me." Truman in his speech taunted Dewey. "He objects to having engineers back up. He doesn't mention that under the great engineer, Hoover, we backed up into the worst depression in history." On the same day Barkley said that Dewey is a ruthless man who considers "shooting at sunrise" as a cure for inefficiency. Harold Ickes jibed that the engineer had been listening to too many Dewey speeches. "Every speech he listened to sounded as though Dewey was going to turn the clock back to the days of Harding, Coolidge, and Hoover. . . . He honestly thought that Dewey wanted the train to run backwards, too." Democrats beat a tattoo on the hasty remark for the rest of the campaign.

William S. White in the New York *Times* sometime later (January 8, 1950) commented that while Dewey had cause to be exasperated at the engineer, "It cannot be said certainly that Mr. Truman would not have responded likewise; but it can be said with the next thing to certainty." In White's opinion, Truman would not have exploded because he has the elusive quality called "the human touch."

There is no mistaking Dewey's warmth to his personal associates. While Dewey seems to be haunted by bitter regrets about 1948, he is careful to shield his associates from blame. On the other hand, a stranger on meeting Dewey is struck by his brusqueness—he has the incisiveness of mind of a man who makes quick decisions, the lack of humility of one who became a brilliant success on his own early in life and the imperiousness of one accustomed to command. These qualities were sensed by the electorate in 1948 and the "lunatic engineer" remark fitted the image.

Dewey's labor committee was headed not by a labor man but by a utilities and corporation lawyer, Barak Mattingly, of St. Louis, national committeeman from Missouri—an example of obtuseness. Dewey picked up little new labor support besides that of the Building Employees during the campaign. Alvanley Johnston, head of the Brotherhood of Locomotive Engineers, came out for him, but if he could have delivered his whole union membership (and he did not commit the union) it would have amounted to only 80,000 workers, about the same number of block workers the PAC had working in the election. John L. Lewis came out for Dewey. At the Cincinnati convention of the United Mine Workers in October he attacked Truman as thoroughly unfitted for the position of President. "His principles are elastic. He is careless with the truth. He is a malignant, scheming sort of individual dangerous not only to the UMW but to the USA." Lewis, referring to the labor leaders who came out for Truman after a White House conference, said he would never sell out the UMW "for a lunch." Truman was so cowardly he did not recommend prison for Lewis' contempt but only a fine. The Mine Workers' endorsement damned Dewey with faint praise, by saying, "He has not uttered any statement that reflects on the integrity or objectives of the UMW." Although the miners voted to double Lewis' salary from $25,000 to $50,000, interviews showed that the majority of miners did not follow his political advice, and in the closing session when a speaker arose to praise Dewey he was shouted down.

The second major group fighting for Truman were the farm leaders and US Government farm officials. The Des Moines *Register* (October 3) said that Dewey was told by Kansas and Missouri politicians boarding the campaign train that agents of the Department of Agriculture were engaging in a "whispering campaign" to the effect that no matter what he said he was really against the "support program." On October 18 Raymond Brandt reported in the St. Louis *Post Dispatch,* "The reported switches of farm voters from Republican to Democratic were said to have been caused by a 'whispering campaign' started by Federal employees, particularly those of the Department of Agriculture to the effect that Dewey and the Republicans were not sincere in their promises of stabilized farm prices by the parity program and of other subsidies and benefits."

The key factor in the farm picture was the nose dive in the price of corn in the fall of 1948. The prices per bushel as reported by the Department of Agriculture were:

January 15	$2.46
March 15	2.11
July 15	2.02
August 15	1.91
September 15	1.78
October 15	1.38
November 15	1.21

Other farm prices had dropped sharply, too. On October 15 wheat was $1.98 a bushel compared to $2.66 a year before; oats were $0.69 a bushel compared to $1.09 a year before.

The Democrats stoked the fire. At Danville, Illinois, on October 12, Truman devoted his whole talk to the change in the CCC charter by the Eightieth Congress, which prevented the farmer from storing his corn and getting support payments. "The grain speculators don't like this [storage program] because they make their killings when the farm prices go up and down in a hurry. They don't care what happens to the farmer." So they got Republicans to change the CCC charter. "Farmers all over the country are being forced to drop their grain as distress grain or let it rot on the ground because the CCC no longer has the power to provide emergency storage space for bumper crops." In Springfield, Illinois, Truman said, "While you sat here on a powder keg waiting for prices to blow up they lit the fuse." Barkley throughout the Midwest and Paul Douglas, Senatorial candidate in Illinois, hammered hard on the storage issue.

Since Truman had backed flexible supports he could not tear into Republicans for the principle which was causing uneasiness among farmers of corn, wheat, oats, barley, soybeans, and other support crops, who saw the possibility that the supports might drop from ninety per cent to sixty per cent of parity in 1950. Local Democratic organizations, however, printed advertisements in papers in the farm belt denouncing the Hope-Aiken Act as the beginning of the end for supports. At Springfield, Truman attacked Congress for not doing anything about supports for a year and a half and then waiting until five o'clock on the morning of adjournment before passing the bill; he implied that Congress might have failed to pass support legislation altogether, which was absurd.

Truman repeatedly said that the Republicans were out "to strangle cooperatives" even though the Eightieth Congress had voted far more for the Rural Electrification Administration than the preceding Congress. Government officials and employees and employees of cooperatives fanned out over the farm belt spreading the gospel that a Dewey victory meant the end of the tax-exempt status for cooperatives and an all-out attack on REA cooperatives. Democrats pointed to the attack on cooperatives in the Eightieth Congress by some Republicans, such as Representative Walter Ploeser of Missouri.

Some Republicans, but only a few, saw the danger. Representative Karl Mundt, a Senatorial candidate in South Dakota, spoke to Len Hall, who was Chairman of the Republican Congressional Committee. "Len, the farmers are getting disenchanted with Dewey. He has to come out here and make a farm speech. He can't win without the farm vote, and the farmers think they have a problem." If Dewey were merely to show that he was conscious of the problem that would be a big help. Hall, who was as deceived as anyone else about the campaign, tried to soothe Mundt's fears. Representative Clifford Hope voiced his misgivings to fellow Republicans. Senator Taft was concerned about the farm vote. His relations with Dewey being as distant as they were, he asked Senator Butler of Nebraska to relay his feeling that a stronger pitch should be made to the farmer.

Dewey failed to understand the urgency of the situation. A farm leader says, "He was told repeatedly in all the Midwestern states that he must make some positive pronouncements on agriculture. He always answered that he had dealt with it before. Dewey had an irritating way of arguing with Midwesterners about the importance of agriculture in New York State and frequently gave the impression that he thought all agricultural wisdom began and ended at Cornell."

This indifference was compounded by what farm authorities considered an act of unbelievable stupidity. For years the party had a farm division as a part of the campaign setup, usually in Chicago. Nothing was done this time to establish one. Finally, a month before the election Dewey yielded to entreaties and sent the head of the Dairymen's League of New York out to Des Moines to set up a division. He died within a week of a heart attack. Then Dewey sent out the Assistant Commissioner of Agriculture of New York to take his place. This man was completely lost in the tall corn and nothing was accomplished. The only other gesture made by the Republican high command was the organization in the last weeks of the Dewey-Warren Farm Committee—it met once in Chicago and ate breakfast with Dewey.

Dewey was so completely misinformed on the farm problem that on October 25, Tom O'Neill of the Baltimore *Sun* wrote from the campaign train, "There is a trace of concern that high prices and abundant markets may influence Western farmers to vote for the status quo—the Democrats."

Then there was the veteran vote. At Fresno, California, Truman had obliquely attacked Dewey for not being in the war, pointing out that although he (Truman) was thirty-three at the time he had left the plow and volunteered in World War I. The Democratic National Committee, by pointedly stating that Truman had vetoed the use of this issue, managed to give it more currency. Chairman McGrath hinted at the issue by saying that Truman hated war because he had fought in a war. The Republican National Committee was peppered with letters demanding the facts about Dewey's war record and whether or not it was true that he had claimed an agricultural exemption. Mrs. Mathilda Burling, head of the Gold Star Mothers, wired him as to this charge. General Bonner Fellers as head of the Veterans Division of the Republican National Committee prepared a chart showing that because of changes in selective-service age rules Dewey was at no time subject to the draft. Brownell decided against using it, and so there was no answer.

The Civil Service lobby was another group which lined up against Dewey. The "housecleaning" statements, of course, induced widespread fears that workers would be turned out wholesale. Newspaper columns for Civil Service workers in Washington said that Dewey couldn't mean to eliminate more than 150,000 workers. The Democratic National Committee claimed that in a fit of rage Dewey had told representatives of the Veterans of Foreign Wars in New York before the session of the legislature that Civil Service workers were "mediocre" and that, "You would have me pay these sons of sea cooks for just breathing. If I had my way the present Civil Service system would not exist." All publications for Civil Service employees printed the story. Dewey's press chief, Jim Hagerty, called the story "rubbish." A Veterans of Foreign Wars Vice-Commander, who attended the meeting, issued a public statement that it was "a damn lie." Denials never caught up with the accusation.

Dewey was most unpopular with the teachers of New York, and the Democratic National Committee claimed that at the Governors Conference in August Dewey had called propaganda for teachers' pay "the biggest lie since Hitler," and said that the teachers had "the most vicious and dishonest lobby in the country." Truman accented the attack. At Springfield, Massachusetts, he said that Dewey in the presence of nine governors had denounced the teachers' lobby as "more vicious than the power or real estate or oil or liquor lobbies." When he reached New York a week before election Truman spoke to a throng including Civil Service workers at City Hall Park and, referring to Dewey by name for the first time, brought up the charge that he had called Civil Service workers "mediocre."

Almost all the liberals were in the Truman camp though not enthusiastically so. An ADA manifesto supporting Truman could wax enthusiastic only on the ground that he was the candidate "on the most liberal platform ever adopted by a major political party in the United States." Of the thirty-six signers it was interesting that only two had survived as members of the Truman Administration—Under Secretary of the Interior Oscar Chapman and Governor Ernest Gruening of Alaska. Three liberals pursued diverse courses. Max Lerner found in the end that he could not vote for Truman since he was "the man who waited three years before he put on the heat against the gluttons of privilege." He would therefore vote for Norman Thomas. Dorothy Schiff Thackrey engaged in a public debate in the columns of the New York *Post* with her co-publisher, her husband, Ted Thackrey (soon afterward they were divorced) because of his support of Wallace and then decided reluctantly to vote for Dewey. "I cannot vote for candidate Truman because he has proved himself to be the weakest, worst informed, most opportunistic President ever to hold the highest office in the land." He had used the Taft-Hartley law often although he had vetoed it, state delegations under his thumb had voted against the strong civil-rights plank in the Democratic convention, and "his record on Israel is disgraceful."

Harold Ickes vacillated for some time. He criticized Truman on many counts. Then he claimed that the Republicans had deliberately tied up Hollywood Bowl on September 23 to prevent Truman from speaking there. "This trickiness is all too likely to confirm in the minds of many that suspicion they have had that he is just that kind of man." (It turned out afterward that the Bowl had been offered to Truman.) When Dewey didn't answer his wire quizzing him on several issues, he decided that Truman was at least "comfortably earthy and without cant." Warming up at last he came out firmly. "Thomas Elusive Dewey, the candidate in sneakers, is for unity, *Alice in Wonderland,* and *Grimm's Fairy Tales,* to say nothing of home and mother." His motto was "I want to be an angel and with the angels stand, a crown upon my forehead, a harp within my hand."

An important phase of the operation of the Democratic National Committee was its appeal to the foreign born or those of foreign origin through its Nationalities Division headed by Michel Cieplinski. Jack Redding in *Inside the Democratic Party* discusses this in detail. A committee was made up with members from twenty different language groups and stories were translated for publication in the foreign-language newspapers. The position of the Democratic Party on the displaced persons problem was emphasized. Among the coups were a widely-printed portrait of Truman by the famous Polish artist Styka and seventy-two lectures in behalf of Truman among German Americans by Dr. Gerhart Seger, publisher of the *Deutsche Volk-Zeitung.* This work among minorities paid off in overwhelming majorities for Truman. There was no such activity in the Republican National Committee.

Careful research by the staff of the Democratic National

Committee paid dividends. Truman in his Western tour quoted from an article by Republican Representative Dondero on public power, "We can stop the trend toward increasing the number of publicly owned power facilities. . . . The Government should follow the policy of selling at the bus [source] to all comers without favoritism and discrimination. . . . On this issue we [presumably Republicans] are all of one mind." Someone from the Amalgamated Clothing Workers spotted some quotations in a book written by Fred Hartley, co-author of the Taft-Hartley Act. GOP leaders had decided, Hartley wrote, that "no more legislation to which organized labor could possibly object" be passed until after the 1948 election. "Republican leaders had an election to win, sound legislative principles were cast aside." Truman often read this aloud as proof of GOP antilabor plans if Dewey won.

While the Democratic National Committee and the campaign train worked together in unity, there was disunity in the Republican machinery. The Republican National Committee at Dupont Circle was located across the street from campaign headquarters headed by Brownell in the Dupont Circle Building. A vehicular underpass was being constructed and the street was impassable—Committee officials often commented that the physical barrier was symbolic of the fact. National Chairman Hugh Scott was ignored. He attended only five or six meetings across the street and says that his presence was required only once. For appearance's sake, he was brought together with Dewey a couple of times. Brownell, himself, counted for little in the strategy. His suggestions on the conduct of the campaign (in general he was an advocate of a stronger line) were disregarded by the Albany brain trust, which viewed his job as mainly "to keep the fat cats of the party happy." The bad feeling reached a high point two weeks before the election. While Brownell glosses over the point, there are several highly placed Republicans who claim that he wrote out a letter of resignation, before Dewey smoothed out the situation.

Let us return now to the Truman campaign. When a reporter commented to him about his hard-fisted campaign he answered, "This is no parlor game." While Truman was in awe of Taft, which would have made campaigning against him difficult, he had no such compunctions about Dewey, whom he held in disdain, calling him in private "China Doll." He would slap his thighs in merriment at Dewey jokes, "You have to know him well to dislike him," and "the bridegroom on the wedding cake." He kept with him a photograph of Dewey and Warren at Pawling in which he said that the farm gate on which they were leaning was upside down. At Terre Haute someone called out, "Dewey can't build a cow stable"; Truman showed the photo and said, "That's how much Dewey knows about farming." It was a "fake" like Dewey's campaign.

Returning to New York after the Vinson affair, Truman said at Buffalo, "The leopard has not changed his spots; he has merely hired some public-relations experts. . . . They've taught him to purr sweet things about unity." In Albany he said, "Why in the world would you want to upset the apple-cart now and throw out an administration that brought about this prosperity." As for unity, "We don't believe in the unity of slaves or the unity of sheep being led to slaughter." At St. Paul he attacked Dewey as a recent convert to internationalism pointing to the scorn he had poured on 50,000 planes a year in 1940 and his demand for speedy discharge of troops in 1944. Unity cannot be produced by "mealy-mouthed issues," but by a definition of issues. "I do not seek unity by concealing the issues between me and the special-privilege groups that control the Republican party."

In Milwaukee he accused Dewey of dragging the atom into politics. "Powerful, selfish groups in the Republican Party are determined to exploit the atom for private property.

Atomic energy cannot and must not be another Teapot Dome for private exploitation." At North Judson, Indiana, he attacked Charlie Halleck, whom he liked personally, but "he faces backwards instead of forwards; he has tried to turn the clock back ever since he got to Congress." At Indianapolis he disputed the Republican claim that talking about depression is playing into the hands of the Communists. Which reminded him of the saying, "Don't talk about rope in the house of one who has been hanged." The GOP had been playing checkers instead of doing something about inflation—as for social security, they took a million off the rolls. "The Communists are rooting for a GOP victory because they know it would bring on another great depression."

The receptions that Truman was getting were now tremendous. Chairman Frank McHale of Indiana said that "a ground swell" was developing for him and that "this election could be the greatest upset in political history."

Truman set forth again from Washington. At Miami, to an American Legion convention, he said that there would be no Munich. The purpose of the Vinson mission was to convey to the Kremlin the "seriousness and sincerity of the people of the United States in their desire for peace." In North Carolina he said that GOP rule meant first "rule by the carpetbaggers, then it means rule by the money-baggers. Either way it means rule that treats the South and West as colonies to be exploited commercially and held down politically." As for the economic threat of GOP rule, "You remember first came the Hoovercrats and then you had the Hoover carts. One always follows the other." He dedicated a monument to Presidents Jackson, Polk, and Johnson. Referring to the Dixiecrats, he said that "Andrew Jackson knew the way to correct injustice in a democracy was by reason and debate, never by walking off in a huff."

In Pittsburgh Truman attacked Dewey's campaign tactics as an insult to the intelligence of the American people. He was using "soft talk and double talk, crafty silence and misrepresentation." As for approving Democratic reforms, "It sounds like the same old phonograph record but this year the record has a crack and the needle gets stuck in it. . . . The crack was provided by the Republican Eightieth Congress. In 1948 every time the candidate says 'I can do it better,' the crack says, 'We're against it.' "

As Dewey saw it, his main job was not to answer Truman vituperation. From Dewey's campaign train, Robert Albright wrote, "Right now Democratic strategists are pinning their hopes on a nationally dramatized slugfest—the kind that Mr. Dewey ran against Mr. Roosevelt in 1944. They figure Dewey is thin-skinned, that he can't take the personal abuse that Truman has been pouring on in his major speeches. Four years ago the champ needled Dewey into the ring and floored him in one round. Then when Harold Stassen tried it last May it was the big Minnesotan who hit the hay." *Time* wrote that "Candidate Truman is most infuriated by Candidate Dewey's refusal to get into a slugging match with him." *Newsweek* wrote, "Dewey's adroit managers figured that Mr. Truman was flailing wildly trying to provoke Dewey into a rough and tumble fight preferably over the 80th Congress' record."

What was in Truman's mind? Clark Clifford, who was closer to Truman than anyone else, says that as a matter of fact Truman was slugging away on a day-to-day basis. In the mad campaign hurly-burly of shaking hands and preparing for the next speech, the man had hardly time to think—much less to brood about whether Dewey would come out of his shell to argue with him. But the Dewey silence gave Truman's attack clear sailing. It is McGrath's belief that Dewey's strategy produced the least complications for Truman.

Dewey started a second swing with a labor speech at Pittsburgh. He defended the Taft-Hartley law explaining how it came about. It was "not perfect," he said. "It can always be improved and whenever and wherever it needs change it will be changed." He recalled how Truman had used the injunction provisions six times to end strikes. Among his pledges were those to "end the log jam in housing," "overhaul the social-security system for the unemployed and aged," and adjust "the present minimum wage [which] is too low and it will be raised."

Earlier in the day, for the one and only time in the campaign, Dewey showed how he could fight with the gloves off. At Erie he was heckled about Taft-Hartley. What was wrong with the law, he shot back, since the lack of a labor policy had cost 166 million work days lost in 1946, and "this miserable administration proposed that men be drafted into the Army because they were on strike?" The veto message Truman sent was "the wrongest, most incompetent, most inaccurate document ever put out of the White House in 160 years." Under the law strikes had been cut fifty per cent and the discharge rate of union members was down twenty-five per cent.

In Louisville, Dewey attacked our foreign policy as full of "clumsiness, weakness, and wobbling." He claimed credit for initiating the bipartisan approach. "I first proposed to Secretary Hull during the election campaign four years ago that we have cooperation between our two parties to win the peace. That was the beginning of our bipartisan foreign policy." The Democrats took all the credit for accomplishments such as the UN and the Marshall Plan, overlooking the contribution of Republicans like Harold Stassen, John Foster Dulles, and Senator Vandenberg. Republican delegates to the San Francisco conference were responsible for important changes in the draft of the UN charter worked out at Dunbarton Oaks.

Former Secretary Hull answered Dewey, saying he was "incorrect" about initiating the bipartisan approach. Dewey insisted it was so. At St. Paul, Dewey by way of answer inserted a statement in his speech that he had a choice in 1944 on whether "to expose to the American people some or any of the blunders and tragedies" of the Roosevelt Administration. Instead, he chose to send a representative [John Foster Dulles] to work in creating the UN. Hull had "accepted his [Dulles'] co-operation handsomely and we succeeded in lifting the whole problem of the United Nations out of the partisanship of a political campaign. I'm glad that I did it and I would do it again."

Among "blunders," Dewey meant that we had broken the Japanese Naval Code before Pearl Harbor, and in 1944, as an act of patriotism, he did not reveal this. It is puzzling that Dewey did not spell this out in 1948. Several years after the war there was no reason for silence. The voters would have been interested and Dewey would have scored.

The question as to who deserved credit for the initiation of the bipartisan foreign policy could not excite the electorate. But as far as the record stands, from Cordell Hull's *Memoirs* it seems that Dewey is entitled to the credit for Republican participation whether or not Hull is justified in disputing that "his [Dewey's] party had taken the initiative." Hull's talks with John Foster Dulles in August 1944 took the United Nations agreement out of the political arena. Hull writes, "Be it said to the credit of Governor Dewey that from the date of this agreement he uniformly rendered excellent service to the nonpartisan approach toward the United Nations."

At St. Paul, Dewey made his closest approach to a farm speech. "There are some people who would like to inject politics into the necessities of food raising in our country. But I don't believe in that." It appeared that Dewey viewed the farm issue, like foreign policy, as nonpartisan. As for the Hope-Aiken Act, "I am wholeheartedly and unequivocally for it and don't you let anybody tell you anything different." Dewey believed that in endorsing supports he was settling the issue. He did not realize that the flexible supports in the Act were what was worrying the farmer. He was for soil conservation and for REA. The Eightieth Congress had voted $244 million more for REA than any Democratic Congress. The livestock population had gone down in the previous few years causing a rise in the price of meat, and Dewey offered

Tom Little in The Nashville Tennessean

"What did you say?"

a typical solution. "It's time we got an Administration which understands the importance of livestock to the diet necessary for a healthy America." There was no mention of the dive in farm prices or the grain-storage problem.

In Kansas City, Dewey made a typical "high-level" speech about the need for good government. "You have known how bad a bad government can be. You rose up and threw it out."

Since Dewey was alluding to the Pendergast machine and Truman's link with it, he might have said so directly. "As never before we need a rudder to our ship of state and we need a firm hand at the tiller." The Government needed teamwork. "We are going to have that kind of a team." He sorrowed over the Administration. "It's tired. It's confused. It scolds and complains, it runs off in a dozen different directions at once. It divides them [the people]. It's coming apart at the seams." The keys to good government were unity, faith, purpose, integrity, and competence. Dewey's sermon on good government was an uninterrupted string of generalities. Returning to New York again, he made speeches, as a reporter said, "just to be courteous and give the crowds their money's worth. . . . He talked like a man who knew that the jury had made up its mind but simply wanted to give them a summing up." At Buffalo on October 18 he said, "There isn't anything more that I could say to you. You are all going to vote for me anyway or I couldn't persuade you." A few days later he urged his supporters to look four years ahead and if they believed in bringing unity to the country "not to respond in kind at any time under any circumstances, whatever the provocation."

On October 25 there was some agonizing re-appraisal on the part of Dewey. Truman in Chicago made a vitriolic attack on the Republican Party. There were three forces of evil in it—those who wanted concentrated power in their hands, those who wanted unbridled inflation in order to profiteer, and those who sought "to stir up religious and racial prejudice." He charged that Dewey was the "front man" for special interests. "When a few men get control of the economy of a nation they find a front man to run the country for them." He cited Hitler, Mussolini, and Tojo, thus insinuating that Dewey was in their class. Marquis Childs, who was friendly to Truman, wrote that the Chicago speech was a "crude appeal to the fears and suspicions of racial minorities that live in

Chicago's vast slums." As "crude" as it was, the speech was a much toned-down version of earlier drafts.

Dewey decided at this point to take the gloves off. The Chicago speech was too much for him to take lying down—let the predetermined strategy go hang. He sat down and wrote on three sheets of foolscap paper a scathing answer to Truman.

Dewey says he felt at this time that he was losing ground. The Dewey advisers always laughed off Truman attacks. "It's only Truman," they would say. But Dewey had been listening on the radio to Truman speeches and became convinced that Truman was winning votes. Brownell had advised Dewey of a noticeable slippage of Republican strength reported to him. "I wish the campaign were over," Dewey told associates.

Dewey was argued out of replying to Truman. Elliott Bell's advice was—who believes that nonsense? Should we get into the gutter with Truman at this late date? Jim Hagerty took a poll of newsmen on the train and found that all agreed that Dewey was in, so why shift. Ben Duffy of BBD&O in New York was aghast at Dewey's lapse into amateurism and warned—don't rock the boat. "At that late date," says Dewey, "it was too late to reverse the gears." So the car went over the cliff. In a Chicago speech the next day Dewey said in aggrieved tones, "And now, faced with failure, with their party split in all directions, its candidates have spread fantastic fears among our people. They have scattered reckless abuse along the entire right of way from coast to coast, and have now, I am sorry to say, reached a new low in mudslinging. . . . That is the campaign I have refused to wage and I never will." At Elkhart, Indiana, a woman in the crowd asked Dewey if he was going to answer the charges and he said, "Nobody believes that stuff, including the people who are saying it, do they?"

There was another argument for continuing the "high-level" campaign. At this time Brownell spoke by phone to the national committeemen from about thirty-six states. They were hooked up on a grid so that Brownell could talk to four or five at a time. The interviews were recorded, Brownell says, to facilitate a report to Dewey. The interviewees were advised of that. "They competed in optimism and sycophancy," says Hugh Scott, who has listened often to the recordings. "It was a wonderful campaign," "Just fine, Herb," "Couldn't be better." The one dissenter, Harry Darby of Kansas, a non-professional politician, said, "I don't know what has happened here with the farmers. I think that Dewey will be lucky to get by with 10,000." These recordings were used after the campaign to vindicate Dewey's campaign. It should be borne in mind that these men were top politicians who believed that they were dealing with the new national power and knew that a record was being made of their views. There were many published reports that local leaders felt differently about the campaign.

It is an interesting facet of history that both men who had the most to lose had misgivings as to the strategy. Warren never thought much of the sweetness-and-light approach. One Sunday in October he was run in from Baltimore to Brownell's home in Virginia for a get-together of campaign officials. Warren said to the group, "I wish that I could call someone in this campaign an S.O.B."

Dewey believes he was ahead until the last two weeks and then lost the election. Brownell states his belief that if Dewey had staged a blazing finish he would have won. Dewey was the victim of his own twentieth-century "teamwork." The team was against him when he wanted to change the strategy. But greatness consists in the strength to follow one's instinct and judgment—not following a team opinion.

In Truman's final campaign week he appealed to three groups—Catholics, Jews, and Negroes. The main target was New York, which McGrath believed Truman could carry.

McGrath believed that Truman's only hope was in the big-city vote in the East.

In Boston, Truman appealed to the memory of Al Smith, naming him no less than eleven times, pointing to the vicious attacks on him by the GOP, which had beat him in 1928. Most of the speech in this Catholic stronghold was about Truman's fight against Communism and why Communists hated him. The Communists were supporting a third-party candidate to defeat him. "In state after state the Republicans have worked to get the Communist-supported candidate on the ballot in order to defeat me." The real Red threat "grows out of the Republican policies of the Eightieth Congress, which threaten to put an end to American prosperity." Within a few days, Truman had labeled the Republican Party as both fascist and pro-Communist.

In Harlem, Truman addressed the biggest open-air rally ever held there. Before 65,000 he accepted the Franklin D. Roosevelt award of the Harlem Ministerial Alliance and reaffirmed a ten-point civil-rights program. He pledged to work for the program "with every ounce of strength and determination I have." It was the first time in the campaign that Truman had discussed civil rights. In several places it had been pointedly brought up, as by Senatorial candidate Archibald Alexander at Camden, New Jersey, but Truman had always ignored the subject.

The final appeal was for the Jewish vote. Israel was in turmoil. The UN mediator, Swedish Count Bernadotte, proposed in September that the partition plan be changed so as to give West Galilee in the north to the Jews and the Negev in the South to the Arabs, which would have reduced the area of the new state substantially. In his *Memoirs* Truman says, "Secretary Marshall informed the United Nations that it seemed to him that it was a fair and sound proposal." As in his statements regarding his recognition of Israel in May, it is difficult to reconcile Truman's explanations. He says in his *Memoirs* that "Zionists, who saw a pro-Arab behind every State Department desk, at once claimed that this [Marshall's stand] was another reversal of United States policy." But on the following page Truman says that he decided that the Bernadotte proposal could not be accepted because it "was so different from the original partition plan."

Again Truman took the Israel question out of the hands of the State Department. The British and Chinese had introduced a resolution in the UN for a cease-fire and an implied threat of sanctions against Israel if it did not withdraw from the Negev. The Palestine Emergency Council published advertisements, "Mr. Truman, where do you stand?" Truman reveals in his *Memoirs* that on October 17 he ordered that no member of our delegation take any action or say anything on Palestine without clearing it with him. Dewey had already come out for the original partition plan. On October 28 in a speech sponsored by the Liberal Party at Madison Square Garden Truman announced, "I have never changed my position on Palestine or Israel." According to Under Secretary of State Lovett, Secretary Marshall had not been consulted, but was told afterward.

Throughout the campaign Dewey never attacked the New Deal since the Bell strategy called for winning with Roosevelt votes. Charlie Halleck prepared a speech for a nationwide broadcast. In a session at Albany, Elliott Bell went over it. "This will never do," said Bell. Halleck had mentioned the New Deal seven times, so Bell went through it, penciling out every derogatory mention of the New Deal, "ripping the guts out of it," as Halleck says. Brownell, who was present, demurred. "Maybe that's what we should be doing, attacking the New Deal."

Mindful of the party "schizophrenia," Dewey had made his own New Dealish predilections known in only a few sentences. In the last days before the election at Boston, Dewey became more outspoken.

He called for increased social security benefits, a higher minimum wage, better public-health services, improved veterans welfare, extension of liberalized security payments to Government employees, farm workers, household domestics, professional people, and self-employed small businessmen. He did not mention how much the increases would be. "There will always be some who say these proposals are costly. To them I say they are not costly compared with the gains in human happiness." He inserted into his prepared speech that this "lays practically no further financial burdens on our country." He promised "enthusiastic support of the next Republican Congress."

Dewey's concern about "unity," meaning the unity within his own party when he became President, became more evident. When he was in Indiana in the closing stage he made a 150-mile detour to Rensselaer to pay his respects to Charlie Halleck. At Boston, Speaker Joe Martin applauded tepidly when Dewey made his welfare proposals. The next day Dewey visited Martin's home at Attleboro and lavished encomiums on Martin and his mother. The fifteen-minute speech was clearly directed not at the audience but at Martin. "As Speaker Martin has said, Republicans have kept their promises." Put on the spot, Martin agreed that the GOP would redeem its pledges.

The rapture of the embrace was marred by an editorial the day before in Martin's newspaper, the North Attleboro *Chronicle,* which said that Dewey's speeches "are designed for tonal effect. . . . Sounds good and brings the applause. But promises nothing." Martin explained this away by saying that it was a canned editorial bought from a syndicate, and his regular linotype operator had been off the job.

At Madison Square Garden, Dewey delivered his windup with the theme of "unity" on which he had started the campaign. He said the times call for "competent, warm-hearted stable government." As for Truman's wild charges, they were "cheap wisecracks, circuses, and side shows." He had conducted a "goblins-will-get-you" campaign but "Halloween will be over tomorrow night."

The contrast in appeals was pointed up by the election-eve speeches. Dewey said the issue is "whether America is going to be a strong united nation." Truman departed from the precedent of delivering a nonpartisan election-eve speech. The election would decide what kind of government Americans wanted. By voting for him all citizens would protect themselves against reaction and against inflation, and would get the best insurance against going back to the dark days of 1932.

[XIII]

PRE-ELECTION ILLUSION

IN RETROSPECT 1948 is often referred to as an "exciting election." That applies more to the shattering climax than the campaign itself. At the time there was agreement that the Truman-Dewey contest had failed to stir up the voters. A false impression has been conveyed of Truman's rousing of the public emotions at the whistle stops. Richard Rovere, who was on the campaign train, wrote, "I would say that the decibel count [of the applause] would be about the same as it would be for a missionary who has just delivered a mildly encouraging report on the inroads being made on heathenism in Northern Rhodesia." James Reston of the New York *Times* concluded, "He [Truman] is not conveying the one thing he wants to convey, a conviction that something really fundamental is at stake in this campaign. . . . The crowds do not really seem quite to believe it. . . . Mr. Truman is a mild man. He has the words but doesn't get the melody. He says he is mad at everybody, but he doesn't look as if he's mad at anybody."

But compared to Dewey, Truman was a "hot" public attraction. The fine Dewey baritone intoning platitudes put everybody to sleep and as it became apparent that his speeches would not change, his audiences, visible and invisible, slimmed out. Truman's speeches were colorful, they had punch, crispness and were organized around facts. They had lots of humor.

Clifford says that there was a definite plan, which Truman approved, to use ridicule as a weapon, not only because it built up audiences but because of an awareness that ridicule unifies audiences who are in on the joke. In Pittsburgh, for example, Truman conducted an imaginary dialogue. Doctor: "You have been bothered much about issues lately?" Patient: "Not bothered exactly. Of course, we've had quite a few." Doctor (tugging an imaginary mustache): "You shouldn't think about issues. What you need is my brand of soothing syrup, I call it 'unity.' " Patient: "What is wrong with me?" Doctor: "I never discuss issues with a patient. But what you need is a major operation—nothing very serious. It will just mean taking out the complete works and putting in a GOP administration."

At Cleveland, Truman called the public-opinion polls "sleeping polls . . . but most of the people are not being fooled. They know sleeping polls are bad for the system, they affect the mind. An overdose could be fatal." Twirling an imaginary mustache, he said that the same doctor he told about at Pittsburgh was passing them out. "He [Dewey] is having such a high-level tea party with the voters that he is horrified when anyone mentions the facts of life. And here I am proposing to drag out that old reprobate, the Eightieth Congress, out of the back room and disclose him to the guests as the candidate's nearest and dearest relative. I'm going to tell the folks exactly how I gave the old sinner a chance to repent at the special session and to mend his ways, only three weeks after he had taken the pledge at Philadelphia . . . and how he refused and backslid again into the gutter of special privilege." At Boston he said, "The Republicans tell us they stand for unity. In the old days Al Smith would have said that's baloney. Today, the Happy Warrior would say that's a lot of hooey, and if that rhymes with anything that's not my fault." At St. Louis he told a fable about a potentate in the ancient city of Albany who appeared before a crowd and asked them if they knew what he favored. In order not to offend him, they said yes. Thereupon he replied that if they knew, there was no point in telling them. The next day he asked the same question; this time they said no. Thereupon he replied that if they didn't know, they were too ignorant to be told.

Newspapers were not deceived by Truman's campaign and made their judgment on the relative competence of the two men. Dewey won considerably more newspaper support than he had in 1944. The New York *Times* swung behind him, as did the Cleveland *Plain-Dealer*. Many Missouri papers switched to Dewey—The St. Louis *Post Dispatch* said that the President didn't have "the stature, the vision, the social and economic grasp, the sense of history required to lead the Nation in a time of crisis." The Oregon *Journal* in supporting Dewey said that "President Truman in descending to his Missouri training in campaign vilification has lost leadership of the Nation." The Scripps-Howard newspapers said the question was whether "competence, wisdom, understanding and teamwork under firm and skillful leadership shall guide the United States." Dewey did not lose the support of a single paper he had behind him in 1944 though conservative papers in the Midwest were unenthusiastic. The powerful Chicago *Tribune* said he was "the least worst" of the candidates. Dewey had sixty-five per cent of the dailies behind him with seventy-eight per cent of the circulation compared with sixty-four per cent of the circulation in 1944. Truman had only fifteen per cent of the papers. But there are the papers and the people—and 1948 showed again that they can go in opposite directions.

Were there no signs of the impending Republican catastrophe? That has been asked often and the answer is that there were omens for all to see but which none saw. The terrific crowds that Truman drew was one omen. *Time* reported, "Politicians and columnists seem puzzled by the phenomenon." Democratic strategists say that they first took heart when in mid-October Truman was greeted by 5000 at 8:00 AM in the rain at Albany and by 7000 at Auburn later in the day in a cloudburst. At Akron, Truman commented on the outpouring of people, "The Republicans have the propaganda and the money. But we have the people, and the people have the votes." He said that his drive was a "crusade to wake the people up. I'm telling you I'm succeeding." When he returned to Washington from the Midwest at the end of October, Truman pointed to the huge crowds in GOP strongholds in Indiana as a sign of victory. Early-morning crowds were never below 1000; the night crowds were always too big for armories and ball parks to hold. In Indianapolis 50,000 heard Truman on a chilly night; Dewey's St. Paul speech in an auditorium seating 12,000 attracted only 7000. Truman had drawn 21,000 in St. Paul. On Truman's campaign train Robert Albright of the Washington *Post* wrote, "Now and then a particularly large crowd or a noisy ovation starts a mighty surge of hope in the rear staff car. Some of it filters forward to the press car and hardbitten reporters ask themselves, Could we be wrong?"

The underdog psychology was playing a part in the closing weeks in mustering sympathy for this man who kept on fighting in the face of seemingly sure defeat. Louis Johnson says that several Truman broadcasts were cut off intentionally to dramatize the lack of funds. On one occasion a broadcast representative turned to him and said, "We'll have to cut him off in a minute unless you agree to put up X dollars," and Johnson replied, "Go ahead, that will mean another million votes."

A warning that foreshadowed the upset was that the Congressional races, particularly those for the Senate, were swinging in favor of the Democrats. In 1956 although a Democratic Congress was elected, Eisenhower won easily, but few in 1948 had any illusions that Dewey had Eisenhower's personal popularity. Len Hall, who was Chairman of the Republican Congressional Committee, says, "We had what we thought were fleabites all over in that campaign, but we didn't realize that they were a cancer." William "Rudy" Reutemann, who was Hall's administrative assistant, said to me shortly after the election, "It was a strange experience. Congressional candidates all over the country were begging us for help, saying they were in trouble. But if Dewey was going to win by a landslide, that was impossible. So we figured that they must be only nervous."

The Senate seemed almost certain to be Democratic. The Washington *Post,* while predicting an easy Dewey victory, said that the Senate would be Democratic forty-eight to forty-seven with one in doubt. Frank Kent, while seeing Dewey in, saw the Senate Democratic fifty to forty-six. The Washington *Evening Star* said of the ticket-scratching that it was a "freakish situation." The *Wall Street Journal* said quizzically of the House and Senate forecasts, "We have no basis for saying that the predictions of that character will turn out wrong. We can say that if they prove correct it will be a most unusual occurrence." *Life* referred to the possibility that the Democrats might capture the Senate as "amazing." The New York *Post* referred to the imminent Congressional gains of the Democrats as the "strangest anomaly of the campaign."

After reviewing reports from different states that state Democratic candidates would win, but Truman would not, McGrath said to his aides, "You can't win all the things they say they're going to win and not elect a President, too. After all, he's at the top of the ticket." On October 26, Leslie Biffle told Defense Secretary Forrestal that the Senate would go Democratic by a margin of five. Forrestal consulted Arthur Krock of the New York *Times* and recorded in his diary, "So far as the Senate and House are concerned, he thinks that 'the hair will go with the hide,' in other words, Dewey's strength will counterbalance local tendencies." Krock was right that the hair did "go with the hide." Krock's paper, the *Times,* on the basis of reports from its local correspondents, saw forty-seven Democrats in the Senate, forty-six Republicans, and three doubtful.

Let us review some of these state campaigns since they were important in determining the national result. Generally speaking, the Democratic candidates had greater appeal than the Republicans. Illinois was a good example. There the Democrats went out of their way to get fresh faces—Adlai Stevenson for Governor and for the Senate Paul Douglas, a University of Chicago economics professor who had enlisted in the war as a Marine private. He campaigned as an internationalist against Speaker Wayland "Curly" Brooks. Since Brooks refused to enter the debate, he kept an empty seat on the platform for him. The Governor Green machine was assailed because of the Centralia mine disaster and the immunity to inspection which was supposedly bought. The Chicago *Sun-Times* exposed a big highway racket.

The St. Louis *Post Dispatch* claimed that state, county, and local leaders had participated in widespread gambling and vice activities in Peoria. Carl Shelton of the Shelton gang had been murdered in 1947 and then Bernie Shelton was murdered on July 26. After the second slaying Big Earl Shelton and the other members of the gang cooperated in naming government officials who "stumbled over each other" the first and fifteenth of each month to be paid. Ace reporter of the *Post-Dispatch* Theodore Link claimed that there was a phonograph recording of a shakedown attempt for $25,000 and that the man who asked for the money claimed to represent the State's Attorney, Roy P. Hull. As a result of these revelations, Hull, the sheriff and his investigator were indicted. Then the State Attorney General of Illinois, George Barrett, stepped into the picture and, lo and behold, a grand jury indicted reporter Link, who had uncovered the scandal, on charges of kidnapping, conspiracy, and intimidation against a minor hoodlum who denied that he had been kidnapped. The *Post-Dispatch* paid to have its editorials on the Peoria scandals reprinted widely in the Chicago and downstate newspapers. It also claimed that gamblers gave $100,000 to Green in 1944 for his campaign and were told that they need fear no interference.

Stevenson campaigned on a clean-government platform. "I don't want a single billboard or poster that is paid for by dirty money." The billboards for Green proclaiming him as a "good Governor" were treated by his opponents as a standing joke. The Republican Chicago *Daily News* came out for Stevenson on the ground that Green "nourishes a swarm of grafters, chisellers and racketeers." The graft issue undoubtedly was a major factor in the Illinois result—in Peoria County a smashing majority expected for Dewey turned out to be only 4000. Dewey had hailed the Governor as "the grand Pete Green."

In Minnesota popular young Minneapolis Mayor Hubert Humphrey seemed a cinch against Senator Joe Ball. Ball had incurred labor wrath by advocating measures which seemed more antilabor than the Taft-Hartley law. Although he had bolted Dewey in 1944, because he felt he was more internationalist than Dewey, he had opposed the Marshall Plan in the Eightieth Congress. His stand on these issues cost him the friendship of Harold Stassen, who had "made" him. Humphrey called Ball an "unthinking bedfellow of the Reds." The stiff ungainly Ball found it difficult to campaign against the glib Humphrey, from whom came a never-ending flow of facts and statistics, and who would dance with the ladies at the drop of a hat. Ball says that the labor organizations did not hurt him so much in the cities as they did in rural areas by distributing leaflets denouncing him in every farm mailbox in the state. An effective issue used against him among veterans was his vote against Civil Service preference for Gold Star mothers.

It was the same story in many other states. In Iowa, Senator George Wilson was up against a popular Democrat, former Senator Guy Gillette, who had successfully resisted Roosevelt's "purge" attempt in 1938. On personal grounds Wilson seemed headed for defeat. In Wyoming, Senator E. V. Robertson, the incumbent, seemed to be losing out to Governor Hunt. In Oklahoma, Democratic Governor Robert Kerr seemed sure to take the GOP seat being vacated by Ed Moore. In Tennessee, Carroll Reece was trailing Representative Estes Kefauver, who won the primary against Boss Crump's candidate while wearing his coonskin cap. There were huge crowds at Republican rallies since their candidate for Governor was Roy Acuff, the "Grand Old Opry" entertainer—but this wasn't enough. Reece, whose feelings as ousted Republican national chairman were supposed to have been appeased by a gift of $38,000 from the national committee for his campaign, wanted Dewey to come to his state to save him, but waited in vain. Seats held by Democrats, such as Ed Johnson of Colorado and Jim Murray in Montana, seemed reasonably safe.

From the standpoint of the Republican Party, the most significant election was that held in West Virginia. Senator Chapman Revercomb was fighting an uphill fight against former Senator Matthew Neely. Revercomb had bluntly refused Dewey's plea in the special session to amend the Displaced Persons Act and Dewey refused to campaign for him or even to endorse him. In view of the expected Dewey landslide, it seemed necessary that Dewey should appear in West Virginia as *deus ex machina* to rescue Revercomb. Walter Hallanan, national committeeman, went to New York City to see Brownell, who said he was unable to help. Hallanan then waited to see Dewey, who came down from Albany to register—but Dewey said no. Senator Capehart tried to persuade Dewey and said he had "no doubt" Dewey would go to West Virginia—but Dewey said no. Warren came into the state and in six speeches said only once that he hoped for the election of a GOP Congress. The desperate Revercomb declared that was a plea for his election. "I have no reason to believe that Governor Dewey is mad at me." Chairman Scott did go into West Virginia and said that the GOP was for Revercomb and for the ticket from "top to bottom." He did this on his own initiative since he had personal ties with Revercomb's family. On his return, Brownell advised him that he better stay clear of Dewey.

Dewey says this of the Revercomb affair. "West Virginia was hopeless anyway. Then Revercomb had walked out on the Republican platform and did not deserve my help." But Dewey was considered to have a better than even chance at the time to carry the state, and it was believed that he might be able to carry Revercomb in with him. As for the platform, there is nothing in it but praise for the Eightieth Congress for passing the Displaced Persons Act. Moreover, in spite of their views on our commitments abroad, which differed from the spirit of the platform and Dewey's own views, Dewey had campaigned hard for Joe Ball, although he had been at first reluctant to do so, and for Brooks in Illinois, whom he hailed as "the distinguished Curly Brooks," and he had endorsed Senator Dworshak in Idaho, who said of the Marshall Plan that "it would make the international situation worse."

Regular Republicans could not forgive Dewey's attitude toward Revercomb. He was endangering the control of the Senate for his own reasons. With his mental orientation to New York State, was he overly concerned about the Jewish and Catholic vote because of the discriminatory features of the Displaced Persons Act? (Actually, few understood them.) Or was his position a matter of personal pique? Was he going to make an object lesson of a Republican legislator who refused to go along with him? The latter view has many adherents among Republicans.

The prospect that the Senate would be Democratic raised

a good deal of doubt as to the "unity" prospect. Walter Lippmann saw the real fight in the campaign on the organization of the Senate. Lippmann urged some Democratic Senators to announce that if the House went GOP they would permit the GOP to organize the Senate. "What is the election about? It is about whether the Government of the United States, divided between the parties, and stalled by an administration that is helpless because of the division within its own party, is to be made capable again of governing. That is why the people will elect Dewey."

We have stated two omens of Democratic victory, the Truman crowds and the Congressional races. There was a third, the elections that took place in the fall of 1948. In the September elections in Maine everybody was excited by the record percentage of the vote cast for Margaret Chase Smith for Senator. But everybody ignored the fact that the vote for the three Republican Congressmen who won, went up compared to 1944 by nine per cent, while the vote for the Democratic candidates went up by thirty-four per cent. Also, the October elections in Alaska had in the past been a good forecaster of the national results. In the elections on October 12, the Republican legislature elected in 1946 was turned out in favor of an overwhelmingly Democratic one, and all four territorial offices at stake went to Democrats. Bob Bartlett's majority of 6700 for territorial delegate in 1946 climbed to 12,800. These votes were ignored.

There were only bouquets for Dewey before the election. Drew Pearson wrote, "As a technician I would say Governor Dewey has conducted one of the most astute and skillful campaigns in recent years." *Newsweek* said Dewey's campaign was "the accepted model of how a probable winner should conduct himself." Bert Andrews of the New York *Herald Tribune* said, "Dewey has waged the most effective campaign of his political career." The *Herald Tribune,* leading Republican paper in the East, the day before the election

praised Dewey for his "plane of restraint and fai
said that he "wisely avoided too great a detail in h

All polls agreed. Roper had stopped polling mc
when Dewey had 52.2 per cent of the vote, Truman 37.1 pe
cent. On election eve Roper said, "I stand by my prediction. Dewey is in." The Crossley poll had 49.9 per cent for Dewey and 44.8 per cent for Truman with 1.6 per cent for Thurmond and 3.3 per cent for Wallace.

The Gallup Poll, which showed Truman inching up during the campaign, had 49.5 per cent for Dewey, 44.5 per cent for Truman and 2 per cent for Thurmond and 4 per cent for Wallace. Chairman McGrath attacked the Gallup Poll results, saying that it had previously erred in favor of the Republicans. Adjusting state by state by this error and eliminating the undecided there was practically a tie. As for the undecided McGrath said they would go mostly for Truman. Gallup replied, "Either he [Truman] is wrong or we are. We will know in a week." McGrath's doubts, he added, were "part of politics."

Newspaper polls were just as widely off the beam, giving states to Dewey which Truman carried in some cases by wide margins. The Chicago *Sun-Times* gave Illinois to Dewey decisively, and the Chicago *Tribune* gave him not only Illinois by 400,000 but also Iowa and Wisconsin; the Des Moines *Register* showed Dewey far in the lead (48 per cent to 32 per cent for Truman); the Boston *Herald* showed Massachusetts Republican for the first time in a generation; the Salt Lake *Tribune* gave Dewey Utah; the Spokane *Spokesman Review* gave Dewey Washington, Montana, and Idaho; and polls by the Cleveland *Plain-Dealer* and Columbus *Dispatch* showed Dewey bettering his lead in 1944 when he had carried the State. The laurel goes to the Ft. Lauderdale *Daily News* of Florida—in a state where Truman beat Dewey 3 to 2, its poll showed Truman 23 per cent, Dewey 62 per cent.

No national observer can take credit for having predicted

the outcome. Louis Bean, an economist for the Department of Agriculture, is given credit for predicting the result, but the reputation is undeserved. In the book *How To Predict Elections,* which was touted after the election, he claimed that the GOP had reached high tide in 1946 and the pendulum was swinging back. The Democrats would be in the ascendancy for the next twelve years (which would have included the two Eisenhower Administrations). But three days before the election Bean forecast to Peter Edson, who wrote a column about it, that President Truman would need an all-out turnout of sixty million voters to win. "That is what he is fighting for." If the vote were as low as fifty-one million, he said that Truman would carry only nine states. The vote was forty-eight million. Bean made the same prediction to Drew Pearson.

Former Governor Ellis Arnall of Georgia wrote an article in the *Atlantic Monthly* for October 1948, "The Democrats Can Win." He started out, "The opinion that the United States will embrace conservatism for a long period beginning with the election of 1948 requires the rejection of almost all the facts available and the adoption of an illogic that is stupendous. Since V-J Day in no country except the Union of South Africa has a conservative party won at the polls in a free election." Note that Arnall argued against defeat only "for a long period." He went on to say that Truman's victory was "possible." As far as labor strength he said, "It is impossible for labor organizations to get their members to the polls in the Congressional races without getting them to the polls to vote for Presidential electors." He belittled the strength of the Dixiecrats, noting how heinous treason to the party was in the South. As for Truman, "His final speeches lack the polish and the masterful delivery of his predecessor, his informal speeches sound like George Babbitt addressing a luncheon club. Then suddenly the realization arises that this man is very typical of America and that the criticism of him is the self-criticism of Americans and that on election day they are very likely to vote for one of themselves. They do not feel that way about the present Governor of New York." While Arnall did not make a flat prediction, he deserves credit for stating the correct reasoning behind victory.

All experts were agreed. *Newsweek* polled fifty top political writers who were unanimous in predicting a Dewey victory with an average of 366 electoral votes, exactly 100 more than he required. However, they saw a Senate with forty-nine Republicans and forty-seven Democrats. The New York *Times* prediction from reports of its correspondents gave Dewey 345 electoral votes. *Life* had a full-page picture of Dewey captioned, "The next President travels by ferryboat over the broad waters of San Francisco Bay." Drew Pearson predicted, "I predict he [Dewey] will be a first-class President." His column the day before election said that Truman's election was "impossible" and his column printed the day after election began, "I surveyed the closely-knit group around Tom Dewey who will take over the White House 86 days from now." The Alsops' column, printed the day after election, began, "The first post-election question is how the Government can get through the next ten weeks," since events would not wait till Dewey took over.

"How long will the Ice Age last?" asked Max Lerner. The US correspondent for the Manchester *Guardian,* Alistair Cooke, captioned an article, "Harry S. Truman—Study of a Failure." The *Wall Street Journal* said, "Government will remain big, active and expensive under President Thomas E. Dewey." *Kiplinger Magazine* published a special issue, "What will Dewey do?" In the introduction it said, "You've got to live with him for four years, possibly eight. He will influence your life, your thinking, your work, your business." On the last page it said that this first close-up of Dewey policy "will have historical value in the future. Perhaps you should put a copy away for your children or grandchildren."

No newspaperman was so hardy as to predict Truman's election. They did see Truman closing the gap. David Lawrence predicted that the popular vote would be closer than the polls indicated. Doris Fleeson wrote, "In Illinois, Wisconsin, Iowa and Minnesota, Democratic leaders predict that the size of the Truman vote outside the cities will be astounding." Marquis Childs in late October wrote, "With some objective evidence to support their claims Democratic strategists believe that a trend has set in away from candidate Dewey and in the direction of candidate Truman. A Dewey landslide in popular votes looks a lot less likely than it did a month ago." But he accepted the Dewey victory. "The Victory Special should be called the Destiny Special for over it hangs an air of destiny and great events to come." His column printed after the election said as to the Democratic Party "it hardly seems possible that Humpty Dumpty can be put together again." The political writer for the Boston *Post* which claimed to be the only large metropolitan daily supporting Truman, said Truman "had a fighting chance"—which is the closest anyone came.

The conviction held here was mirrored abroad. An observer at the meeting of the UN Assembly in Paris says that foreign diplomats swarmed all over John Foster Dulles, the prospective Secretary of State, while General Marshall was given less personal attention.

It would be impossible to recreate the mood of absolute certainty that prevailed. A great victory party was held by Republican headquarters in Washington the Thursday before election. Dewey had heard "Hail To The Chief," reserved for the Chief Executive, many times in the closing weeks. Democrats had moved out of the Government or had arranged to do so. Fred Othman wrote in his column, "We'll miss lil' ole Harry." Washington hotels were heavily booked by Republicans for the inauguration. Dewey aides were reported to have rented homes and booked their children in schools.

Dewey assured the people of New York that his aides would stay on in their jobs till January.

Everything was ready for Albany to move to Washington, that is all but a minor detail. The people would have to vote.

Dewey was in New York City to await the results. Despite extreme provocation he had succeeded in maintaining his strategy from start to finish, the strategy of self-repression. It was alien to his natural aggressiveness, and he admits that he would have preferred a fighting campaign. Opening his campaign in Des Moines in September, Dewey had said he would be giving specific details as to his program. In the closing week he said, "Governor Warren and I have fully and frankly stated our views on the issues of the campaign." He had done so only in the framework of broad promises. The New York *Times* said editorially that Dewey had promised housing, no more dust bowl for farmers, better roads, better housing, better schools, and better health protection, to develop and conserve natural resources, and develop the country's great river systems on a broad regional basis. "Is he overpromising?"

There had been a few stray twinges of concern in the *Victory Special* that all was not going well—as we have noted, Dewey knew that Truman had gained ground with his slam-bang attack, the "slippage" of the Republican Party candidates was an accepted fact, Elliott Bell had been disturbed by the lack of campaign buttons in the crowds, and also by the lack of youngsters in the crowds, whom he regarded as an index of the interest of their parents. But all these were forgotten in pre-election euphoria. There were discussions about the Cabinet. Three days before the election Dewey relaxed with his associates in the Hotel Roosevelt and talked about his behavior at the big moment and the day after. He asked, what should he do with his mother and sons. Someone suggested—"Have them with you." So that problem was solved and they were on hand to accompany Dewey back to Albany.

And as for Truman? Continuously, from one whistle stop to the next, he had pumped the hands of local politicians and said, "Of course, I'll be elected, of course, I'll be elected." Mrs. Truman in perplexity asked Clark Clifford, "Does he really believe that he'll be elected? He acts that way." If Mrs. Truman didn't know, Clifford could give no better answer. Truman made no predictions to his associates. To Chairman McGrath he said only, "Howard, after this election there will still be a Democratic Party and you can be sure of that." Two weeks before the election he told Senator Kilgore, "If Joe Ball, Curly Brooks, and Revercomb are beaten, I'll take my licking with a smile." He showed the true state of his feelings when he went to Excelsior Springs, a resort close to Kansas City, to spend election night by himself. He had written the campaign off the books but he had the personal satisfaction of his favorite epitaph that "he done his damndest."

Gould Lincoln, political writer for the Washington *Evening Star,* wrote, "The campaign now closed marks the passing of the strange political alliance which served to elect the late President Franklin D. Roosevelt four times." The Washington *Post* editorially said that the coalition in the Democratic Party fell apart "because of the natural tendency of such movements to disintegrate once the purpose that had called them into being has been served."

[XIV]

SHOCK

ELECTION DAY—November 2, 1948.

The Dewey people had worked long on the preparation of a victory statement which the press was informed would not be issued until after Truman conceded defeat. Brownell jumped the gun by announcing at four-thirty in the afternoon that a record vote had been cast and that Dewey had been overwhelmingly elected. The ballroom at the Hotel Roosevelt with six hundred capacity was jammed early and there was an overflow crowd of three hundred in the lobby. Amid the screams of sirens Dewey returned from dinner with an adviser, Roger Straus, at 8:00 PM and went to his suite on the fifteenth floor from which he would descend later in the evening to the bannered balcony. Six secret-service men were on hand to guard the next President.

From the beginning the returns were not encouraging. Truman went into the lead in popular and electoral votes and was never to be headed off. He was strong in early returns from Southern States like Texas, Florida, and Tennessee, and unexpectedly strong in Massachusetts. When the Massachusetts vote was posted on a huge scoreboard, a girl worker with an orchid and four strings of pearls asked a newsman if the result could hold up her eight-thirty dinner date. That was one date missed in a young life. On a television network there was a seesaw on a wheel with a donkey on one side and an elephant on the other. A commentator pushed the donkey up to show Truman ahead but then smiling archly to the audience reminded them, "Soon the elephant may be up," and flipped it to show how. The demonstration was repeated twice more in the evening and then the demonstration and the arch smile disappeared for good.

The radio networks had alerted stations for a 9:00 PM announcement of victory. The 9:00 PM deadline passed and Dewey had not yet been elected. Truman had carried Southern states where he was the regular Democratic candidate by convincing margins; he had clearly won Massachusetts and Rhode Island and was making a strong race everywhere—surprisingly in the Midwest—including Ohio and Illinois. The newsreel people in the Roosevelt Ballroom asked for a "dry-run" victory cheer and then for a second one. "Cheer louder." Democratic headquarters at the Hotel Biltmore, a few blocks from the Roosevelt, which had been bleak and deserted, showed signs of life. At 9:30 PM Brownell claimed 295 sure electoral votes, a safe majority.

It was 10:00 PM and the donkey was still up. Dewey was leading in the large Eastern industrial states of New York, New Jersey, and Pennsylvania, but the New York vote was the first event to spread discouragement in the Republican ranks. At 10:30 PM it appeared that despite Wallace, the President would carry New York City by over half a million. This was unexpected. "We are in for trouble," the Dewey people said to each other. In Illinois the downstate vote which had been expected to erase easily the Truman lead in Cook County was failing to do so. In Ohio, Truman had twice lost the lead but now was nosing ahead again by a razor-thin margin and holding on. Radio and TV commentators had interviews scheduled with GOP bigwigs, but no one would appear so they had to interview each other.

It was 11:00 PM. The President was ahead not only in Illinois but in the supposedly safe Dewey farm states of Iowa and

Wisconsin, and he was still hanging on like a bulldog to that razor-thin lead in Ohio. Despite the apparent loss of Indiana, New York, and Pennsylvania, he was ahead in electoral votes. At 11:15 PM Brownell said that a "pattern indicative of Republican victory is developing," but there was no proof. George Gallup, who had beamed in the early hours, now glowered.

It was midnight in New York. Whether or not Truman had been elected, it appeared likely that Dewey had failed to get an electoral vote majority. Elmer Davis announced "Henry Wallace can go to sleep tonight a happy man. Because the Wallace vote defeated Truman in New York and Pennsylvania [he was wrong about the Wallace vote in the latter], the election will be thrown into the House of Representatives." Republican after Republican had been toppled—Joe Ball, Chapman Revercomb, George Wilson, and Wayland Brooks would not be back in the Senate. Adlai Stevenson had been elected Governor of Illinois by the biggest margin in history. The UAW had shown its strength in Michigan by replacing Governor Kim Sigler with a newcomer to politics, thirty-seven-year-old G. Mennen Williams. Chester Bowles admitted he was "flabbergasted" to be elected Governor of Connecticut. In Washington Chairman Hugh Scott surveying the carnage turned to Joseph Harsch of the *Christian Science Monitor* and said, "It's a good thing. Those mastodons wouldn't listen to me. They had to learn their lesson."

At 1:30 AM Brownell was heard from for the last time. New York was Republican by 50,000 and Dewey "will be the next President of the United States." But the Roosevelt was emptying out. One would-be celebrant turned to another and said they were "pollbearers" for the Republican Party.

The President, in Excelsior Springs thirty-two miles from Kansas City, after taking a Turkish bath had retired in the early evening with a ham sandwich and a glass of milk. He awoke at midnight and turned on the radio. H. V. Kaltenborn reported that the President was 1,200,000 votes ahead but not elected since the rural vote might turn the tide. The President turned off the radio and went back to sleep. At that time he was losing only in a few GOP strongholds west of Indiana and had carried the whole of the South except for the four Thurmond states and all the border states except Maryland.

Into the early hours of the morning the lights were on all over America. The pattern of the vote remained unchanged. Adjectives like "fantastic," "incredible," "amazing" were on everybody's lips as the greatest political surprise in American history was unfolding.

At 1:00 AM in Independence, Missouri, a crowd assembled around the Truman home and Margaret came out on the porch to announce, "Daddy isn't here." Henry Wallace perused the shambles of his party with a vote of about a million. There was no gracious statement from him but only harsh words. "The cup of iniquity of both the old parties will overflow and one or the other will disappear." At 2:00 AM he went to congratulate his only supporter who had won, Vito Marcantonio. At 2:20 AM, when it appeared that Truman might lack a majority of electoral votes and the vote would be thrown into the House, Jim Farley said, "The South always supported the Democratic Party in its darkest hour. It would do so again if the proper approach were made." At 2:35 AM Senator Knowland, Warren's campaign manager, said that he would settle for a 100,000 lead in California, but the state was going in and out of the Truman column. At 2:50 AM George Gallup said it was probable that Truman had won a majority of electoral votes. A reporter said that he looked "like an animal eating its young."

Through the years a tale has spread by word of mouth and been widely accepted that Dewey flew into a rage that night and hit Brownell with a lamp or a wastepaper basket. This seems to have originated with a gossip squib by "Cholly"

Knickerbocker in the New York *Journal* that Dewey had to be forcibly restrained from punching Brownell in the nose. It is an invention. No one around Dewey in those poignant hours when his chance to write his name in history dimmed out saw anything resembling rage. "He was crushed," says one member of the group, J. Russel Sprague.

The President awoke again at 4:00 AM and turned on the radio. He heard Kaltenborn say that he was now 2,000,000 votes ahead, but it looked like the election would be decided in the House. He said to Jim Rowley, his secret-service aide, "We had better get back to Kansas City. It looks like I've been elected." At 6:45 AM he appeared at a penthouse suite in the Muehleback Hotel where Matt Connelly, Charlie Ross, and other aides were staying. His first jubilant words were "Labor did it." He had little to say to the press. "When you win, you can't say anything. You're just happy."

At 11:14 AM Dewey conceded, after it appeared that Ohio was definitely in the Truman column. He appeared before the press two hours later. "I am as much surprised as you are," he said. "I have read your stories. We were all wrong together." His show of good spirits in the face of disaster brought genuine applause from the press. "Governor Warren and I are both happy that we waged a clean, constructive campaign, and I have no regrets in the world."

The New York *Times* had a record 25,000 phone calls between 9:00 AM and 6:00 PM seeking confirmation. Thirty-four employees and a number of job applicants were pressed into service to say "It's true." Confetti streamed down from garment houses on near-by Seventh Avenue. The stock market fell with a resounding crash. Liquidation was so heavy that many leading stocks did not open till noon. The loss in stock values during November was to total $8 billion.

The producers of a movie running on Broadway, *June Bride,* took steps immediately to change a line "from McKinley to Dewey." It was a time for quips and double-takes. Bob

Hope had one word to say, "Unpack." Groucho Marx said, "The only way a Republican will get into the White House is to marry Margaret Truman."

Fitzpatrick in the St. Louis *Post-Dispatch*

At the How-Did-It-Happen Club

Truman had won states with 304 electoral votes—38 more than he needed. He had carried all three of the close major states on election night—California, Illinois, and Ohio, the last one by 7000 votes. Thurmond's total was 38, carrying the four Southern states in which he was the official Democratic nominee and no others. Two electors on the Truman ticket in Tennessee and four in Florida had announced that they intended to exercise their constitutional privilege and vote for Thurmond, but only one elector finally did—giving Thurmond a total of 39 and reducing Truman's electoral vote to 303. On the issue of "unity" Dewey might be satisfied. The Congress was unified behind the Democratic Party. Democrats in the Senate increased from 45 to 54. In the House the Democrats went up from 188 to 263. Republican Senators Dworshak, Buck, and Robertson had joined the departed. In the House, GOP stalwarts like Harold Knutson, Chairman of the Ways and Means Committee, Howard Buffett and Bertrand Gearhart were gone.

The return of Truman to Washington was a triumphal parade. In the St. Louis station he held aloft an early edition of the Chicago *Tribune* which headlined, "Dewey Elected President." The Washington *Post* invited Truman to attend a "crow banquet" in which the main course would be breast of tough old crow *en glace,* while he would eat turkey. The Democratic National Committee had agreed to furnish toothpicks since it would take months to get the crow out of everybody's teeth. The President declined saying, "The fellow who lost feels bad enough without being crowed over." The words of Truman were exemplary. He said, "I bear no malice or feel badly toward anyone."

On reaching Washington the President was greeted by a crowd of 750,000—the greatest since the visit of George VI in 1939. Bands played "I'm Wild About Harry" and "Missouri Waltz." It took twenty-two minutes to get from the train to the line of cars. Senator Johnston of South Carolina, who had administered the snub to Truman at the ebb of his fortunes at the Jackson Day dinner months before elbowed his way onto the train to greet Truman. He said that he was for Truman all along, had intended to vote for him but somehow had not managed to get to the polls. When the procession passed the Washington *Post* Building the President in merriment pointed to the sign "Welcome Home From the Crow-eaters."

Louis Johnson says that he was deluged with checks right after the election—predated to the day before election. Among them was a check from Henry Morgenthau, Jr., who had previously declined to chip in.

There was no doubt in the minds of the liberals of the significance of the victory. Harold Ickes wrote exultantly, "It was not an election last Tuesday, it was a revolution. That the revolution was to the left, but not too far, there can be no doubt. The rush to sell stocks the next day attested to the direction." Jack Kroll said, "The Democratic Party has rid itself of the lunatic fringes, the extreme right represented by the Dixiecrats and the extreme left represented by those who voted for Henry Wallace." Mrs. Roosevelt called for a purge of the Dixiecrats from the party. J. R. Wiggins in the Washington *Post* saw a "fourth reincarnation" of the Democratic Party.

Labor took credit for the victory. The *CIO News* said, "Frankly, we don't intend to be a bit modest about the part organized labor played in the Democratic victory. . . . It revealed that labor can become a potent political force." The *New Republic* said, "The main credit goes to organized labor." Freda Kirchwey in the *Nation* said, "He owes his election to labor and its liberal allies." The ILGWU *Justice* carried David Dubinsky's statement, "The only great force in the community that stood firmly with the President from the start of the campaign to its glorious finish was the organized labor movement." *Advance* of the Amalgamated Clothing Workers read, "Truman said 'Labor did it' and he is right. Labor is responsible." *Pilot* of the National Maritime Union had in big type on its front page, "Labor Did It." No one took issue with labor on its claims. *Fortune* congratulated Sumner Slichter for his insight in his recent book, *The*

American Economy, in describing our capitalistic economy as "laboristic."

Wallace did not congratulate Truman but sent him a warning that his pledges must be kept. He blamed "the capitalist press," for the fiasco. He took some of the credit for the victory for himself. "They voted for the Democratic candidate only after we had forced him to compete with us in the peace program, in civil liberties and in the revival of an expanded New Deal with emphasis on lower prices and housing." Glen Taylor said that Wallace's candidacy had been responsible for the Administration's not taking a direct hand in China. "The Chinese would be better off under the Communists than under Chiang." The Nanking government of Chiang Kai-shek did not conceal its disappointment. Molotov in Moscow said that the Dewey defeat was a defeat for a program of aggression. The *Daily Worker,* however, was unhappy. "The vote for Wallace fell below not only the unrealistic quotas assigned to him by certain forces, but even below what his most sober supporters, including this paper, had expected." Eugene Dennis explained the low vote for Wallace. The "masses remained confused and misled" about the Marshall Plan and foreign-affairs issues.

Communist publications pounded away at the theme that the Wallace party must remain in existence to see to it that Truman delivers and also as a refuge for those who would be inevitably disillusioned. "Try to collect" was the theme. Wallace was supposedly the candidate of peace and Truman the warmonger but by November 18 the *Daily Worker* had found that Truman had already betrayed his pledge as the peace candidate, "There is no longer any need to wear the mask of peace. There is no longer any need to kid the American people. . . . Truman has found no difficulty in dishonoring the mandate of the American electorate less than two weeks after he was chosen by it to move for peace in the spirit of his pre-election Vinson mission."

In March 1949 in *The Progressive,* Dr. Tugwell wrote that Communists were so prominent in the Wallace campaign because progressives boycotted the Wallace movement. "I ought to have left the Party in August." He was "truly thankful" for the Truman victory. Senator Humphrey in reply said that this was the "first public admission of a prominent member of the Progressive Party that the Communists dominated the campaign" and it was amazing that "he is grateful for the colossal failure of the campaign to which he contributed his name and reputation."

The "experts" took a trouncing. As a Christmas gift *Newsweek* sent bottles of Old Crow bourbon to the fifty leading Washington correspondents who had unanimously predicted the Dewey victory. How had they all gone wrong? Arthur Krock of the New York *Times* said, "We didn't concern ourselves with the facts. We accepted the polls unconsciously." The New York *Times* quizzed its local correspondents. One answered, "I believe the widespread publication of public opinion polls was largely responsible for the opinions given me. Correctly or incorrectly usually reliable political dopesters simply let Gallup do their thinking for them." Another wrote in the same vein, "My forecasts were based on opinions of party leaders, opinions of a few individual observers who have been good before and the feeling engendered by numerous conversations with all sorts. All of these opinions were influenced by Gallup, Crossley and Roper." The mortification of all experts was typified by the column in the New York *Daily News* that John O'Donnell wrote immediately after, which wound up with a note to the editor: "I feel like hell."

Even though no one in the United States had predicted the result, it developed that an expert abroad had done so: Joseph B. Keenan, the war-crimes prosecutor in Japan, revealed that General MacArthur had predicted the election in July. He told Keenan that those who were selling Truman's chances short would be very surprised the morning after the election and he had advised the White House to that effect.

It appeared that pollsters had been discredited for good. Newspapers like the St. Louis *Globe-Democrat* canceled the Gallup Poll. The Indiana State Senate rose for a minute in silent tribute "to the memory of George Gallup." Wilfred Funk of the *Literary Digest,* which was put out of business after it predicted Landon as the winner in the 1936 election, said, "I do not want to seem malicious, but I can't help but get a good chuckle out of this." Gallup's first reaction was "which voters stayed home?" He later put the blame on the last-minute shift of voters and said that the error was in taking the last reading ten days before the result and assuming that the undecided would not vote. Roper said, "I could not have been more wrong and the thing that bothers me at the moment is that I don't know why I was wrong." Later he said that there had been too much reliance on direct questions and too little on attitude scales. Crossley blamed the polls for ruining the polls, "I am convinced that the widespread publicity given the polls findings served to redouble Democratic efforts to bring out the vote and may have created overconfidence among Republicans." Explanations in any case seemed to be inadequate. As the Chicago *Daily News* said, "The pollsters may say that the error was not great but when a man breaks into a dance after he has been pronounced dead the doctor can reasonably expect to lose a few patients."

It appeared that some poll results had not been published. The last minute poll of the Chicago *Sun-Times* which showed a Truman surge was not published because it was distrusted. The Staley Milling Company polled farmers by giving them a choice of a donkey or an elephant on chicken feed sacks. When the results among 20,000 farmers showed up as fifty-four per cent to forty-six per cent in favor of the donkey, the poll was abandoned.

Republican leaders found no common ground for agreeing on the cause of the disaster. Senator Taft said, "It is almost impossible to put an administration out of power at the very peak of a prosperity boom." Senator Vandenberg had a five-word explanation, "Harry got the most votes." Joe Martin said, "We offered too many Brahmins, too many plutocrats." Senator-elect Mundt gave a penetrating explanation, "The rural vote was decisive. If Dewey had gotten it he would have won in Ohio, California, and Illinois. Farmers failed to accept his support of farm support prices as enthusiastic, as genuine, and as vigorous as that of President Truman. . . . We have failed to focus attention on the mistakes of Yalta and Potsdam. Very little was made of the Vinson-to-Moscow travesty."

The Republicans couldn't agree on whether they had been chastised because Dewey was too far to the left or the Eightieth Congress was too far to the right. A group of 520 Republicans in southern California in a public statement said, "We should be sure candidates who run for office on the Republican ticket should subscribe to the principles of real Republicanism." Harrison Spangler, Republican National Committeeman from Iowa, said, "The wide-open highway leading to success was before them. To the astonishment of the people and the despair of Republicans they took the left side of the road, littered with New Deal traffic, and ran off into the ditch, sending the occupants of the car to the hospital with Henry Wallace." The Chicago *Tribune* said, "For the third time a Republican convention fell under vicious influence and nominated a 'me too' candidate who conducted a 'me too' campaign. For the third time the strategy failed."

But on the liberal side Senator Henry Cabot Lodge saw it in the opposite light, "The American people in effect said to the Republicans, 'You have made some real progress in liberalizing yourself, but you have not gone far enough. We are still afraid you may backslide. Go out and try again.' " Senator Aiken called for housecleaning the Old Guard. "The Old Guard is a self-perpetuating board of trustees who would rather see the party go down to defeat than lose control of the machinery."

Chairman Scott made available to correspondents a cross-section of letters that the National Committee received as a result of its self-analysis program. The preponderance of letters reflected a view that the party should reject the "me too" attitude in favor of "reasonable conservatism." A St. Louis party contributor wrote in, "The records show that we have lost repeatedly by acting as a weakened, watered-down imitation of the New Deal, so why not come out as a militant, fighting conservative body?" A Lynn, Massachusetts, man said that the party "must understand that the growing stay-at-home vote is obviously sound and conservative and disgusted."

At the end of November in a letter sent to the 22,000 party workers Chairman Scott urged them to "audit and police the Truman New Deal." He said the GOP "cannot compete with the Democratic Party in pressure bribery nor in appeasement of the radicals of the far left." The letter brought a jab from Democratic Chairman McGrath that the "Republicans like the Bourbons had learned nothing and forgotten nothing." The New York *Herald Tribune* attacked the Scott letter—"Representative Scott is apparently among those to whom the last elections and indeed the whole political history of the last 20 years has taught nothing. . . . There is a legitimate competition which the Republicans must take part in. . . . They must compete for the allegiance of the younger voters who have come close to being convinced that the Republicans can offer them no inspiration and goal. They must compete for the support of labor which has tended to be drawn into the Democratic orbit. . . . To do this something more than negatives is required."

One month later in his newsletter Scott had another theme, "Republican policy must continue to be something more than blind opposition to whatever may be proposed or to whatever has been proposed by the Democratic opposition. There are many laws on the statute books today written during the 16 years of Democratic control of the Federal Administration which undoubtedly would be there if a Republican President had been in office."

There was now a move to oust Scott from his job, which was in a sense flattering since he had been a figurehead during the campaign. The Taft and Stassen forces joined hands to oust him as a symbol of Deweyism. At the Omaha meeting in late January of 1949, which was dubbed by Harold Ickes a meeting to find out "who killed cock robin, or rather cocky robin," the anti-Dewey forces put up Roy Dunn of Minnesota. Clarence Buddington Kelland labeled Scott a "political ghost looking for another campaign to haunt." Scott was attacked for having taken the job although he was not to run the campaign. There was not a kind word spoken for Dewey except from the National Committeewoman from Vermont. Scott joined in the criticism of Dewey saying that he should not become a candidate again. Len Hall had called Russ Sprague from Omaha one hour before the discussion and told him that it would cost Scott his job if Dewey were to be defended and Sprague told him to use his judgment. The vote was close but Scott got a reprieve.

In the Forrestal *Diaries* there is an entry for December 20, 1948, that in a conversation with the President he was told that Senator Taft had sent a congratulatory letter that "as the President might gather, neither he nor his wife were particularly disappointed in the results of the election." The Dewey faction has used this as proof that Taft did not want Dewey to win and made only the most halfhearted efforts in his behalf. When the *Diaries* were published, Taft asked the President for a copy of the letter. Members of the Taft staff who saw it say that it merely congratulated Truman and said that Taft would extend cooperation where cooperation was possible. It is hard to believe that even if Taft had harbored this sentiment he would have been so careless as to put it in writing to a political foe. It is very perplexing—and the only reasonable explanation is that Forrestal confused Truman's comments about Taft's feelings and the contents of the letter.

On February 18 Dewey addressed the Lincoln Day dinner in Washington. Dewey announced that he had been elected after all—as leader of the party for another four years. Dewey said the party was "split wide open." If reactionaries got control the party would be buried as "the deadest pigeon in the country." The GOP must recognize that Government must be "more than a cold, impartial umpire." In talking to Joe Martin by phone about the arrangements before the dinner, Dewey took exception to the radio arrangements. A Congressman visiting Martin at the time commented, "Did he dictate the menu, too, or is he going to let us eat what we want?"

The excitement over the election simmered down. Whittaker Chambers produced his pumpkin papers in early December, giving the Hiss case its final charge of interest. Discussion was published about the possibility of shooting a satellite into space. The stock market started upward in December. Merrill Lynch published ads pooh-poohing the fear as to the effect of the Truman program, "General McAuliffe said 'Nuts.' " The National Retail Dry Goods Association in a meeting found the lesson of the election, "If you find out what the people want you can sell it."

Republicans, including Dewey, showed the American spirit of sportsmanship. The philosophical way in which Dewey took defeat brought admiration even from his enemies. At the Gridiron Club dinner in Washington in December he told a joke about the man who awoke at his wake, finding himself in a coffin with a lily in his hand. He said to himself—if I'm alive, what am I doing here, and if I'm dead, why do I want to go to the bathroom? That's what I said to myself, said Dewey, at ten-thirty the morning after election. He laughed when a chorister representing Dewey sang, to "Songs of

Araby," "I sang thee songs of Albany, and tales of my great team; of unity that lovely word, I really let off steam; with nice platitudes I tried to make, sweet White House visions rise; but all my speeches seemed to make, was wonder in their eyes." An engineer sang to "Rambling Wreck from Georgia Tech," "Oh, come you wise Republicans, and listen to all my strains, and never trust yourselves again aboard a Victory train; I hope you've learned your lesson, the meaning's mighty clear; I'm a rambling wreck, but what the heck, I'm a lunatic engineer."

There was merriment but bitterness, too. The resentment by Congressional leaders toward Dewey was not, as it has been pictured, so much about the "high-level" campaign technique. That was a legitimate error in judgment. But they could not condone his coolness toward the Eightieth Congress and its members, and particularly what they regarded as an attempt to "purge" Senator Revercomb. They would take no chances in the future. The Republican Congressional Committee had been merely a mechanism for channeling funds. Now it would have its own research and propaganda personnel. Robert Humphreys, national affairs editor of *Newsweek,* was brought in as first director of public relations.

The gloom in Republican headquarters was pitch-black. If the party could not win in 1948, when could it win? The turning point came on September 13, 1949, when John P. Saylor won a House seat in a special election in the Twenty-second District of Pennsylvania. Spirits picked up and the reconstruction of party morale began which culminated in the election of Eisenhower and Nixon in 1952.

[XV]

1949—DISILLUSION

CAREFREE DAYS for Truman followed the election, including a rest at Key West. He had little to say about the election except, "I'm through giving them hell," and "You not only have to be good but be lucky." He never claimed that he expected the result. He was reliably reported to have said, "Anybody who comes around here saying he knew I was winning will get tossed out fast."

In the revelry of victory no one doubted that the Truman Revolution was on hand and that he would have his way with the wayward Congress. Had not the people spoken with a mighty voice? Speaker-to-be-ousted Joe Martin saw a six weeks' honeymoon period with repeal of the Taft-Hartley law and the passage of civil-rights legislation. Senator McKellar, who had voted for Taft-Hartley, said he would now vote for repeal. President William Green of the AFL saw a possibility that the Taft-Hartley law might be off the books by March 1. Vice-President-elect Barkley saw selective price controls and civil-rights legislation with a ban on filibusters. As for the Dixiecrats, their day was done. Informed sources said that Truman would meet with Congressional leaders to cut them down to size—he would deprive Senator Eastland and in the House the dozen Southerners who had deserted to Thurmond, including influential Eugene Cox of Georgia and John Rankin of Mississippi, of their patronage and their seniority rights on committees.

Then doubts began to creep in.

Had the election given Truman the stature of a Roosevelt? Hardly. The cold statistics showed that he was actually a minority President with 49.3 per cent of the vote. It was evident that while he had won by a nose his party had won far more impressively in both Houses. And as Truman was to say in February at the Jefferson-Jackson Day dinner, "Campaigns and elections are just preliminary exhibition matches—the fight in Congress is the main bout."

Revolutions need lieutenants. The new majority leader in the Senate was Scott Lucas, who had voted for the Taft-Hartley law and had led the fight in the Resolutions Committee in the Democratic Convention for a mild civil-rights plank. Conservatives headed the powerful committees—Representative Doughton, who was the new chairman of the House Ways and Means Committee and Senator George, who was chairman of the Finance Committee, immediately announced that they would oppose any excess-profits tax; Senator McKellar would head the Appropriations Committee and Senator Maybank would succeed Senator Wagner as head of the Banking and Currency Committee. Liberal newspapers were grieved at the failure of Truman to purge his Cabinet. The conservative John Snyder would remain in the Treasury post and Charles Sawyer would remain in Commerce, though Sawyer had said in May, "The less Government controls of inflation or anything else the better."

Max Lerner voiced his doubts two weeks after the result. "The trouble with Truman's New Deal is that the war economy may not even let it get started. . . . Even a $15 billion war budget means that the American people will be spending more than one-third of total Government expenditures on production for death instead of production for life." Thomas Sancton in the *Nation* asked how the character of the

Administration could change since it was composed of Forrestal-type men, bankers, corporation lawyers, and big men in industry. "Almost every aspect of our domestic political life has become a reflection of our military involvement."

Labor became less exuberant and took a more sober view. The annual AFL convention in Cincinnati in mid-November was disappointed by the matter-of-fact letter it received from the President. There was no word of thanks. He merely promised "full support for carrying forward a program for the benefit of all the people of our nation." The President on reflection or advice had decided that he must not regard himself as the bondsman of any interest group. Walter White of the NAACP visited him on November 28 and reported that Truman said that he felt no obligation to anyone but that he would live up to his campaign pledges, including civil rights. Victor Riesel on December 9 wrote, "The labor men who expected to have Harry Truman measured for shining armor by the pre-Christmas merriment are finding their blitz balked by what they're sanctimoniously referring to as 'Government by crony.' The President is genial, almost hilarious with the union chiefs who come to see him. Still he's promising nothing but that he'll keep his campaign promises."

The Inaugural was a jamboree marked by a reunion with his Battery D pals, such as had not been seen in Washington since the inauguration of Andrew Jackson. ". . . Victory had been snatched from a predicted disaster and I thought the party was entitled to have its day of celebration," Truman writes in his *Memoirs*. At the Inaugural banquet he did his famous imitation of H. V. Kaltenborn on election night when he predicted first that Truman would be defeated and later that the election would be thrown into the House. The Inaugural address had nothing to say about the campaign promises or their redemption—it was about the fight against Communism. At this time the "bold new program" was set forth, including the famous Point Four for helping underdeveloped nations with our technical skills.

Two weeks before the inauguration the President in a State-of-the-Union Message to the Eighty-first Congress discussed the domestic program. He coined the phrase "Fair Deal" in saying, "Every segment of our population and every individual has a right to expect from our Government a fair deal." He asked for repeal of the Taft-Hartley law, but with restrictions on secondary boycotts and jurisdictional strikes, endorsed without comment the civil-rights program, asked for construction of a million housing units by the Government in seven years. He put forth the radical proposal that the Government build facilities to turn out materials in short supply, specifically mentioning steel. His messages showed, the President commented to a Democratic Party reception, that he did not regard his campaign pledges as "scraps of paper."

The move to chastise the errant Southerners faded out. Chairman McGrath said that the President could forgive "venial" but not "mortal" sins and he put the revolt in the former class. Thurmond had taken the view the day after the election that the split was only a "family quarrel." In December the President used a classic post-Civil War phrase, "the late unpleasantness," to characterize the Southern revolt, and many viewed this as a signal that all would be normal. There was certainly no forgiveness in his heart; passing the reviewing stand in the Inaugural parade Thurmond saw him pull down Barkley's arm which was raised in greeting. But McGrath's influence prevailed and bygones were left to be bygones. There were no patronage reprisals, and no committee posts were lost, which distinguished this from the punishment meted out to the La Follette rebels in 1924. At a party caucus Speaker Rayburn said, "There is only one kind of Democrat." (Months later, after McGrath had become Attorney General, and William M. Boyle, Jr., had taken over, national committeemen were purged from the four dissident Southern states.)

The Eighty-first Congress started auspiciously by curbing the powers of the House Rules Committee to throttle legislation. But then came a period of stagnancy—this obviously was not going to be like the "Hundred Days" of 1933. In two Jefferson-Jackson Day dinners at the end of February Truman assailed the Eighty-first Congress, saying that "special interests" were "on the job." He hinted that he might take the case to the people. "I may even get on the train." Representative Donald Jackson, a Republican said, "I'm glad Truman called the Eightieth Congress the second worst in history. It looks like you fellows will make the grade for top honors."

The Senate came to grips with a ban on filibustering to pave the way for civil-rights legislation. Under Rule XXII of the Senate, cloture could be imposed on debate on a measure by a two-thirds vote of those present. Vice-president Barkley ruled that Rule XXII applied to a "motion" to take up a measure as well as the measure itself. He was reversed by the Senate 46 to 41. So the filibuster of two weeks against the motion to take up the anti-poll tax bill could go on. Walter White of the NAACP, holding McGrath responsible for the vote, accused him angrily of forgetting "the oldest law in politics, taking care of the people who took care of you on election day." Senator Lucas admitted that civil-rights measures were "practically dead" and he was right. Bills to end lynching, to repeal the poll tax, and to establish an FEPC all died in the Eighty-first Congress.

Congress then passed a rent-control measure, which was far weaker than the one passed by the Eightieth Congress in protecting tenants. It provided that rent control might be taken over by local communities which the Administration had called a "gutting of controls"; it also increased rents by providing for "a fair net operating income" for landlords. Charlie

Halleck in the House said that Congress had revised the Administration proposals and "This sets the pattern for what is going to happen from this point on in."

Then came the fight to repeal the Taft-Hartley law. The cards were so heavily stacked against the Administration that only by gross delusion could there have been hope that it could be done. While heads had toppled because of the union drive, thirteen Senators and two hundred and fifty-seven House members who had voted for Taft-Hartley had been re-elected. Was this a mandate? In the Senate there were fifty-four Senators who had voted to override the veto. Roscoe Drummond during the campaign wrote that a plan had been presented to Truman to get a pledge from a majority of Democratic candidates for Congress to vote for repeal, but it had been abandoned because the pledges could not have been obtained. It is interesting to note that a *Fortune* poll showed that only nineteen per cent of Truman supporters favored repeal of the Taft-Hartley law.

The generals of the Administration did not agree among themselves. The President himself had endorsed certain features of the Taft-Hartley law. Labor Secretary Tobin was against the injunction in national-emergency strikes because moral suasion was enough, a view for which he was derided by other Democrats; Attorney General Clark felt that there was an inherent right of the Government to ask for an injunction. Tobin was against the non-Communist oath provision in the Taft-Hartley Act, but for the more drastic provision that Communists should not be able to hold union posts. Senator Taft in amusement said, "No one today is proposing repeal of the Taft-Hartley law in substance—only in name." The attempt to write new legislation was finally abandoned.

The President kept repeating that stand-by price controls were needed, but the economy was slipping into the recession of 1949 and the program was obsolete. The proposal for increasing taxes was junked. It was evident that the Eightieth

Congress had shown statesmanship in cutting taxes since the increase in consumer purchasing power was helpful in pulling the country out of the recession.

The Eighty-first Congress was dubbed the "Eighty-worst" Congress. Liberals expressed their disgust. Thomas Sancton for the *Nation* said, "The Eighty-First Congress taken as a whole is as much an instrument of monopoly-Main Street-plantation reaction as was its predecessor." The *New Republic* said, "Even the most naïve voter can see by this time how little the Truman victory last November meant. . . . Truman really heads a minority third party depending for its success in Congress on how many votes he can attract from his rivals."

The accomplishments of the Eighty-first Congress, which was engulfed by the problems of the Korean War in June 1950, finally earned the sobriquet, "The do-little Congress." It passed an enlarged housing program on the pattern of the Taft-Wagner-Ellender bill, enlarged the coverage of the social-security program, and raised the minimum wage from forty cents to seventy-five cents an hour. But on the whole Truman was unsuccessful. There was no new labor law, no civil-rights legislation, no national health insurance, no Federal aid to education, no cash subsidies to farmers proposed by the Brannan Plan. (Congress postponed the date when flexible supports would go into effect.) Reviewing the record when Congress went home before the Congressional elections of 1950, Arthur Krock wrote in the New York *Times,* "The foregoing suggest that if the Eighty-First Congress like its predecessor had been in Republican hands, Mr. Truman would have assailed its record as vehemently."

Louis W. Koenig, in *The Truman Administration: Its Principles and Practice,* says, "After all his untiring persistence, only a fraction of what he meant by the Fair Deal was enacted into law by the Congresses of his Administration. From the point of view of practical politics, narrowly construed, he was a failure as a legislative leader." He saw

Truman's contribution in a "delayed action" in creating a new "climate of opinion."

> "And everybody praised the Duke,
> who this great fight did win."
> "But what good came of it at last?"
> asked little Peterkin.
> "Why that I cannot tell" said he;
> "But 'twas a famous victory."

In his *Memoirs* Truman, after discussing the election, does not allude again to his campaign program and what happened to it in the Eighty-first Congress. This is a striking omission. He dwells at length on what he regarded as the notable accomplishment of that Congress, the ratification by the Senate of the North Atlantic Treaty on July 21, 1949.

His personal triumph lingered long in Truman's mind as evidenced by his repeated jabs at detractors and skeptics of 1948. In July 1949, he took to task Arthur Hays Sulzberger, publisher of the New York *Times,* for having told Pope Pius XII in June 1948, that he was sure to be defeated. Mr. Sulzberger admitted that he had erred with everybody else. The Washington *Post* said editorially of this, "We hope that whatever triumphs and pleasures he can extract from these admissions, he will now allow the subject to rest. For though amusing for awhile, it has long since become rather tiresome to everybody except Mr. Truman himself."

There is no doubt that the event brought about a metamorphosis in the Truman personality. The former diffidence and humility were gone. The new confidence and assurance were displayed in his role as Commander in Chief during the Korean War. The election welded his bonds to political machines, made him less sensitive to press opinion, and increased his loyalties to the associates who stood by him in his hour of travail. These effects colored his reaction to the scandals, uncovered by Democratic-controlled committees in Congress, which rocked Washington in his second Administration.

[XVI]

WHAT WENT WRONG?

	Popular Vote	*Electoral Vote*
Truman	24,105,695	303
Dewey	21,969,170	189
Thurmond	1,169,021	39
Wallace	1,156,103	—

Every event in human experience results from the convergence of many forces. It is futile to identify a single force as the effective cause of the final result. It is also futile to say that if such and such had happened differently, then the final result would have been such and such. Such speculation collides with the inescapable fact that the final event alone is within human knowledge. Even if the film could be rerun and any step in the progression of events eliminated, something else might have occurred the results of which we cannot assess.

This applies to the "ifs" and "maybes" that have been voiced about the great fiasco of 1948. It is impossible to identify a single factor as responsible, whether it be the bungling of the farm issue, the attack on the "do nothing" Congress, labor-union activity, the "whistle stops" or any others, including the "lunatic engineer." No one can say with assurance that if any one event had happened differently Dewey would have been elected. All that is within our knowledge is that in the inscrutability of fate all did converge to produce the final event.

But politicians are not philosophers and there is a universal feeling among them that the victory was thrown away. The quip attributed to prominent New Dealer Paul Porter that "Dewey snatched defeat out of the jaws of victory" sums up that feeling. The result was extraordinarily close. If Dewey had carried Ohio, California, and Illinois, he would have been elected with 267 electoral votes. If he had carried two of them the election would have been decided by the House. A shift of 3500 votes from Truman to Dewey out of 2,898,000 would have given Dewey Ohio, a shift of 16,500 votes out of 3,955,000 votes would have given him Illinois (if Wallace had not been ruled off the ballot, Dewey should have carried the State), and a shift of 9000 out of 3,808,000 would have given him California—or a total shift of 29,000 votes out of 10,661,000 votes would have elected Dewey. It is hard to believe that a strong Dewey campaign would not have captured one out of 367 voters.

The prime cause of the upset was the switch in the farm vote. The loss of Ohio, Illinois, Iowa, and Wisconsin because of the desertion of the traditionally Republican farm vote was a shock. Minnesota, which was lost, had been considered in the doubtful category. While Dewey's total vote was 37,000 less than it had been in 1944, his vote dropped by 585,300 in the ten Midwestern states of Ohio, Illinois, Indiana, Michigan, Minnesota, Nebraska, Kansas, Missouri, Iowa, and Wisconsin. It dropped in all these states but Illinois.

Dewey says candidly, "If the farmer had been reassured that the Republican Party would continue the farm-support programs the result would have been different." Elliott Bell puts at the top of the reasons for Dewey's defeat the drop in the price of corn just at the time when bin storage space was unavailable because of the Eightieth Congress—some devilishly bad luck in timing by Mother Nature.

Dewey did not know what hit him until it was over. He admits that he did not know the farm issue in 1948. As an Easterner Dewey knew little about parity. He did not know about the uneasiness caused by the scheduled introduction of flexible supports in 1950. He did not know of the drop in the price of corn. He did not know of the grain-storage issue.

None of these matters was written up in the New York papers. No one explained them to Dewey. The members of the Dewey brain trust traveled in blissful unawareness of this dagger being thrust in their vitals, though their campaign was supposedly the acme of twentieth-century scientific expertise. In private conversations afterward Dewey blamed his Midwest adviser, Everett Dirksen, for this staggering failure in intelligence, calling him "that damn baker from Peoria." Dirksen's own alleged failures in 1948 were behind the howls from Eastern delegations in the 1952 Convention when Senator Dirksen, pointing at Dewey, said, "You led us down the road to defeat."

The Dewey brain trust blamed national headquarters in Washington for the lapse, saying that phones and teletypes were hooked up at every train stop during the campaign trips, but no intelligence of any real value was ever relayed. There was a good deal of time, however, spent in New York between trips. Then Republican farm politicians are blamed for not giving their wholehearted thought and energy to the Republican cause because they cooperated on a nonpartisan basis with the Department of Agriculture. When Brannan talked of a "sinister conspiracy" against the farmer, they were so farmer-minded rather than Republican-minded that they joined in the chorus.

If Halleck had been Dewey's running mate, he would have grappled with the farm issue which he understood. Warren did not understand it. In the spring of 1948 Warren felt that he needed some education on national issues. Raymond Moley sent Dr. Julius Hirsch, an economist who is a specialist in agricultural economics, to spend some weeks with Warren. On his return East, Hirsch reported the failure of the mission. He told me among others that Warren did not grasp the parity concept or the complexities of the farm problem.

Donald R. Murphy, Research Director for *Wallace's Farmer,* points out that in 1948 "a good many farmers were ready to be scared." In a poll published by the paper on January 3, 1948, the question was asked, "Do you think there will be a serious depression in the United States in the next ten years?" Fifty-four per cent of the farmers said "yes" and thirteen per cent said "no." When the "yes" voters were asked, "When do you think the depression will come?" fifty-eight per cent replied, by 1950. With "anti-Hoover attitudes still strong under the surface, with some stirring up by Congressional action, especially on corn storage," says Murphy, "the corn-price drop made enough farmers apprehensive so that they made a last-minute switch to Truman." Thus, they voted for parity rather than unity.

If Dewey had known the issue and been alive to the danger, it could have been readily met. The flexible support principle was a bipartisan proposal, had logic and justice behind it, and was in the best long-range interests of the farmer. As for the grain-storage issue, Dewey could have hit back hard on that. It was the Department of Agriculture, not the Eightieth Congress, which had pulled a boner. Of the 292 million bushels of bin space at the end of the war, the Department had liquidated 246 million bushels of space before the CCC charter was changed. Misled by poor previous crop years, it made a grievous miscalculation about 1948. A confidential CCC report in October 1947, "Grain Bins and Equipment Report," had criticized the liquidation at a fraction of cost. Even after the new CCC charter took effect in July, 1948, the Department sold another 4 million bushels of bins.

Reciting these facts in a speech to the Senate on April 22, 1949, Senator Williams said, "No one in Congress had been made aware that additional storage facilities were needed." The Administration never mentioned the matter at the Special Session. Even if the need had been discovered by July and the CCC had had the authority to buy bins, it would have taken eight to ten months to get delivery, due to the scarcity of steel, which would have been too late for the 1948 crop. As for the nefarious activity of grain speculators, as Truman alleged, Dewey could have pointed to the Congressional investigation in January, which had involved high Democrats in grain speculation.

If Dewey had given convincing assurance as to price supports and a quick change in the CCC charter, that might of itself have stemmed the drop in the price of corn since dumping corn due to panic had a lot to do with the price situation. A charge by Senator Williams, which has not been explored, is that the Government did not buy a single bushel of corn for six weeks while the price was plummeting during September and October, but in November with the elections over, it bought 3,850,000 bushels.

Labor-union activity is hard to assess as a factor in the final result since we cannot judge how great a defection from the Roosevelt vote would have occurred without it. With the vote as close as it was in Ohio, Illinois, and California, the union vote undoubtedly made the difference. But in spite of the union drive, Dewey carried six industrial states in the East which he failed to carry in 1944—New York, Pennsylvania, Maryland, Delaware, Connecticut, and New Jersey. The CIO-PAC said that it endorsed 144 Congressional candidates who won and 71 who lost, not a glittering record since it gave endorsements in less than half the districts.

An analysis by William Lawrence of the New York *Times* of the Ohio vote showed that in the nine largest industrial counties the Democratic percentage shrank to 52.7 per cent compared with 55.2 per cent in 1944. Thus, in Cuyahoga

County (Cleveland) it shrank to 54.4 per cent compared with 60.3 per cent in 1944; in Summit (Akron) it was 57.5 per cent compared with 58.4 per cent in 1944; and in Mahoning (Youngstown) it was 62.5 per cent compared with 66.6 per cent in 1944. But the farm counties flipped over into the lap of the Democrats. Putnam County shifted from 71.8 per cent Republican in 1944 to 50.5 per cent Democratic; Mercer County from 63 per cent Republican to 52.9 per cent Democratic; and Ottawa from 58.3 per cent Republican to 52.4 per cent Democratic. The conclusion was that the farm vote and not the labor vote gave Truman Ohio.

The unions could not prevent the shift from the Democrats in the cities because of the deep-rooted desire for a change. The Ohio pattern is clearly seen in other parts of the Midwest. Let us take the vote in three other Midwest states compared with the vote in their main metropolitan area. In Minnesota the 1944 margin of 62,448 for Roosevelt was widened to a 209,348 margin for Truman, but in Hennepin County (Minneapolis) Roosevelt's margin was 32,011 and Truman's 30,751. In Michigan Roosevelt won by 22,476 in 1944 and Truman lost the State by 35,147. The loss was due to what happened in Wayne County (Detroit) where Truman's majority fell to 163,220 compared to Roosevelt's majority of 238,400. In Wisconsin we have the clearest picture. Roosevelt lost the State by 24,119 but Truman won it by 56,351. In Milwaukee County, however, the Roosevelt margin of 62,834 shrank to 48,965 for Truman.

Truman might better have said, "The farmer did it," instead of "Labor did it." But labor learned a lot in 1948 and laid the foundation for more successful vote drives in later years.

Ohio illustrates the miscalculations of Dewey's carefully predesigned campaign. He refused to campaign in Ohio, although he crossed it twice in daylight hours, making only the Cleveland speech. It was in the bag. On the other hand, he barnstormed in Minnesota (Senator Ball says that "He did all we asked him to do") but it was all wasted. Another miscalculation—Dewey had always taken the anti-Roosevelt votes of 1944 more or less for granted. But the New York *Times* analysis of Ohio voters showed that a lot of Roosevelt haters, such as Coughlinites and those opposed to a third or fourth term candidate, switched to Truman. In 1944 Dewey reaped the harvest of the Roosevelt hate which was a hate of classic proportions. In 1948 he capitalized on second-grade, second-rate hate—which was not good enough.

This brings up the relative appeal of the personalities. James Roosevelt, who was State Chairman of California, says, "Issues didn't matter in 1948. The people didn't want Dewey." Abe Goff, defeated for re-election to Congress in Idaho, tells of five friends meeting the day after the election, each of whom voted for Truman because he didn't take to Dewey but each of whom thought that he alone had made his choice for that reason. The "lunatic engineer" was a big break. The Democrats played up Dewey's pettiness in taking a plane from LaGuardia Airport eight miles to Idlewild Airport, so that he, like Truman, could land from a plane for the dedication ceremonies. No objective review can ignore the widespread aversion to Dewey's New York mustache. The "Dewey Duster," which was a bit of black chenille to be clipped to the upper lip, appeared on the Chicago market in September but never caught on. In an election as close as this, it can literally be said that Dewey lost by a whisker.

By contrast, Truman was the "square root of America." He was a Lion, Moose, Elk, member of the American Legion, VFW, Regular Veterans Association, Order of Ahepa, Society for the Preservation of Barbershop Singing, and 33rd degree Mason. In the closing stages of the campaign the spectacle of the underdog gallantly fighting on against all odds made a powerful appeal to Americans. Elliott Bell rates this as second only to the price of corn in the result.

While there is room for argument about the effect of various blocs, there is no room for argument about Truman's debt to one bloc—that is the South, which contributed about seventy electoral votes even with the thirty-nine votes for Thurmond. But Truman did not seem to recognize it. In August 1949, the President boasted that he had won without the Solid South. On the contrary, he won because most of the Southern states through party loyalty, which was traditional in the Solid South, stuck by him despite his civil-rights program.

The Southern revolt in the end represented a net gain for Truman. In the North he won smashing majorities in Negro districts, which was the original political object of his civil-rights program. In New York's Harlem he got 108,000 votes as against 34,000 for Dewey and 29,000 for Wallace. His 130,000 majority in Negro wards in Chicago was four times his Illinois majority. These majorities were due to the fact that he was regarded as the Negro's champion. Without Negro support no President would take the risk in the future of offending the South.

His loss of electoral votes in the South was only a temporary loss, and therefore illusory. The best that the Dixiecrats could have done would have been to throw the election into the House, in which case the Southern votes would almost certainly have landed in Truman's column after a deal, as Senator Russell states. The States' Rights movement could have changed the final result only if Thurmond had split the Democratic vote in Southern states so as to give Dewey a plurality and enable him to win the electoral votes.

The Wallace candidacy, however much it was inflated in the newspapers, played little part in the calculations of the leaders of the major parties. In retrospect they can hardly recall it as part of the campaign thinking. The Dewey people ignored it. As far as Democratic leaders can recall, it was regarded more as an asset than a liability. They figured that at least a third of Wallace's vote would come from Republicans, who were Midwest isolationists or "River Baptists." In any event, Truman would gain votes because the Wallace candidacy would insulate Truman from the charge that he wasn't sufficiently anti-Communist. The Communist-spy scare in Government, which Truman had called a "red herring," was very recent in memory.

As it turned out, the total vote for Wallace was below all forecasts. Half of Wallace's nationwide total, 509,000 votes, were concentrated in New York, which enabled Dewey to win the state and its forty-five electoral votes by 60,000 votes. This was quite a jolt to the Democrats on election night. If Truman was to win at all, McGrath had counted on New York. The 9980 Wallace votes in Maryland and the 46,500 votes in Michigan also swung these states to Dewey. But elsewhere his vote did not count. Dr. Gallup writes me, I think correctly, that "the belief on the part of most political observers that Dewey would win was based upon the Wallace vote." Gallup points out that the one per cent vote for him in Ohio compared with a predicted minimum of three per cent or four per cent. In Iowa, his home state, he got only 12,000 votes. In California the vote was half of what was expected.

But the Wallace candidacy won Truman a heavy vote, particularly among Catholics. This was evident in Massachusetts, where a birth control referendum brought out a great outpouring of Catholics and Truman carried the State by 242,000 compared with Roosevelt's majority in 1944 of 114,000. Samuel Lubell in *The Future of American Politics* says, "Throughout the country Truman received a record Catholic vote exceeding in some areas even Al Smith's turnout." In eleven Boston wards Truman set a new Democratic high. His majority in Suffolk County (Boston) was 159,000 compared with Roosevelt's 1944 majority of 95,000. Because of Wallace, Truman got the Al Smith vote without suffering the penalties of being Al Smith. In the close race of 1948, it is conceivable that Wallace elected Truman.

At the start of 1948 Harry Truman was deemed a strong contender. The notion that he was doomed to defeat sprang up in the early months of 1948 when the Wallace candidacy appeared to be formidable and when there was a Southern revolt. As the campaign went on, and it appeared that the Wallace and Dixiecrat threats were not as formidable as they looked and that Truman was actually gaining votes by being anti-Wallace and pro-civil rights, political seers and prophets should have revised their evaluations. But convictions had hardened on the subject even after the original premises for the theory had been weakened. This was the central error of the predictions in 1948.

Since 1948 there has been considerable acceptance of the reverse-coattails idea—that instead of the President pulling local candidates in on his coattails, Truman rode in on the coattails of more popular local candidates. For example, while Adlai Stevenson won the Governorship in Illinois by 560,000 and Paul Douglas was elected Senator by 400,000, Truman squeaked through with only a 33,000 margin. In Ohio, while Frank Lausche won the Governorship by 215,000, Truman's margin was only 7000. Other examples can be cited, where Truman trailed far behind Senatorial candidates. He won by 28,000 in Iowa while Guy Gillette won by 163,000; he won by 28,000 in Colorado, while Ed Johnson won by 175,000; he won in Tennessee by 67,500 while Estes Kefauver won by 160,000.

There were certainly a lot of popular Democratic candidates that year compared with their Republican counterparts, and undoubtedly Senatorial contests had some effect on the Presidential vote. But there is another side to the picture which is always overlooked. Truman carried Massachusetts by 242,000 votes while a Republican, Leverett Saltonstall, won the Senatorship by 134,000 votes. Truman carried Kentucky by 125,000 while Virgil Chapman defeated John Sherman Cooper by only 25,000. Truman carried Iowa while the Republicans won all the eight House seats, carried California while Republicans won Congressional contests by 626,000, and in carrying Wisconsin ran 133,000 ahead of Democratic Congressional candidates.

Statistical comparisons between the Congressional and Presidential votes district by district are full of snags and pitfalls. In March 1949, Southern Congressmen, who were irritated by Truman's assumption that he could boss Congress around, asked Charles Bartlett, Washington correspondent of the Chattanooga *Times,* to make a survey. It showed Truman's vote lagged behind that of Democratic Congressmen. The findings started an argument as to the statistical methods used. The problem is complicated by the fact that Presidential candidates normally receive more votes than Congressional candidates; in many districts there are no real contests at the Congressional level and, most important, in 1948 Truman lost votes to Wallace and Thurmond while Congressional candidates had to contend with only a scattering of Wallace opponents. The most valid comparison is on the basis of the total vote:

	Democratic	*Republican*	*Others*
For President	24,105,695	21,969,170	2,758,815
	(49.36%)	(44.99%)	(5.65%)
For Congress	23,819,943	20,920,315	1,402,115
	(51.62%)	(45.34%)	(3.04%)

This does not show Truman weaker than the Party. Truman's percentage is smaller only because of the greater dent made by the third parties in the Presidential contest than in Congressional elections.

The Social Science Research Council which made a study of the 1948 election polls stated that if the "coattail" theory has any validity, it means that a unified psychological picture of the party reflects on the relative merits of competing candidates. The Presidential candidate, rather than local candidates, usually promotes that picture. The study says, "Hindsight indicates that the Truman vote had a far more solid party basis than Dewey's." There is no reason for believing that Truman owed more to Stevenson in Illinois than Stevenson owed to Truman. As a matter of fact, said the Council, "such large differences in majorities would seem to indicate little or no correlation between the vote for Governor and that for President."

A striking phenomenon was the extraordinarily low vote. The total vote of 48,833,000 was a million below the 1940 vote in spite of the big population increase. It was only 850,000 above the 1944 vote. Since the population increase, including the Armed Forces overseas, was 8.5 million, and the G.I. vote in 1944 was not considerable, a far bigger vote had been expected in 1948, particularly since labor had staged a big get-out-the-vote drive. It is a remarkable fact that 683,000 persons who voted for local offices did not bother to vote for President.

Did Republicans or Democrats fail to vote? There were many statements from individual Republicans that Dewey's pallid campaign and open embrace of New Deal measures in the later stages of the campaign gave them the feeling, "If this is all he has to offer, then what difference does it make?" Statistics tend to bear out an assumption that Republicans failed to vote because there was no incentive. The total vote in Ohio, Illinois, Iowa, and Wisconsin, four Midwest states which Dewey had expected to carry but lost, fell off compared to 1944. It fell off also in three states which Dewey carried thanks to the Wallace vote—New York, Maryland, and Michigan. In Iowa the decline in the vote occurred in the heavily Republican counties. Howard Buffett, who lost his seat in the second district of Nebraska by 3244 in a vote which was 9714 lighter than 1944, writes me, "The regular Republicans of deep convictions stayed away from the polls in large numbers in Nebraska in 1948."

Dewey stated after the election and states today that "overconfidence" of Republicans kept a large number from voting. If overconfidence caused by the public-opinion polls was a factor, it was certainly offset by the band-wagon vote which must have been heavy among the 21,969,000 who voted for Dewey.

Truman had conducted his whistle-stop campaign on the theory he expressed that his only chance to win was to pull out a record vote of 60 million—time and again, he exhorted the crowds that they had no one to blame but themselves if they did not vote. The small total turnout showed he failed in this objective. Nonetheless, the general feeling was that he had pulled the Democratic vote to the polls. As Walter Lippmann commented, "I did not expect the Democrats to bring out their full vote." The Truman vote in 1948 plus the Wallace and Thurmond vote was 26,430,000, which was 828,000 in excess of Roosevelt's vote in 1944.

The general apathy which hurt the Dewey vote was properly chargeable to Dewey, who waged no fight. The Washington *Post* said just before the election, "The campaign has been duller and less significant than any similar contest in recent years." Walter Lippmann wrote, "There is no fundamental conflict of doctrine, no ideological conflict remotely comparable with that which separates parties, say in France or Britain."

It is fair to say about Dewey that never did a candidate have so much to talk about and say so little. Dewey had permitted a Congress which *had* notable accomplishments to be branded as a "do-nothing Congress"; he had allowed a President who had urged that striking railroad workers be drafted to brand the Taft-Hartley law as a "slave-labor act"; he had allowed Truman to take the credit for high prices and high wages and yet blame the Republicans for not controlling inflation; he had not challenged Truman when he called a tax cut which had relieved 7,400,000 from paying taxes a "rich man's tax bill"; he had let Truman blame the Republicans for a grain-storage shortage which was the fault of the Administration; he had not challenged the head of an Administration filled with Wall Street men when Truman labeled Republicans "Wall Street bloodsuckers"; he had skipped the issues of Communists in Government and the errors made by the Administration abroad in dealing with Communism.

Many Democrats felt that Taft would have been harder to beat than Dewey in 1948. Harold Ickes said after the event, "They sent in their bat boy with the bases full; the next time they'll send in their Babe Ruth, Senator Taft."

Fundamentally, there was only one thing that Dewey purported to offer in 1948, that as President he would be a better administrator than Truman. Raymond Moley, seeing that that was Dewey's forte, wrote a speech for Dewey on those lines after being assured that he was not wasting his time. The speech was never used. In that speech Moley set out the tenets of good administration, and analyzed the weaknesses of the Administration under Truman. Moley was specific in citing examples of poor administration, "There will be no grain or stock speculation on Government time. . . . It is bad public service to select men for public office because they are old friends, political has-beens, or because they need a job. . . . There will be no public brawls among Cabinet officers in the next Administration. . . . No Henry Wallace will be announcing foreign policy while the Secretary of State is on a diplomatic mission in Europe. . . . It is bad to appoint two or more people to do the work of one. . . . In the next Administration there will be one and only one Secretary of Defense and he only will speak for the Army, Navy, and Air Force." Hard punching along these lines directed to the most vulnerable feature of the Administration might have convinced a majority of the electorate that there was some good reason for switching to Dewey. As it was, the New York *Post* was right in commenting in October on the noticeable apathy, "As far as the people can see, the future will be the same no matter which party wins." While Elliott Bell reflects that he has lost faith in the electorate since 1948, he had, in fact, presented no argument to the electorate for Dewey.

[XVII]

THOUGHTS ON 1948 AND TODAY

SOME ELECTIONS in our history have seen important issues drawn between the parties and significant effects. In the last hundred years 1860, 1896, and 1932 immediately come to mind. In other elections there has been no clear-cut contest of issues or principles. The 1948 election is in this class.

The issue of the "do-nothing" Eightieth Congress was mere fantasy and forgotten after the election was over. This was not the era of crisis which produced the New Deal. The Congresses of the Truman Administration reflected the popular will that in a time of prosperity there was no need for more radical reforms. The issue of the Eightieth Congress was probably effective in bringing Democrats to the polls out of fear that gains won through the New Deal might be erased. In the closing days of the campaign Truman repeatedly raised the specter that Dewey might destroy the New Deal.

While its effects on history are conjectural, the election of 1948 has left a deep imprint on current thinking about the process of campaigning and the motivations of the electorate. Surprisingly, in these vital areas there is little sound information. Professor Henry Steele Commager wrote in 1952, "It is indeed a bit embarrassing how little we actually know about voting or nonvoting. . . . What, after all, influences or controls voting? Is it party loyalty, hereditary or acquired? Is it habit? Is it geography? Is it class or group interest? Is it argument or propaganda?"

1948 has elevated the campaign as such to prime importance. Farley's Law that the electorate had made up its mind long before election day has now been deeply buried in the face of clear evidence that Truman won in the last weeks. A premium has been put on the "hard" campaign and on "fight." Robert Humphreys, Republican Campaign Director, believes that modern methods of communication, by which the candidate is brought into the living room, work against a "don't rock the boat" strategy.

"Fight" means not only vigor in attack but alertness in nailing down misrepresentations made by the other side. Vice-President Nixon in campaigning in the Congressional elections in 1958 often referred to the Truman upset; he undoubtedly had it in mind when he said on October 16 that some people argued that the record of the Administration would speak for itself, but "this is never true in the short run. The record never speaks for itself when somebody else is speaking against it and no one is speaking for it."

The GOP acted on the same theory in 1952. On the same day that the White House announced that President Truman would campaign for Stevenson, there was a meeting in the office of National Chairman Arthur Summerfield. A decision was reached to send a group of researchers hot on the heels of Truman to correct his facts. Adopting the suggestion of Senator Mundt, it was called a "Truth Squad," and a "Truth Squad" later followed Stevenson. Since President Eisenhower liked the idea, it became a fixture of the 1956 campaign—a visible legacy of the 1948 experience.

The Truman campaign is something of a model from the standpoint of political propaganda. In the first place, like all good propaganda, it hammered on a single theme, the do-nothing wicked Congress. It was a simple theme and one which commanded general interest. A complex theme or a variety of themes can bewilder the electorate. In the second place, he never discussed his accomplishments to win admiration, but focused on a common object of hate. In his study of mass movements, *The True Believer,* Eric Hoffer says, "Hatred is the most accessible and comprehensive of all unifying agents. . . . Common hatred unites the most heterogenous elements." Truman had found a substitute for Hoover, who had become shopworn as an object of hate. In the third place he was always interesting, which is necessary these days when there are so many distractions from politics, including free entertainment.

Another lesson of 1948 is that it is dangerous for a Presidential candidate to try to disassociate himself from the record of his party. For better or worse, candidate and party must sink or swim together. The Democrats did not commit the folly of dumping Truman because wiser minds knew that the party was saddled with his record. It is safe to say that Dewey's coolness to the Eightieth Congress won him few votes from its enemies but alienated conservatives who felt that the first Republican Congress in eighteen years deserved warmer support.

A turning point in political thinking was Truman's victory on a small turnout. As we have noted, the goal of Truman's whistle-stop campaign was a big vote in which he believed lay his forlorn hope of victory. The 1948 vote threw a harpoon into the theory cherished up to that time, as stated by Dr. Gallup in his October 5 release, "A small vote turnout hurts the Democrats more than the GOP because a large percentage of the stay-at-homes are Democrats."

Republican strategists examine the Presidential votes of 1940 through 1952.

	Republican	*Democratic*
1940	22,304,755	27,243,466
1944	22,006,278	25,602,505
1948	21,970,065	24,105,812
1952	33,936,252	27,314,922

This tabulation would indicate prima facie that the hope of Republican victory lies in pulling a big vote. The Democratic vote remained steady through four elections. The Truman vote in 1948 plus the Thurmond and Wallace vote, about 26,430,000, is remarkably close to the Stevenson vote. But the Eisenhower candidacy attracted 62.7 per cent of the voting population to the polls in 1952 compared to 51.5 per cent in 1948 and 53 per cent in 1944, and that additional vote went heavily Republican. Dewey did not think in terms of voting potential. In 1952 when General Eisenhower entered New York to campaign, his first advice from Dewey was that he could not guarantee success in New York unless Eisenhower endorsed a compulsory FEPC. Eisenhower said he would not do so, and he would still win. A million more voters went to the polls in New York and he carried the state by 850,000.

This premise, that the Republican vote is more elastic than the Democratic vote, opens the door for the argument by conservatives that if the voters had a clear choice between party lines the stay-at-home vote could be brought to the polls. They argue that that choice presented by the Republicans should be in terms of conservatism. A Republican conservative, James L. Wick, in a thoughtful book published in 1952, *How NOT to Run for President—A Handbook for Republicans,* says, "The Republicans can make no greater mistake than to think that the tactics which win voters in large numbers to the New Deal would, if imitated, win them to the Republican Party. In promising largesse from the United States Treasury, the Democrats will always outbid the Republicans."

There can be no proof of an hypothesis as to the 1948

campaign, although it is plausible that Dewey was hurt by general apathy which came about because he presented no basic difference in principles. The Wick thesis about "outbidding" does seem logical. Did Dewey win votes by promising to raise the minimum wage when Truman named a specific figure of seventy-five cents an hour, by promising to make changes if necessary in the Taft-Hartley law when Truman promised to repeal it, to "break the log jam in housing" when Truman endorsed the Taft-Wagner-Ellender bill, to do something (which he did not specify) about soaring prices when Truman had a program for price controls?

1948 emphasized the psychology of the individual. The voter votes as an individual, atomistically, so to speak, which nullifies mechanistically predetermined assumptions about elections. Henry Hazlitt cited the Jules Verne story about an effort to get all residents of the earth to shout together so that the sound would reach the moon. There was dead silence—everybody was listening to hear the others. The Washington *Post* noted Laski's statement in *American Democracy*. "There is something in the psychological climate of America which resists any ultimate regimentation of behaviour and opinion." Max Lerner said that what linked Dewey and the public-opinion polls was "that they are symbols of the same thing, the effort to supplant human life by the slide-rule, to run the political animal as if he were part not of a biological universe but a mechanical one."

The emotional appeal of the candidate's personality on the individual vote has been upgraded in importance. In 1948 the Republicans presented a candidate with a personality which did not go over with the electorate; in 1952 they presented a candidate with a winning personality. Personality as a recognized factor is, of course, nothing new. In 1860 the Republican Party pictured a successful railroad lawyer as a railsplitter. In 1928 it was recognized that some personal characteristics of Al Smith made him unpalatable to many Americans.

As far as the temper of 1948 is concerned, Dewey was not "common" enough for the common man. Apropos of this, Representative Clarence Brown tells the story of Governor Vic Donahey of Ohio, who used the word "ain't" in a speech. He was criticized by Ohio newspapers which pointed to the many institutions of higher learning and the cultural distinctions in a state of which Donahey was Chief Executive. Donahey at a press conference was asked his reaction. He leaned back, took a chew of tobacco, and said, "Well, I'm convinced that there are more people in Ohio who say 'ain't' than there hain't people who say 'ain't.' " In reference to Truman's undoubted greater acceptance in the Midwest, Homer Hush, farm editor in Des Moines, says, "Strange, isn't it, that people vote for candidates they like more than for candidates that might support policies they believe in. If you like a man and he appears to follow accepted moral codes, he can hardly be wrong on farm policy or foreign relations."

It does seem important for the candidate to establish some rapport with the voter or establish some identification in the voter's mind. Roosevelt was hardly the common man, but it is probably correct to say that he was identified by voters as a "father image," the repository of superior wisdom and sympathetic understanding in those troubled years. The "image" of Dewey could readily have been transposed into one that the voters would have wanted. If Dewey had painted a picture of an Administration filled with incompetents, rascals, and Communists who had to be ruthlessly purged, the same qualities that made him look allergic to a complacent electorate would have made him look like the man to do the hatchet job.

In *The Hidden Persuaders,* a dithyramb to the advertising industry, the author, Vance Packard, says that "voters could not be depended on to be rational. There seemed to be a strong illogical or nonlogical element in their behaviour, both individually and in masses." He cites with apparent approval that "During the 1952 campaign Dr. [Ernest] Dichter announced that all the long-winded talking about issues such as inflation and Korea would actually have very little to do with the outcome. The crux of the campaign, he insisted, was the emotional pull exercised by the various candidates."

It would be a sad day for America if Mr. Packard were right about how Presidents are chosen. But the advertising techniques designed to impress the name of a product on a consumer's mind are not the same advertising techniques used in a political campaign designed to grab the voter's attention long enough so that an argument can be made. Holding the voter's attention is a serious problem in an age characterized by what Clifton Fadiman has aptly called "The Decline of Attention." Campaign Director Robert Humphreys, who introduced visual techniques into the campaign kit down at the Congressional level and used advertising agencies in the last two national campaigns, has always been enthusiastic about facts and factual presentations as a prime campaign tool. "An array of facts," says Humphreys, "gives a feeling of authenticity to the argument." There is nothing "nonrational" for example, about the "father image" that Packard discusses. The issues in Government today have become so complicated that they are beyond the understanding of many voters, the powers of the President have multiplied and the contingencies that may arise are unforeseeable. Such being the case, is it not reasonable for the voter to put his trust in a candidate who seems to possess superior wisdom and sympathetic understanding?

Rather than voting "nonrationally" most people vote in accordance with their feeling as to which candidate will best serve their concept of self- or national interest. Where the voter cannot find an appeal to his interests, the pull of personality or "likeability" becomes dominant. Such was the case in 1948 when it did not appear to many to make much difference who won. On the other hand, history provides a long list of candidates more affable than their opponents who have gone down to defeat because they did not appeal to the voter's interests. The warm John W. Davis who lost to the dour Calvin Coolidge in 1924 is a case in point. Ideally, the candidate's personality should be suited to the temper of the times or should be wedded to a cause for which it is suited. As Professor Commager says, "Candidates are most effective when they appear as symbols for some great principle."

A rational element that played a part in the 1948 election was prosperity. In good times there is a reluctance to change administrations; depressions just about seal the doom of an administration in power. In a study of this subject (New York *Times,* August 24, 1952), Louis Bean found that during fifteen out of seventeen elections in which a party in power was re-elected, there was prosperity. The two exceptions during which there were depressions occurred in 1876 when Samuel Tilden got a majority of the popular vote and lost out in the famous compromise, and 1908 when Taft was assisted by the great popularity of Theodore Roosevelt. During eight out of fourteen elections in which the party in power was defeated, there were depressions. During the other six there was prosperity, but in five of the six cases, the party was split.

There was in 1948 only a dim appreciation of Truman's advantage in riding the crest of prosperity. The New York *Times* did take note of it when it said editorially on the day of the election, "Most Presidents in good times have been elected. . . . It is Governor Dewey, who in race track parlance is carrying the weight in the political race. Only when we take into account the size of the handicap, are we fully appreciative of the strength and meaning of the indicated swing in public opinion." Two professors at one of Governor Dewey's favorite schools, the Cornell School of Agriculture, showed unusual prescience. In an article written on July 15, 1948, for *Farm Economics,* Professors F. A. Pearson and W. I. Myers said, "The public tends to vote for the continuance of administrations that have been in power during prosperous times and to vote against the incumbent administration when depression marks the approach of election. . . . In good times the voters' satisfaction and conservatism makes any change seem inadmissible." Taking the general price level as their prosperity index they found that results in twenty-seven out of thirty-one previous elections bore out their findings. Their theory did not agree with election results only in 1824 when Jackson won in the popular vote but lost to John Quincy Adams in the House; in 1852 when according to them the Whigs should have been returned to power; in 1876 in the famous disputed election; and in 1912 when Theodore Roosevelt prevented a Republican victory by splitting the Party. The 1852 election was the only real exception because the other elections had special circumstances. In the last paragraph the authors said, "The only startling conclusion this reasoning leads to is that Truman will win in November if the price level is stable or continues to rise and provided Wallace and the Dixiecrats get few votes." The general price level did not dip in 1948 and Truman capitalized on the drop in the price of corn and farm products by blaming it on the Republican Congress.

The polls, which reputedly died after the 1948 election, rose phoenix-like out of their ashes. Since it is the most popular one, let us look at the Gallup Poll. Dewey says he believes in the Gallup Poll, but Gallup stopped polling two weeks too soon. Gallup advises me that "the failure to poll up to the very end of the campaign was the greatest mistake" made in 1948. But Gallup in *A Guide to Public Opinion Polls,* published in 1948, said that it was "unthinkable" that polls could make an error like the *Literary Digest* error because for one reason, "polling organizations are aware of the time factor and for this reason usually insist upon polling almost to the day of election."

One person did question the polls in 1948. Robert Cobb Myers of the Psychology Department of Princeton in *Commentary* magazine raised doubts. His article written before the election appeared in the November issue. He pointed to a strange case. In March, 1948, Gallup announced the results of a poll on the question, "Do you think that prices will be higher, lower or about the same in six months?" The results—higher, fourteen per cent; lower, thirty-nine per cent; same, thirty-six per cent. Roper published a poll in April in *Fortune,* asking the question with the one inconsequential change, "prices of things you buy." The results—higher, fifty-four per cent; lower, nine per cent; same, twenty-two per cent.

Myers also referred to Gallup's consistent underestimate of the Democratic vote and an admission that Gallup made before the House Committee on Campaign Expenditures in December 1944 that he had altered his own figures. He had arbitrarily subtracted two percentage points from the Roosevelt vote in his August, September, and October 15 polls because he guessed there would be a low turnout which would reduce the Democratic vote. But he did not inform his readers about what he had done; for this he was criticized by a Technical Committee of eminent statisticians. His estimate of the 1944 New York vote was based on what the committee called "nonpolling evidence," meaning his own judgment.

Gallup has a method of computing his errors which no statistician could accept. He subtracts the forecast percentage from the actual percentage vote, which minimizes the error. Thus, he predicted 51 per cent for Eisenhower in 1952. Since

Eisenhower got 55.4 per cent of the vote, Gallup calls this a 4.4 error. It is actually a substantial 8.6 error (4.4 divided by 51). A 40 per cent error on the Wallace vote in 1948 is turned into an error of 1.6 per cent by subtracting the actual 2.4 per cent from the predicted 4 per cent.

Gallup's errors have been on the majestic side. In 1944 he underestimated the Democratic vote in forty states. He underestimated Roosevelt's total by one third, 140 electoral votes. In 1948 he gave Dewey 170 electoral votes which he lost, almost a third of the total electoral vote. While an error of two per cent is critical in a toss-up state, he underestimated Truman's vote by eighteen per cent in Massachusetts and twenty-four per cent in Minnesota. In the runaway 1952 race his last release said that Eisenhower and Stevenson were "coming down the homestretch in a tight race" and he could not predict the result.

The basic problem with polls is the sample, which must be an accurate cross-section of the voting population. In 1948 Gallup used 61,674 interviews over a period of two months. In Massachusetts in 1948 the interviews used only 968 persons out of a vote of 2,155,346. Gallup tells me that his samples are even smaller today. The decisive factor in Massachusetts was the Catholic vote. Gallup listed religion among the eight named and "other factors" used as controls in quota sampling, but certainly the 968 ballots could not have given proper weight to that factor and the fact that because of the birth-control referendum more Catholics than non-Catholics turned out to vote. The case of Massachusetts in 1948 illustrates that to draw an accurate sample the pollster must make his own value judgment as to what the impact of the various issues will be. That is opinion, not science.

The sample technique requires that the pollster, or his interviewers choose the voter who is the common denominator, a process which can be a subject of endless argument. He has not solved the problem as to what to do with the undecided vote. He does not know who will turn out to vote. Then there is the problem of interviewing at the lowest economic and cultural level, of which Gallup has said, "When you get down to the foreign-born and so on you have one devil of a problem interviewing."

Then consider the problem of interviewing to the last minute, which practically must mean up to the last five days. The 61,674 interviews of 1948, which we have mentioned, had to be spread over a two-month period, since Gallup's operation is a commercial one and he must have several poll reports. Let us assume that as many as one fourth of the interviews could be crammed into the final poll. (Gallup used the whole sample for his final prediction unless the last wave of ballots showed a new trend.) That means only 15,418 interviews over the nation to ascertain the final result. Dividing the actual number of interviews in 1948 by one fourth, we would have 241 in Massachusetts, 454 in California, 266 in Iowa, and 280 in Minnesota. Can any sound conclusions be drawn from these tiny numbers in a vast voting population?

The ditty sung by a character representing Dr. Gallup in a parody at the Gridiron Dinner in 1948 stills holds true,

> Ah, sweet mystery of life, we have not found thee,
> Ah, we do not know the secret of it all.

In retrospect the 1948 campaign seems bizarre since the campaign focused on domestic questions while the real crisis was our foreign policy. In Truman's *Memoirs* the campaign is almost like "time out" from what was paramount in his mind, the winning of the peace.

During the campaign his administration was wrestling with the life or death problem of the Berlin airlift and the chance of war. The *Forrestal Diaries* tell of a meeting on September 14 at the home of Philip Graham, publisher of the Washington *Post,* at which newspaper publishers and editors were briefed by Marshall and Forrestal on Berlin. "Roy Roberts expressed the strong belief that the policy of our

Government should be so conducted as to make sure that there would be no chance of any overt act prior to November 2." The others dissented. Then Forrestal posed the question as to whether the bomb should be used in the event of war. There was "unanimous agreement that in the event of war the American people would not only have no question as to the propriety of the use of the atomic bomb but would in fact expect it to be used." While this was going on, Truman was barnstorming the country for votes by denouncing Congress because it did not grant enough social security benefits or irrigation projects.

Today, as in 1948, the foreign policy issue, the issue of survival, overrides all others. If future campaigns are to be conducted around domestic matters, they will be ignoring the core issue. Since security facts are involved, foreign policy is not well suited to the forum. However, it is legitimate to inject a question into the campaign, as to whether peace has been maintained or threatened, and whether any vital interests of the nation or the free world have been sacrificed. Despite criticism Vice-President Nixon in the 1958 Congressional elections brought foreign policy into the campaign by claiming that the Administration had managed to keep peace without appeasement.

As in 1948, inflation is today the paramount domestic concern and as in 1948 it is bound up with the dimensions of our commitments abroad. Neither party in 1948 talked in terms of what a real war on inflation might entail: holding down money incomes, farmers' prices, workers' wages, and business profits. Truman's invitation to all interest groups to share more freely in the national cornucopia could hardly be reconciled with his professed desire for price controls or measures to protect the consumer, fixed income groups, and others who suffer by inflation. Chairman Hugh Scott said only after the election was over, "If you can keep farm prices high, cut the cost of foodstuffs, encourage labor generally to seek higher wages and still give lower building costs, Mandrake the Magician will have to take a back seat."

As in 1948, votes may be won by promising benefits and subsidies from the public trough and through Government action. The only corrective lies in appealing to the sound common sense of the people. Even in a political campaign they can be educated to the fact that the piper must be paid, that only by restraint or even sacrifice can the inflationary spiral ever be halted.

A political campaign is an opportunity for educating the public as to public issues by giving them the facts. It is wrong to assume as Dewey apparently did in 1948 that the public knew the facts, for example, as to the benefits of the Taft-Hartley Act. If Dewey had conceived of the campaign in terms of public education Truman would not have been able to get away with the issue of the Eightieth Congress. It is also wrong to assume that the public cannot understand the issues if the facts are given. Lord Bryce said that politics ranked fifth among the interests of the common man; today during a Presidential year the contest for the Presidency ranks even higher as a conversational topic. A candidate should articulate the arguments that his supporters can use. James L. Wick in *How NOT To Run for President,* says that one of the little-understood principles of political persuasion is that the undecided turn to others to make their decisions for them. "These 'leaders'—minor as well as major—who are so anxious to become 'salesmen' for the party are the persons the candidate in his speeches should try to influence and stimulate."

There is a final observation to make about 1948. The mass hallucination that Dewey was sure to win deserves a place in the list of "Extraordinary Popular Delusions and the Madness of Crowds." Unlike the South Sea Bubble and the Tulip Craze it is recent. Unlike the Florida real-estate madness of the Twenties, it was not a delusion of the man-in-the-street. It was a delusion of the *cognoscenti,* pumped through all the channels of communication to the masses. The lack of any dissent among the professionals makes it possibly unparalleled in history.

The press on which the public relied was guilty. There was a note of indictment in Dewey's words to the press the day after the election, "I am as surprised as you are. I have read your stories." In many cases friends and relatives of the Dewey staff who boarded the campaign train had reported that it was strange that they could not observe any Dewey sweep in their areas. Yet, on this same train, says Elliott Bell, he was repeatedly asked by leading correspondents why Dewey bothered to campaign at all.

I was as guilty as anyone else of propagating the delusion. As an oracle for a business advisory service, the Research Institute of America, I participated in writing "What Dewey's Election Means to Business," which reached our clients before election. The day after, in a state of numbed shock, I wrote a much less lucid account of "What Truman's Election Means to Business." To me as to all others the flimsy evidence for the delusion was open for examination. It consisted of a premise that sprang into life nine months before election day as to the strength of the Wallace movement and the Southern revolt. It consisted also of three polls, based on probability samples, which had been tested in only three Presidential elections, and in the main badly underestimated Democratic strength. There were also, I have noted, omens in the two months before which should have been evaluated.

There is a lesson in this and a warning. In these perilous times a delusion like that of 1948 can arise again with more serious consequences to the nation than the defeat of Thomas E. Dewey. To know the truth we must be wary of blind acceptance of assumptions, no matter how widely they are held. The individual skeptic must be bold in exploring his doubts and there must be an unceasing search for the facts.

BIBLIOGRAPHY

BIBLIOGRAPHY

The author has utilized many newspapers of the period. The principal ones were the New York *Times,* the New York *Herald Tribune,* the New York *Post, PM* later the New York *Star,* the Washington *Post,* the Washington *Evening Star,* the Chicago *Tribune,* the St. Louis *Post-Dispatch,* and the Wall Street *Journal.*

The Congressional Record was consulted for the period. Also, Senate Report #1775, "Investigation of Federal Employees Loyalty Program," Eightieth Congress, Second Session.

Books to which reference was made included:

Coit, Margaret. *Mr. Baruch.* New York: Houghton Mifflin Co., 1957.

Eccles, Marriner S. *Beckoning Frontiers.* New York: Alfred A. Knopf, Inc., 1951.

Gallup, George. *A Guide to Public Opinion Polls.* Princeton: Princeton University Press, 1948.

Hull, Cordell. *Memoirs.* New York: The MacMillan Co., 1948.

Hyman, Sidney. *The American President.* New York: Harper & Brothers, 1954.

Koenig, Louis W. *The Truman Administration: Its Principles and Practice.* New York: New York University Press, 1956.

Laurence, William L. *Dawn Over Zero: The Story of the Atomic Bomb.* New York: Alfred A. Knopf, Inc., 1947.

Lubell, Samuel. *The Future of American Politics.* New York: Harper & Brothers, 1952.

Macdonald, Dwight. *Henry Wallace: The Man and the Myth.* New York: Vanguard Press, 1948.

Millis, Walter, ed. *The Forrestal Diaries.* New York: The Viking Press, 1951.

Moon, Henry Lee. *The Balance of Power*. Garden City: Doubleday & Company, Inc., 1948.

Mosteller, Frederick, and others of the Social Science Research Council. *The Pre-Election Polls of 1948*. New York: Social Science Research Council, 1949.

Packard, Vance. *The Hidden Persuaders*. New York: David McKay Co., Inc., 1957.

Redding, Jack. *Inside the Democratic Party*. Indianapolis: The Bobbs-Merrill Co., Inc., 1958.

Rogers, Lindsay. *The Pollsters*. New York: Alfred A. Knopf, Inc., 1949.

Sherwood, Robert. *Roosevelt and Hopkins*. New York: Harper & Brothers, 1950.

Stassen, Harold. *Where I Stand*. Garden City: Doubleday & Company, Inc., 1947.

Truman, Harry S. *Memoirs*. Garden City: Doubleday & Company, Inc., Vol. 1, 1955; Vol. 2, 1956.

Tugwell, Rexford Guy. *A Chronicle of Jeopardy*. Chicago: University of Chicago, 1955.

Wick, James L. *How NOT to Run for President—a Handbook for Republicans*. New York: Vantage Press, Inc., 1952.

Magazines consulted for the whole period were *Time, Newsweek,* the *Nation,* and the *New Republic.*

Articles in periodicals that were used included:

Arnall, Ellis. "The Democrats Can Win" in *Atlantic Monthly,* October, 1948.

Bean, Louis. "Do Eelctions Follow the Business Cycle?" in the New York *Times Magazine,* August 24, 1952.

Commager, Henry Steele. "Is it the Man or is it the Issue?" in the New York *Times Magazine,* October 12, 1952.

Davis, Elmer. "President Dewey's Strange Bedfellows" in *Harper's,* September, 1948.

Hale, William Harlan. "What Makes Wallace Run?" in *Harper's,* March, 1948.

Hatch, Alden. "Men Around Dewey" in *Harper's,* October, 1948.

Jackson, Gardner. "Henry Wallace: A Divided Mind" in *Atlantic Monthly,* September, 1948.

Myers, Robert Cobb. "Opinion Polls and Public Policy" in *Commentary,* November, 1948.

Pearson, F. A. and Myers, W. I. "The Price Level and Elections" in *Farm Economics,* September, 1948.

Rovere, Richard H. "Letter from a Campaign Train" in the *New Yorker,* October 9 and October 16, 1948.

Smith, Alice Kimball. "Behind the Decision to Use the Atomic Bomb: Chicago 1944-1945" in *Bulletin of the Atomic Scientists,* October, 1958.

Tugwell, Rexford Guy. "Progressives and the Presidency" with a reply by Hubert Humphrey in *The Progressive,* March, 1949.

INDEX

INDEX